GENDER
JUSTICE

GENDER JUSTICE

David L. Kirp, Mark G. Yudof,
and Marlene Strong Franks

The University of Chicago Press
Chicago and London

DAVID L. KIRP is a professor in the Graduate School of Public
Policy and lecturer in the School of Law at the University of
California, Berkeley. MARK G. YUDOF is dean of the
University of Texas Law School and holds the James A.
Elkins Centennial Chair in Law. MARLENE STRONG FRANKS
is a policy analyst completing her Ph.D. in public policy at the
University of California, Berkeley.

The University of Chicago Press, Chicago 60637
The University of Chicago Press, Ltd., London
© 1986 by The University of Chicago
All rights reserved. Published 1986
Printed in the United States of America

95 94 93 92 91 90 89 88 87 86 5432

Library of Congress Cataloging in Publication Data

Kirp, David L.
  Gender justice.

  Bibliography: p.
  Includes index.
  1. Sex discrimination—Law and legislation—United
States. 2. Sex discrimination—United States.
I. Yudof, Mark G. II. Franks, Marlene Strong. III. Title.
KF4758.K57 1985   342.73'085   85-5885
ISBN 0-226-43762-0   347.30285

If I am not for myself, who shall be for me? If I am for myself alone, what kind of person am I? And if not now, when?

Hillel, *Ethics of the Fathers*

Contents

Acknowledgments   ix

Introduction   1

Part I. Conceptualizations

  1. Choice and Justice   9

  2. Pedestal or Prison? The Historic Consequences
     of Paternalism   29

  3. Neither Oppression nor Naturalism: Why the
     Prevailing Paradigms Distort the Present   46

  4. Gender in the Context of Community   67

Part II. Elaborations

  5. Gender, Justice, and the Justices   85

  6. Gender in the House of Policy   124

  7. Gender Policy and the Marketplace   140

  8. Gender Policy and the Forms of Family   173

Conclusion   202

Notes   206

Index   241

Acknowledgments

Some books seem to write themselves, the authors driven by a single and consuming idea. William Empson, for instance, is said to have finished *Seven Types of Ambiguity* in little more than a month. Others are endless years in the making before reaching the promised land of completion. That has been the case with this volume.

As students of public policy are fond of pointing out, the decision to ask a particular question often leads to a particular kind of answer. And, in a domain as capacious as gender justice, the right question to ask does not come engraved in stone. The senior authors began this study a decade ago, focusing on gender issues in primary and secondary education. But educational policy seemed a too narrow cut, one specific instance among many broader claims of substantial and consequential sex-based discrimination that deserved to be treated together. The draft we produced was a massive tome exploring many facets of the claim of discrimination. "Did discrimination explain the present state of men and women?" we asked. Our answer, predictably enough, was a weasel. "Yes, but." When the "buts" turned out to be more interesting than the "yesses," we reformulated the question, discarding a thousand pages of typescript in the process. The concern that animates this volume is a normative one—"What should be the aims of gender policy?"—and we rely on description not as an end in itself, but in the service of argument. In working through the particulars of this approach, we added a third contributor, Marlene Strong Franks.

A volume that has been so many years in the making acquires numerous debts along the way. A number of colleagues—among them Susan Appleton, Mary Jo Bane, Patricia Brown, Owen Fiss, Judith Gruber, Barbara Heyns, Douglas Laycock, Sanford Levinson, William Powers, Michael Sharlot, Ann Swidler, Elisabeth Hansot, Janet Flammang, Deborah Rhode, and Sanford Unger—have offered detailed appraisals. Gail Lapidus, who cotaught a 1980–81 seminar on gender policy at Berkeley, has been particularly giving of her time and energy. Such scrutiny does not, of course, imply agreement. It has made our argument clearer in presentation.

Graduate students at Berkeley and Texas have also had a hand in the enterprise. A gender justice seminar, taught intermittently at Berkeley since the mid-1970s, has yielded two articles and many more useful ideas. Andrea Altschuler, Deborah Bloch, Susanne Donovan, Janie Franks, Rosemarie Haffner, Martha Hardwick, and Eileen Soffer served as research assistants at various stages, helping us to locate and somehow to tame the masses of material. Marleen Fouche, Bette Francis, Alice Daniels, Cydney Hill, Alyce Lottman, Rannah Burns, Elisabeth Keyser, and Brian Harvey turned our scribbles into readable copy.

Gender Justice has been on the road, with portions presented in lectures delivered by David Kirp at Washington University School of Law, the University of Chicago Department of Public Policy, and the Murphy Institute of Political Economy at Tulane University. The responses to those presentations have also enabled us to sharpen particular elements of the argument.

We are especially grateful to the Russell Sage Foundation and to its president, Marshall Robinson. The foundation offered financial support at a critical stage; without that aid, the book would not have seen the light of day. The patience of the foundation's officers, their reliance on good cheer and sound counsel rather than on nudges and goads, has appreciably eased our task.

In the end, though, responsibility for the volume rests squarely on our shoulders. That is a familiar sentiment. But it is meant as more than the usual boilerplate prose, since writing about gender justice is an unavoidably personal enterprise. There is far more of the authors' personae in these pages than one might find in a book dealing with, say, microeconomics or the technics of bridge-building.

Introduction

What kind of world is this? What has happened to justice?
  Heinrich Böll, *Group Portrait with Lady* (1973)

When a subject is highly controversial—and any question about sex is
that—one cannot hope to tell the truth. One can only show how one came to
hold whatever opinion one does hold. One can only give one's audience the
chance of drawing their own conclusions as they observe the limitations, the
prejudices, the idiosyncracies of the speaker.
  Virginia Woolf, *A Room of One's Own* (1929)

Public policy and gender are tightly intertwined. Sometimes gender is what
policy is all about—laws relating to equal employment opportunity, for
example, or sexual preference or access to credit. But these, the obvious
cases, represent only the smallest part of the pertinent policy universe.
Because gender influences so many aspects of our lives, policies that ostensibly aren't about gender at all nonetheless have evident relevance. Day
care, for instance, while directed to the needs of children, creates options
for working parents. The availability of job training for heads of households receiving welfare—almost always women—affects women's possibilities for liberation in quite different ways. The income tax code, social
security, divorce and custody arrangements, health benefits, military conscription, housing policy, educational opportunities: each touches upon
gender, even if only lightly and inadvertently.

At all its levels and in all its branches, government is linked with gender. Congress considers abolishing sex-based differences in pension plans.
State legislatures debate the ramifications of a maternity leave law. The
United States Supreme Court weighs the permissibility of different minimum drinking ages for men and women. The Department of Education
gives substance to statutory proscriptions against discrimination in educa-

1

tion. Municipalities increase the wattage of city street lights to discourage would-be rapists. The policy debate often centers on consequential problems, but the question being considered sometimes seems trivial, as when the federal government ponders the acceptability of mother-daughter and father-son school functions or six-person women's basketball teams (as contrasted with five-person men's teams).

Only in the past decade have we become attentive to this dimension of policy. That newfound concern partly derives from a more general realization that policies connect, and that inexplicit and indirect effects are important: if government prepares paperwork impact and environmental impact statements, why not gender impact reports too? Gender has also become a hotly debated policy arena, for the disputes reflect sharply conflicting views of contemporary social mores. Attention to gender can be attributed, on the one side, to a heightened sensitivity to gender-based justice in all its nuances, brought about by the revival of feminism as a mainstream political movement.[1] With the discovery of the "gender gap"—the fact that women disagree with men not only about policies that affect them directly, such as abortion and child care, but also on such matters as the nuclear arms race and foreign policy—women are being taken seriously as an important political force.

On the other side, the New Right has excoriated government policies related to gender—most prominently, those concerning abortion and sex education—as undermining family values and social stability.[2] It was no coincidence that a task force appointed by President Reagan and charged with eliminating excessive regulation singled out rules about sexual harassment on the job—trivial items, really, in the paperwork jungle—as prime offenders. The campaign for the Equal Rights Amendment offered the occasion for pitched battle between the partisans; even with the failure of that campaign, the conflict will endure.

With such heightened attentiveness, one might assume that the meaning of gender-based justice has by now become clear, and that what remains is only a "struggle against archaisms,"[3] putting into practice what is known to be right in principle. Two thoughtful commentators, approaching gender-based justice from very different ideological perspectives, have insisted that this is the case. Sociologist Jessie Bernard, writing about equal employment opportunity, confidently claims that

> Job discrimination as an issue is by now old-hat and can be relegated
> to the more conventional reform-oriented women's organizations.
> The emphasis of movement women is on what they see as deeper,
> more revolutionary changes. They aim their attack on the subtler

rights denied them not by law or administrative rules, but by mores, custom, tradition, and convention.[4]

Public policy, as Bernard sees it, entails a mopping-up operation. Bernard denies that there exist significant disagreements concerning these matters. Factional disputes give way to a commonly held public interest capable of securing objectives that, having been won, no longer seem to matter; the newer and more exciting challenges reside elsewhere.

Midge Decter's dismissal of gender inequity as a source of substantial concern is more pointedly framed:

> No doubt women are far from having attained a full parity of opportunity. . . . These are issues of injustice that lend themselves not to the large-scale analyses of a liberation movement but to the particular and practical application of pressure against the wrongdoers. . . . [T]here is no disagreement as to what constitutes an injustice. . . with respect to issues bearing on the rights of women today.[5]

These propositions are tempting, in part because they sound like what might be said about race policy. Concerning race, the republic has made up its mind: what is wanted, in the long run, is a society in which race counts for naught in the public sphere of life. Should we not be similarly clear-headed with respect to sex? Moreover, a great deal of gender policy has been made, and one might well imagine that a common understanding of fairness concerning gender informs that policy.

The facts are otherwise. The profusion of policy masks an uncertain and problematic sense of what gender-based justice means. As so often happens, particular policies have been shaped in response to need, occasion, or the gentle application of suasion; there has been little concern with consistency or generalizability. Taking the proliferating legislation and court decisions as our guide, discrimination means one thing with respect to the military, and something quite different in the marketplace and schoolhouse. Traditional maternal responsibilities are here encouraged, there apparently penalized, again for no apparent reason.

These specific inconsistencies point to more general puzzles. Are policies that favor women, purportedly to overcome past disadvantage, such as quotas for jobs and schools, themselves discriminatory? How should an interest in sexual privacy be reconciled with a desire for equal treatment or with a moral concern for the sanctity of life? Is it acceptable to rely on sex-linked characteristics when these are based on demographic fact, not stereotype, and appear suited to the task at hand: using the different life expectancies of men and women to determine life insurance premiums and pension payments, for instance? (And does one's answer to that question depend upon whether reliance on the characteristic helps or harms women?) Varied resolutions of such issues dot the statute books. Taken together, they reveal that an underlying issue of principle—the meaning of gender-based justice in the sphere of public influence—remains unresolved, the bases for policy incoherent.

Each of these matters, as well as a great many other policy conundra, surfaces in these pages. But they arise by way of example, not detailed inspection, for this is not a book about educational opportunities, the Equal Rights Amendment, the conscription of women, or equal pay. Instead, our aim is to suggest a frame for thinking generically about the proper aims of policy and law, as these bear on gender.

We pose, as our central question, whether government should aspire to alter societal *outcomes,* as these vary by sex, or—very differently—to free up the *processes* by which individuals make life choices for themselves. This is an ambitious and problematic undertaking. Any serious discussion necessarily borrows from a host of conceptual lenses: on history, for some sense of the aims and impacts of past sex roles; on psychology and sociology, for an understanding of how individuals act on their own and as members of groups; on politics, as a test of feasibility; on economics, to discern the marketplace implications of gender policy approaches; on philosophy, for normative benchmarks; on biology, for hints concerning the limits of human malleability; and more, including importantly our own common sense.

Some preliminary disclaimers are in order. The inquiry does not purport to make pathbreaking contributions to philosophy or history, but instead draws on these and other domains with the ambition of better understanding what good policy and law might look like. It is necessarily selective, for our aim is to test an argument and not to produce an encyclopedia; along the way, some matters of substantive importance undoubtedly receive short shrift. The argument does not take shape in neat sequence, rising like the floors of a building, but rather presents particular and partial perspectives of the whole. The frustrating thing about this approach is that, logically, everything should come first. In a discussion that ranges in level of generality from statements about the nature of the society to illustrative specification of sensible day care and tax policy, from ruminations about the aims of the law to pointed critiques of particular court decisions, questions and puzzles necessarily remain. Short of writing many more books, we cannot hope to be complete.

The book has two parts: Conceptualizations and Elaborations. Part I lays out the framework of the argument for equal liberty as a benchmark of gender policy, presents an historical overview of the treatment of women, examines the paradigms presently in use by thinkers of the Left and Right, and finally considers the place of community in an approach centered on individual choice. Part II descends to particulars. First we examine the implicit framework the Supreme Court has used in its gender cases, and illustrate that the liberty-based framework has more coherent results. We then outline the framework for policy making and take up specific topics in the realms of the workplace and the family.

The two parts of the book inform each other: part I is not a theoretical tract but an attempt to fashion a consistent framework grounded in real problems; part II examines selected cases in the light of that framework. Throughout the book, we take up controversial topics over which the partisans are eager to do battle. Words become chameleons in such a context, changing their meaning; or tigers, ready to assault the unwitting passerby. It is easy to be misunderstood in these circumstances, particularly when one's perspective cannot comfortably be assimilated into the conventional categories. Our aim is to shift somewhat those categories of thought, inviting a new look at a venerable issue.

I

Conceptualizations

1

Choice and Justice

People have tirelessly sought to prove that woman is superior, inferior, and equal to man. . . . If we are to gain understanding, we must get out of these ruts; we must discard vague notions of superiority, inferiority, equality which have hitherto corrupted every discussion on the subject and start afresh.
Simone de Beauvoir, *The Second Sex* (1952)

Very dangerous things, theories.
Dorothy Sayers, *The Unpleasantness at the Bellona Club* (1926)

I

What does justice in the realm of gender imply about the shape of public policy? We begin unravelling the strands of that question with a not-so-farfetched story, for stories have a way of making arguments come to life.

Slightly before once upon a time, in the state of Civitas, all workers labored at one of three occupations: they were butchers, bakers, or candlestick makers. The details of this economy, how Civitas developed such specialization and the like, need not detain us. What is relevant for our concerns is that, though all citizens above the age of sixteen were employed, the proportion of men and women who busied themselves at particular tasks varied widely. Nine out of every ten butchers in Civitas were men. The bakers were equally divided between the sexes (though some said that women concentrated on such chores as fancy-topping making). Just one candlestick maker in ten was a man.

No one paid much attention to these differences—indeed, no one was really aware of them—until a survey published by Civitas State University converted guesses into data. Reaction to the findings was strong and varied. One group, the Levellers, read the evidence as confirming the abiding sexism of Civitas. "Justice requires that men and women divide themselves equally among the occupations," they opined. "So long as differences remain, discrimination will spring up; in these matters, men and women should be as alike as peas in a pod." If this equal division didn't happen naturally, the Levellers said, government should step in and order it.

The Naturalists saw matters very differently. "This variation," they announced, "is in the nature of things." Although no one in Civitas knew about genes, the Naturalists purported to understand God's will. "Men were made to slaughter, even as women turn base metal into things of beauty," they thundered. "Justice means leaving well enough alone."

A third group, the Liberals, had no fixed conclusions but only questions. "How did this distribution of occupations come to pass?" they wondered aloud. "Are men and women making real choices based on their own life needs and circumstances? If so, those preferences deserve to be honored, for there is no 'right percentage' of male bakers or female butchers in all times and places. Or have pesky prejudices and powerful pressures effectively forced men and women into the jobs they now hold? If that's the case, justice demands that government intervene to remove these barriers to choice."

How do we go about choosing among these alternative conceptions of just policy, both generally and in the specific context of gender? Whatever the particulars, any policy approach may be conceived as accomplishing one of two goals: specifying a particular outcome, a desirable state of affairs, or mandating procedures that enable people to make decisions for themselves.

These two approaches carry with them different assumptions about what we know to be good. Requiring a particular result affirms that the outcome is desirable, even as prohibiting some activity affirms the opposite. Such declarations require agreement that the outcome is a good one. As a society, we value healthy workers and despise murder, and these values find a home in our laws. The mandated results are often less than absolute, as when government calls upon polluters to take all reasonably feasible steps to purify the environment, rather than taking a costs-be-damned approach. They are also fixed by political compromise, as when government determines how tightly to weave the social safety net in the light of available revenues and competing needs. In each instance, though, whether through consensus or compromise, we decide upon a good outcome, a desirable result.

With regard to other issues, however, the proper outcome is not so clear. What we care most about is the process, not the result. Our criminal justice system is premised on fair assessment of guilt or innocence. Our schools reward those who can pass impartial tests, not those who present pedigrees. A well-functioning market is indifferent to whether one is a congressman or a cab driver, as long as the individual's credit reference checks out. In these instances, the outcomes of transactions are not given in advance, but left to the processes of the institutions. There is no best result, no standard to predict who will be Fiat owners or who convicted felons.

The two approaches, process- and outcome-oriented, make different assumptions about the characteristics of those who are subject to the policy. In setting the engine of process in motion, as in the paradigm case of the marketplace, we imagine rational individuals who pursue their self-interest and posit that such personal calculations benefit society generally. Market mechanisms rely on particular expressions of preference, and the market aggregates individual preferences differently from political processes that rely on one person/one vote weightings. Other processes assume other things: that students will not cheat on tests, that jurors and judges will fairly evaluate the evidence, that drivers will obey traffic signals. The common assumption is that individuals are capable of reasoned and consistent choice—or at least more capable than those who would act on their behalf.

A result-oriented policy, on the other hand, acknowledges that individuals will not arrive at the desired outcome without prod or push. Sometimes it is technically too hard to devise a procedure that produces the hoped-for results, as when people are too dispersed to negotiate or lack needed facts. At other times, people will systematically spend too little on such "public goods" as police protection or public schooling, knowing that they will benefit when others take up the slack.[1] In these instances, procedural approaches are unavailing. If there is to be policy, the collectivity has to determine the good outcome and find a way of mandating it.

Any rule aimed at securing a particular result rejects all the alternatives, and that causes problems. To be sure, there are times when the society is very sure about the result that it wants to reach: when the desired outcome is empirically fixed, as when parents are required to feed their children who otherwise would starve, or when basic moral values are being expressed, as when assault is prohibited. But when a rule rests on a shaky consensus or has weak factual supports, different and maybe better possibilities are denied without good reason.

As the story of Civitas suggests, the idea of justice in the domain of gender may be understood either in terms of process or result. The result-oriented approach specifies the attributes of a good society as these relate to gender, and proposes rules aimed at bringing about that good society. This conception presupposes that the collectivity knows what it wants concerning relations between the sexes and, more broadly, the relevance of gender in our public lives; it conceives of government action as spiriting us away from a flawed present to a substantively happier future.

Since no wise philosopher lives among us to chisel the proper roles of the sexes onto stone tablets, those who take such an outcome-oriented view of gender justice hold conceptions of the good society at least as varied as those prevalent in Civitas. Some claim that gender should be socially irrelevant; their antagonists maintain that the profound differences between males and females rightly and inexorably reassert themselves in law and custom. Yet whatever the details of their position, the partisans are united in identifying justice with a specific result.[2]

The contrary approach, process-oriented in character, attends less to what the society becomes than to how we arrive there. It focuses primarily on how individuals exercise choice and the limits imposed on choosing. In this view, rules are needed to purge procedures of all unnecessary impediments, leaving individuals as free as possible to determine for themselves the relevance of gender. Choice itself, not some specified social arrangement, becomes the yardstick of goodness.[3] The outcome-oriented approach imposes a particular conception of justice on the polity, while the procedural alternative encourages individuals to vote with their feet.

We are not neutral in these matters. Our aim is to elaborate the argument for comprehending gender justice primarily in procedural, not substantive, terms. In our view, justice means enhancing choice for individuals, securing fair process rather than particular outcomes for the community. By opting for process over outcome, we value self-determination over collective determinations of sex roles.

The reality of social policy is, of course, more complex than this simple statement suggests. Competing concerns—among them the recognition of other liberties, an interest in efficiency, attention to the equity-rooted claims of those least well-off, a desire to foster forms of community, the press of politics—have a way of messing up neat formulas. Life is murkier than art—or intellectual models. These concerns can be smuggled in on an ad hoc basis and relabelled as liberty, but we prefer to be more direct, to complicate the tale where necessary by indicating how choices among these concerns might best be made, while still paying deference to the values of liberty.

The preference for individual decision in matters trenching on gender remains our touchstone. We begin with the philosophical underpinnings of this liberal position, the understanding of human beings as distinguishable from other species by their capacity for autonomous action, and the commitment to liberty as a way of honoring this core human trait. Traversing this sometimes swampy terrain lays the groundwork for the more spirited debates about gender justice between the radical feminists and naturalists.

II

People differ from one another in all sorts of ways, "in temperament, interests, intellectual ability, aspirations, natural bent, spiritual quests, and the kind of life they wish to lead."[4] But what makes humans fundamentally alike, and sets us apart from animals, is our ability to follow our "own law," the literal meaning of autonomy. Human beings define goals and move toward them; we write our own scripts and act them out. Rather than following the dictates of instinct, we self-consciously choose how we will live, thus reigning, in Kant's memorable phrase, as sovereigns in the kingdom of ends.[5] Our autonomy affords us "the capacity for second-order, independent judgment and choice. . . . One paints one's own idea of the good life, self-critically deciding, as a free and rational being, which of one's first order desires will be developed and which disowned, which capacities cultivated and which left fallow, . . . and what goals to strive toward. The development of this capacity for individual choice is central to becoming a person."[6]

This assertion makes a profession of faith, for there is no proof that *only* humans act autonomously or that *all* humans do so. To believe that people but not dolphins cultivate their capacities or strive for self-fulfillment may be to slip into the trap of anthropocentrism, regarding man as the premeditated aim of the creation of the earth. At the least, the proposition of human uniqueness is not readily tested, for the calipers that would enable us to probe the psyches of dolphins are not at hand. All we can say is that the proposition comports with a widely held view of the world.

If one credits the notion that everyone—or everyone *else*—resembles the Stepford wives, cleverly disguised machines controlled from a central source, then one can be persuaded that humans are not autonomous. Yet the opposite assertion is hardly outrageous. Our laws hold individuals responsible for their own actions, except under unusual circumstances; so too do our widely shared moral norms. This is not to say that humans consciously govern themselves at every moment. We often opt to do things because they are habitual or because they are mandated by an institution whose authority we have accepted. It is the *capacity* for choice that is crucial.

Each person ultimately affirms either determinism or autonomy according to the beliefs held about himself or herself, since "proof" is not to be had. To accept determinism is to abandon the quest for good rules altogether, for if the mechanism of decision is in someone else's hands, the laws we impose on ourselves are meaningless. The assertion that people are autonomous rests on our preference for believing that we endow our actions with significance. We sense our own autonomy and consequently affirm it in others.

The assumption of autonomy needs to be qualified for those incapable of acting responsibly on their own behalf, either because of age or mental deficiency.[7] But the idea of autonomy will admit of no distinctions between men and women. Although the point seems intuitively obvious when stated so boldly, some present policies treat one sex or the other as having a lesser capacity for choice, and this falls just one step short of treating them as inferior members of the species.

III

How autonomous beings might best be organized into a society is an ancient philosophical problem.[8] If all persons have the capacity to govern themselves, then they are capable of choosing their own life plans; but if they possess that capacity, what is the use of government? Because the wishes of some collide with those of others, government needs, at the least, to make rules that shape public interactions. "All that makes existence valuable to anyone," John Stuart Mill wrote over a century ago, "depends on the enforcement of restraints upon the actions of other people."[9]

What principles should undergird these laws? We argue that government should interfere as little as possible with individual choice, and that any laws imposed on the society should be imposed on all, regardless of caste or class. Although this liberal position carries an impressive philosophical pedigree—Kant tells us to treat people as ends, not means; Rawls asks us to don a veil of ignorance in designing rules for the society[10]—

there are, of course, other and more interventionist conceptions of the state that value individual liberty less. The preference for a government that fosters individual liberty needs to be appreciated, not as the logical consequence of our perception of humans as autonomous, but rather as a second leap of faith.

Autonomy states a claim of potential individual power, but what is to be made of that power? Edmund Burke once remarked that "if the effect of liberty to individuals is, that they may do what they please, we ought to see what it will please them to do, before we risk congratulations."[11] To those who believe that leaving individuals to their own devices invites anarchy or who share Plato's dour view that registering individual preferences in a democracy leads to tyranny, the reality of human autonomy is cause for concern—and government check—not celebration. The justifications for constraint are many, and include promoting greater equality of result, protecting individuals from their own stupidities, advancing the collective welfare, and nurturing the innocent young.

The form and persuasiveness of these rationales depend on the circumstances in which they are advanced. No single, simple value fixing the limits of liberty seems plausible; and when philosophers claim otherwise, they overreach themselves. We are skeptical about philosophical schema that purport to derive the primary importance of liberty from supposedly neutral principles or simplified social orders. Such devices as the reasoned dialogue, the original position, the social contract, or the state of nature, such conceptions of human beings as bundles of aggressive drives or unalienated labor, would seem more persuasive if they did not regularly turn up enlightened Englishmen, laissez-faire capitalists, socialists, libertarians, or whomever the philosophical model-builder had it in mind to praise.[12] The real world is more disorderly than these schema admit.

Our own commitment to liberty is less universalist in its derivation.[13] Liberty offers a plausible account of what gives human life meaning and significance, with roots in our own cultural and political traditions. It finds its expression in the statements defining our nation's mission: the Declaration of Independence, with its paean to life, liberty, and the pursuit of happiness; and the Bill of Rights of the Constitution, with its guarantees of free exercise of religion, freedom of speech, and protections against state deprivations of life, liberty, or property. Liberty conforms to widely held notions about the fitting relationship between government and the governed. It values tolerance and diversity of life choices; this holds particular appeal in light of fundamental disagreements about the meaning of the good life. Most pragmatically, liberty seems preferable to the alternative of collectivism in its various guises. Respect for individual choice, however mysterious its origins, is a necessary condition of social justice.

In a just society that accepts the primacy of autonomy, governmental interference in people's lives is constrained, both in the kinds of laws that may be imposed and the form of that imposition. "The sole end for which mankind are warranted, individually or collectively, in interfering with the liberty of action of any of their number, is self-protection," John Stuart Mill writes. "The only purpose for which power can be rightfully exercised over any member of a civilized community, against his will, is to prevent harm to others."[14] Mill asserts that because all other rules treat the individual will as properly subservient to the majority wish, they deny persons the liberty to which they are entitled. This view is upheld in our century by philosopher Robert Nozick, who maintains that the only legitimate role of the state is to protect property and persons.[15] Others who share a commitment to liberty will embrace a broader role for government. They will acknowledge the need for protection from without as well as protection within, for instance, and add other circumstances warranting the exercise of state power, such as fixing the grossest imperfections of the marketplace or redistributing basic goods.[16] Despite such differences, these substantive formulations have a common purpose: to insure that government does only what is necessary, remaining respectful of the liberty of individuals.

That persons should be "free from" interference with their lives is the fundamental liberal principle.[17] But all impositions are not equally offensive—thus are liberals distinguished from libertarians. A law that prohibits driving down the middle of the road is of a different order of magnitude from one that restricts who may enter certain professions. The former constrains liberty only a little, with large benefits for the smooth running of society; the latter profoundly affects lives. Most laws that involve gender concern fundamental life choices, because gender is such an important facet of our selves. This is why rules that treat the sexes differently deserve such careful scrutiny: it is almost certain that the government is discounting or delimiting the autonomy that enables persons to make important life choices for themselves.

IV

The claim that gender justice demands respect for the choices of men and women cannot be fully understood without considering the private and public spheres in which individuals lead their lives.[18] The public sphere is the world of political and economic affairs, the private sphere refers to relationships in which personal satisfactions or interests, not the public good, are determinative. The private sphere is one of sexual intimacy, procreation, and childrearing, informed by affection, trust, privacy, and responsibility. In the public sphere, we are individuals sharing a "collective space" that sustains commercial transactions and political interchange, a world where the "infinitely varied interests" of men and women are served.[19] We have rights and responsibilities to the commonwealth; our relations with others are typically formal, conducted at arm's length, dominated by norms of public law. If in the private sphere we are lovers, brothers, mothers, in public life we are citizens, entrepreneurs, consumers, taxpayers. Our "essential" natures matter less in the public world, where we deserve to be treated as rational persons capable of reflective choices about our lives.

The boundary between public and private is blurred, with each domain impinging on the other. Childrearing is generally lodged in the private sphere, but children become a public concern if they are abandoned, neglected, or abused; certain vital aspects of childrearing, such as education, are routinely entrusted to the state. Contracts or formal voting, characteristic of the public sphere, are not unknown in families. Feelings of loyalty, obligation, or sentimental attachment are not confined to one's intimate relationships but are also felt in commitments to larger communities, whether the company, church, union, club, or nation.[20]

A new conception of politics often embodies an innovative effort to redraw the boundaries between public and private. Economic determinism, whether Marxist or laissez-faire, may be conceived as redefining politics in the light of a newly grasped relationship between politics and production. Feminist thinkers extend the public sphere into the private by speaking of the family in the essentially political terms of oppression and inequality; or, conversely, they expand the private sphere into the public, proposing to humanize politics by making it more compassionate.

Despite this fuzziness, fundamental differences between the public and private sphere can be specified. In the public realm, there is little agreement on transcendental values; reason is defined objectively, in terms of the fit between means and loosely specified ends. The private household tends to engage in subjective reasoning. Its ends are those of love, trust, obligation, and moral duty. The public world is more instrumental in character and settles disputes in formal ways, while fair procedures are valued less in the private sphere, where the legitimacy of the household's authority is more likely taken for granted. The public sector turns out goods and services. The contemporary household, rarely engaged in significant material production, produces instead an enclave of intimacy in a world increasingly driven by the ethos of the polity and the market.[21]

Because the private and public spheres are governed by different values, they allow different weightings of the salience of gender. Our commitment to liberalism evokes the expectation that the political, economic, and social systems respect our personal life plans. The market allows each of us to register our preferences without regard to our identity as a man or woman, while universal suffrage is a formal affirmation of our political indistinguishability. Although these arrangements do not function perfectly, we are moving closer to this public ideal. In our private lives, by contrast, sexual identities matter greatly—and rightly so. Two individuals who decide to form an intimate household are not indifferent to each other's sex, for sex bears on one's sense of the physical attractiveness, personality, and emotional competency of the other person. In the liberal ideal, we are properly indifferent to the gender of a candidate for public office. Would anyone ignore the sex of a lover?

The two domains have historically had very different significance for men and women. Men's lives have traditionally been rooted in the public sphere, women's lives centered in the private, with women assuming more of the responsibility for childrearing, emotional nurturance, and housework. While this pattern has not prevented some women from pursuing careers, the competing demands of the two spheres, coupled with women's hegemony in the household, has often led them to adjust their public roles to make them more consistent with their private responsibilities. These adjustments—compromises, if you will—have almost invariably constricted women's freedom in the public domain. For instance, women have been more likely than men to choose careers that have limited prospects for advancement but permit part-time work or allow easy reentry after time off for childrearing. Conversely, men have typically looked to the public sphere for most of their satisfactions. They have traditionally pursued the highest-paying and most prestigious jobs, even if this left them with little energy for household concerns.

The private and the public orders, though governed by different values, shape one another in many ways. The private universe carries primary responsibility for initiating the younger generation into the culture, transmitting values, and preparing the young to assume moral responsibility. To a great extent, our identity as females and males finds its source in the social definition that occurs in the private sphere. If there is a form of liberty associated with individuals in the private domain, it is an affirmative liberty, designed to give children the knowledge and ability to make future life choices.[22] The family may be the ultimate welfare state, granting to each according to his or her needs.

Identities formed in the household carry over into the public arena. If the household fails, the polity may fail. If the household has a sexist or racist bent to it, so may the public sphere. If the household grows less important because men and women devote more of their energies to the public sphere, turning childrearing and even intimacy over to public institutions or the marketplace, we may all be losers. We will have denied ourselves an enclave of affection and caring, and children may reach adulthood ill-prepared to exercise the responsibilities of liberty. Yet even as the private sphere treats individuals as males and females, fathers and mothers, sons and daughters—indeed, it gives meaning and understanding to those identifications—liberal values require that we pay little attention to such characteristics in the public arena.

The commitment to gender-neutral liberty in the public sphere, coupled with the importance of gender in the private sphere, evokes ambivalence, resentment, and personal strain. Because conceptions of the private and public roles of men and women are evolving, these tensions are exacerbated, since the greater the range of options in the two spheres, the more difficult choice becomes. And the reality of choice may also breed unhappiness. The formerly happy housewife may grow discontented because she comprehends new possibilities in the world beyond the family; the career-oriented man may regret his failure to devote more time to his children.[23] With roles in flux, there is also a greater chance of disagreement between men and women as they fix the terms of intimate relationships. Unless each is more accommodating of the other's preferences, unhappiness or dissolution of the relationship is predictable, as the increased divorce rates of the past several decades attest.

This discussion of public and private domains is not a plea to reset the clock of human affairs. It merely points to the abiding and basic tension between the personalistic values of the private sphere and the quest for liberty and equality in the public sphere. Policy cannot ignore private family forms without being radically incomplete, but neither should it aspire to undo the differences between public and private.

This is hardly noncontroversial, for the family is often the target of activist intervention from both ends of the political perspective. From the vantage of the Left, the allure of policies aimed at undoing the influence of the family is understandable, since the family is a conservative institution.[24] The perceptions that men and women have of themselves and each other, their sense of what choices are appropriate for their sex, their attitudes toward procreation and childrearing, their beliefs as to what life choices are possible—all partly derived from experience in the family—powerfully determine the public and private behavior of both sexes. To the extent that these attitudes perpetuate the conventional, repealing sexist laws and policing marketplace discrimination will not suffice as effective counters. Only the most radical intervention in the private sphere, disregarding expressed personal preferences and the need for intimacy and privacy, can promise "true" liberty. Or so Simone de Beauvoir has insisted: "No women should be authorized to stay home to raise her children. Society should be totally different. Women should not have that choice, precisely because *if there is such a choice, too many women will make that one.* It is a way of forcing women in a certain direction."[25]

"Forcing them to be free" describes the blueprint for a New Jerusalem that is totalitarian and alienating, not liberating. It also offers an improbable scenario, since such a policy would necessitate radical alterations in our most basic behavior, and men and women are unlikely to revolt against themselves. Moreover, it is unnecessary, as the private sphere is growing less parochial, for reasons having relatively little to do with official coercion. The cause of change resides instead in countless personal decisions affecting intimate others; it is rooted in individuals' efforts to persuade one another to rethink their lives, in a dialogue that deepens their understanding of themselves as communal beings, even as it asserts their individuality and capacity for autonomy.

The Right's celebration of the conventional family is as misguided as the Left's assault, since convention does not offer the only measure of intimate union. There is no need for the state to try maintaining familiar private orderings in all their particularity, for beyond the most basic acts of mothering, no logic compels one sex or the other to assume particular household tasks or job assignments.[26] Nor can only the conventional family satisfy felt needs for intimacy, childrearing, support of dependents, security, and trust. Rules about private lives generally should uphold the forms of personal relationship that people choose as worthy of support, without assigning persons to roles according to gender, since raising children involves love, discipline, and caring, qualities that are not the province of either sex. Neighborhoods, churches, and clubs are all important parts of our lives, and they will continue to be so, no matter what the sex of the members. Premising relationships on preconceived notions of the roles of men and women renders them stifling rather than supportive.

V

Treating liberty as the preeminent value does not ensure that justice will follow as night follows day. No account could afford to be so simple-minded, but there is a kernel of truth here. What is seen as gender injustice has less to do with the different statuses of men and women in our society than with how those statuses came into being. The idea that women are men's equals in the public realm was slow to be popularly accepted; the conception of women as less than whole beings spawned laws that assumed women could not decide for themselves how to live.[27] Women were excluded from the rigors of the public realm because they were viewed as fragile, in need of protection; in turn, men were regarded as invariably capable of and destined for responsibility as protectors. That some women and some men would not select these roles, given a choice, is the new idea that has entered the public consciousness.

Simply to affirm the liberty of individuals sets us on the road to the just society, although it will not get us there. In a just world, we would not only remove barriers but also give support, for liberty has no appeal when it promises only the freedom to starve. Assuring the basics of life is not antithetical to liberty but rather completes it in a way not comprehended by classical liberal thinking. To leave people entirely to their own devices offers no respect for individuals in a world where the distribution of resources often results from luck, historical accident, family inheritance, or injustice. In deciding what level of help should be universally available in a society, a just outcome would take into account both the available resources and the benefits that any person would request, not knowing whether he or she would ever need to ask government for that minimum level of support. These things cannot be established from first principles, because they depend on the situation at hand; in this country, basic levels of education and income support are determined through the political process.[28]

Coupling basic minimums with governmental non-interference will not remove all barriers to choice, since people will still be powerfully influenced by their upbringing, religion, class, race, or even the region of the country in which they reside.[29] Private lives count—quite properly. Public policies should not aim at undoing the differences between people but rather at allowing them to rise from a certain guaranteed floor of support, leaving the distance they go to their own interests and inclinations. Individuals can usually best decide what is in their best interests, because they are the ones with the greatest incentives to weigh highly personalized costs and benefits. Non-interference will not ensure a just society, nor will provision of basic support, but the lack of either will almost certainly guarantee injustice. When men and women are given the opportunity and the capacity to choose, then justice is possible.

This is not to say that people must proceed alone and in a vacuum. We rightly try to persuade other people of the folly of their ways but we must acknowledge their right to choose. Imposition itself is the bad, not the particulars of what is being imposed. To insist, for instance, that a world where some women stay in their homes and raise children is an unjust world implies that those women have made the wrong choice. Yet if the decisions were reached when women had realistic opportunities to pursue other careers, on what moral basis can anyone stand outside as judge, condemning the mothers for their decision? To remove individuals from an historic era when one's gender stood as a proxy for one's proper role in life, only to impose on them a regime in which one's gender becomes a reason to discard those roles merely reflects a tyranny of the new, a form of stereotyping as debilitating to autonomy as the earlier conventions.[30]

Honoring individual choice ultimately enables the individual to define his or her own identity in one of its most fundamental aspects. The premise is not that individuals will choose well, by some objective external criterion, for we do not know what "well" means in this sense. Individuals will act in what they regard as their own best interests, and that seems justification enough.

This view is congenial to the understanding of humans that underlies welfare economics, with its stress on encouraging the efficient allocation of goods through individual action. It's more sensible to let individuals advance their own cause through private exchanges than to impose some external standard of "better off," the economist argues. It is assumed that individual actions based on preferences will lead ultimately to efficient solutions: individuals are considered capable of bargaining with one another, and because what is required to be better off is a matter of personal preference, such bargains are thought generally to be better than those imposed from without.[31] The efficiency calculation treats society's interest as the aggregate of informed self-interest, not as a collective will. That assumption closely accords with Mill's view that "the interest which society has in [the individual] is fractional and altogether indirect, while with respect to his own feelings and circumstances the most ordinary man or woman has means of knowledge immeasurably surpassing those that can be possessed by anyone else."[32]

Economists cannot explain *why* individuals act. They posit that decisions always entail rational calculation but this need not be so. Rationality is not the issue; self-interest is, as Dostoevsky's Underground Man says:

> Man everywhere, and at all times, whoever he may be, has preferred to act as he chose and not in the least as his reason and advantage dictated. And one may choose what is contrary to one's own interest, and sometimes one *positively ought* (that is my idea). One's own free unfettered choice, one's own caprice—however wild it may be one's own fancy worked up at times to frenzy—is that very "most advantageous advantage" which we have overlooked, which comes under no classification and against which all systems and theories are continually being shattered to atoms. And how do these wiseacres know that man wants a normal, a virtuous choice? And what has made them conceive that man must want a rationally advantageous choice? What man wants is simply *independent* choice, whatever that independence may cost and wherever it may lead. And choice, of course, the devil only knows what choice. . . .[33]

Independent individual choice, even when coupled with basic minimums, does not necessarily lead to happiness. As John Kenneth Galbraith has pointed out, "the notion of happiness lacks philosophical exactitude; there is agreement neither on its substance nor its source."[34] At the least, however, happiness depends on a sense of living a life in accordance with a plan, of moving toward some goal. In the just society premised on choice, there is nothing to keep people from choosing unsuitable goals or mistaking the proper path toward a goal. Processes can be opened up, stereotypes banished, support extended, but felicity cannot be guaranteed.

VI

In contrast to a process-oriented society, where liberty and autonomy are the underlying values, a result-oriented society deliberately defines the good life for its members. Policy then assumes form in the context of this vision of the good; the future must be carefully crafted, not allowed to evolve out of the happenstance of individual choice.

The clearer is our sense of the good future society, the clearer can we be about how to act today in order to attain the desired tomorrow. At the extreme, when all that is desirable has been detailed, no further changes are called for; we behave as we have in the past and will in the future. Utopian visions from Plato to B. F. Skinner have this in common. The imagined societies, whose inhabitants lead planned and predictable lives, are essentially fixed and unchanging. There is no dynamic, no impetus to learn from experience.[35] The utopianist's task is not to determine what we will become—that is given—but how we will reach that objective, how we will manage utopia in its particulars. While implementation is not a mechanical task, it is very different from choosing among competing aims and ends.

If there is concurrence about a society's aspirations, the importance of volition is diminished, for the exercise of individual liberty matters less than achieving the desired collective end. If, for example, it is felt that the good future society is one in which all adult members vote and work and all children are educated, the primary aim of policy will be to bring about these results. The collectivity might wish to do this in a manner that enhanced volition or diminished coercion—assuming that families would educate their children and that adults would work voluntarily, undertaking no collective intervention until that assumption proved wrong—but it need not do so. If constricting choice is essential to achieving the desired end and if the society holds fixed views about what is desirable, choices will indeed be constricted.

Our society values some results so much that coercive measures are deemed necessary: criminals are jailed to produce a safe society, children schooled in order to produce an educated society, and so forth. With respect to the relevance of gender to the good society, however, no shared vision obtains; the public is deeply riven, as are its elected representatives. Nor can philosophers, who search for normative principles to guide their discussions, agree on the proper role of gender. Reasoned defenses of very different end-states abound, but clarity is not to be found.

Philosopher Richard Wasserstrom, who explicitly relies on the concept of the good future society as a way of assessing present policy, suggests that such a society would embody "the assimilationist ideal," with sex assuming no greater importance than eye color and all role-differentiated behavior somehow having been undone. Wasserstrom initially develops this ideal in the context of race, where he entertains no real doubts about its appropriateness. With respect to sex, however, he is less confident. The assimilationist ideal, if implemented, would require "profound and fundamental revisions of our institutions and our attitudes": it is, in other words, far from consensually held. Of itself, that poses no necessary objection; nor is the fact that "the assimilationist ideal would require the eradication of all sex-role differentiation" reason to reject it in theory.[36] If the idea has sufficient normative allure, such dislocations may be justified.

At this point in the argument, Wasserstrom confesses puzzlement. It may be, he suggests, that a more open-ended and pluralist position, premised either on the positive appeal of diversity or the importance of tolerating differentness, makes better sense. And there are additional possibilities:

> Some persons might think the right ideal was one in which substantially greater sexual differentiation and sex-role identification was retained than would be the case under either [an assimilationist or pluralist model]. Thus, someone might believe that the good society was, perhaps, essentially like the one they think we now have in respect to sex: equality of political rights, such as the right to vote, but all of the sexual differentiation in both legal and non-legal institutions that is characteristic of the way in which our society has been and still is ordered.[37]

Elizabeth Wolgast assays a complex understanding of gender justice, one that regards identity of treatment as at best a partial goal.[38] Her approach distinguishes among spheres of human activity,[39] suggesting that abiding differences between the sexes necessitate differing policies for family and child care, employment opportunities, and support during old age.

Wolgast differentiates the public and private aspects of our lives. The concept of rights, she argues, although relevant in the public domain, ill suits the family, where relations cannot be comprehended as ties among peers. In these respects, Wolgast's approach parallels our own, but the points of divergence are at least as noteworthy. Wolgast relies heavily on primate studies and biological findings to assert natural differences between males and females. Although she recognizes that these differences do not necessarily dictate sex roles, for society may opt to emphasize or minimize the salience of the biological inheritance, they do matter. Because women approach the world differently from men, Wolgast asserts, affirmative action is needed to assure that women are involved in "the full spectrum of decisions that affect men and women both."[40]

The leap from biology to policy through an endorsement of affirmative action is great indeed, and there is little attempt to provide an analytic basis for the jump. Even less supported is the claim that "the perspective of one sex cannot be relied on, in general, to represent the concerns of the other." Wolgast begins with the undoubted differences between men and women in procreation, turns to more questionable evidence for a broad array of biological differences, and emerges with a conception of justice that reflects the differentness of women as akin to the claims of "the lame or blind or retarded." Along the way, the claims of persons become less salient; the philosopher becomes a lawyer, writing a brief for women as women. "The wife and homemaker will need some special provisions for her old age; the career women will not need these, but will need equal rights with respect to work. The woman who pursues a part-time career will need both kinds of rights less urgently."[41] Are these not more usefully understood as needs of individuals, male *or* female, who find themselves maintaining a home or working part-time?

Other philosophers introduce different points of view. Alison Jaggar would treat the ideal of "equality between the sexes" as signifying a world in which there exists "no institutional recognition of sex differences,"[42] while Christine Garside holds this position to be impossible in the face of the "inescapable and important fact" of one's sex. "Women will always be different from men as the result of self-determination, because we differ in physical structure, we differ in our present social experience, we differ in our inherited past and so on."[43] Too much distinguishes men and women, argues Garside, for gender ever to be irrelevant. Not so, responds Jaggar, who believes that the past can be overcome, the present remade, a course of action that she regards as only possible but also proper, for distinctly female cultures are not worth preserving in isolation.

This brief foray into contemporary philosophy reveals deep fissures among those who take an avowedly principled approach to gender. Competing visions of good society reflect basic differences concerning what people believe and how they behave; if these shift over time, an ideal end-state becomes impossible to define. Certain matters now mired in controversy may become sufficiently clear to serve as the basis for new substantive policy, either because they are empirically proven or command moral consensus: paying people equally for equal work regardless of their sex, once a heresy, now seems inevitable and right. Individuals speak out or vote with their feet, and those acts translate into collective action.

Society is likely to remain puzzled and divided about basic matters of gender policy, however, since even as today's confusions are resolved, new unknowns arise. It is this circumstance, not just a situation in which the future is unknown but one in which unknowability is a constituent element, that renders individual choice so vital. Concentrating on processes, rather than imposing some unknown and unknowable collective preference, allows society to evolve and enables individuals to continue to transform themselves. Unpredictability and self-transformation: these, taken together, are not just artifacts of our time but represent desirable human traits on which a policy of relying on individual volition can be grounded.

VII

Our aim is a public world where one's sex counts for little. Each person deserves respect for his or her autonomy, and any limits placed on liberty should not reflect the insulting judgment that one sex is less capable of acting autonomously than the other. Liberty is our aspiration but it need not become our fetish. Our commitment to the need for intimacy, privacy, and other values of the private sphere prompts us to propose subordinating gender neutrality on occasion in order to protect our sexually defined selves. These are exceptional occasions, though; and the fewer the exceptions, the more confident the society can be in its successful pursuit of gender justice.

The conception of the good society that we propose makes no claim that some choices are morally more worthy than others and should therefore be induced or coerced. We reject arguments for restoring a natural order, an epoch of "vernacular gender" in which women and men occupy separate spheres, for we find no principled basis for imposing such constraints.[44] We also reject the notion that justice demands that the distribution of life outcomes be identical across sexual lines. The ranks of the butchers may never be half-filled by women, here or in Civitas, and men may remain the primary wage-earners in two-parent families. Or things may turn out differently.

If we believed that discrimination chiefly caused these variations, our position would be different. Yet the evidence reviewed in part II of the book leads us to conclude that variations between the sexes are attributable, not just to noxious discrimination, but also to factors such as personal taste and voluntary obligations that policy has no business disturbing. Policy can hope to enhance individuals' opportunity and capacity to formulate life plans in accordance with their own notion of the good, regardless of gender. But policy will not necessarily revolutionize the way things work. Institutions will remain what people, acting together, make them.

What is essential is that people be empowered to choose how to spend their lives, defining themselves in the process. We uphold volition as a cardinal value, not only because of its stress on the exercise of individual will but also because of the transformation of individuals and communities that may result. As legal scholar Laurence Tribe writes, what is called for is

> the sanctification neither of the present nor of progress but of evolving processes of interaction and change—processes of action and choice that are valued for themselves, for the conceptions of being that they embody, at the same time that they are valued as means to the progressive evolution of the conceptions, experiences and ends that characterize the human community in nature at any given point

in its history. As those conceptions, experiences, and ends evolve through the processes made possible by a legal and constitutional framework for choice, the framework itself—the society's idealized conception of how change should be structured—may be expected to change as well.[45]

In such a world, the intrinsic capacity to act is of paramount importance. Personal choice alters shared values, which in turn reshape the possibilities of choice; the continuing process, rather than some stated set of ultimate objectives, defines the good society. "Public code and private conscience plow together," observes philosopher David Pole. "Each springs from and contributes to the other, channels it and is channeled. Both alike are redirected and enlarged."[46]

This emphasis on choice cannot fairly be bent into an apologia for the present. The commitment to diversity has its roots in the belief that the community as a whole is enriched by variation, both of individuals and groupings, even as individuals are better off if free to pursue their preferred goals.[47] Acceptance of differences will encourage social cohesiveness, for it "may serve to eliminate the cause for dissociation and to re-establish unity. Toleration and institutionalization" of the conflicts brought about by tensions among individuals can be "an important stabilizing influence."[48] But make no mistake: this is not "the politics of liberal complacency."[49] Removing the formal impediments to volition, securing the basic requisites of choice, encouraging tolerance for the divergent choices of others, and attending to those who bear witness to one or another resolution of these basic questions of individual and societal identity will lead to change. Over time, in what George Simmel calls an "infinite rhythm," it will take us far from the present, to places presently unknowable.[50]

Individual choice and social tolerance are not the metric of routine policy discourse. We are used to thinking not about processes but about outcomes, because they are measurable and hence enforceable; not about individuals but about aggregates—workers, minors, aliens—because they offer a definable audience. Yet where the audience is necessarily all of us, addressed as individuals, and right outcomes nothing more nor less than the sum of what each of us prefers, the conventional will not work. Focusing on choice may some day be seen as a transition to some new crystallization of social fairness. Who can say now what form that new society will, or should, assume?

2

Pedestal or Prison?
The Historic Consequences
of Paternalism

With the loss of tradition we have lost the thread which safely guided us
through the vast realms of the past, but this thread was also the chain fetter-
ing each successive generation to a predetermined aspect of the past. It could
be that only now will the past open up to us with unexpected freshness and
tell us things that no one as yet had ears to hear.
Hannah Arendt, "What Was Authority?"
in Carl J. Friedrich, ed., *Nomos I: Authority* (1958)

I

Although the past is a subtle teacher, offering few clear lessons, historical
evidence nonetheless gets deployed in the service of arguments addressed
to contemporary concerns.[1] Such uses are appropriate so long as one bears
in mind that the intention is not purist but pragmatic, to give life to the tale
of the past and to relate it to the present.

Historical discussions of the relevance of gender to policy sometimes
demonstrate how shabbily women have been treated—more pointedly,
how similar has been the condition of blacks and women—in order to
justify different and better present-day treatment of women. Special benefits programs directed exclusively at women have been defended in this
fashion, and the Supreme Court has used such logic in upholding preferential treatment of women. Our purpose is importantly different, as is the
way we approach the past.

That women have historically been disserved by public policy seems
beyond dispute, but it is the nature and not the fact of this disadvantage that
has continuing relevance. To summarize the argument that this chapter
develops, women were victimized by policies designed to protect them—
policies that, for this very reason, denied them the chance to make basic
decisions for themselves. That proposition is true of both the common law
understanding of women which persisted through much of the nineteenth

29

century, and the view of women embodied in twentieth century rules about working conditions. Men too were victimized by these laws, which imposed upon males the burden of the provider role.

The conventional policy wisdom of the eighteenth and nineteenth centuries regarded women as appropriately dependent on men. Women were thought incapable of determining important matters for themselves, too virtuous to be exposed to the rough and tumble of the larger world. Men, by contrast, were seen as naturally able to deal with mean reality. Male self-interest doubtless contributed to this perception: there is no other good explanation for the fact that wives could not legally deny their husbands the privileges of the bedchamber. Yet the historical evidence suggests that the dominant reason for sex-differentiating rules was neither self-interest nor animus towards women, but something altogether more laudable: concern and affection. Rules governing the conduct of women were adopted in what was honestly seen as women's best interest, obliging women to behave just as they would have if they had been able fully to appreciate what was best for them.

The protective labor laws enacted in the twentieth century, which fixed maximum hours, set minimum wages, and determined working conditions for women (but not for men) were in good measure pushed through by women themselves. In this respect, they differ from earlier gender policy. But the image of women embodied in such laws and the argument advanced by their advocates closely resemble the common law conception: because they were frail and readily exploited, women needed to be protected from the vicissitudes of the marketplace, while men were able to act effectively on their own behalf.

No longer is it taken for granted that paternalism embodies wise gender policy, for while some paternalistic policies, such as rest periods for women workers, did yield tangible benefits for women, others, such as credit restrictions, have had the opposite effect. Yet, regardless of short-term gains, paternalism inherently creates disadvantages, because it treats women as a class, rather than as workers or married individuals or would-be borrowers, and because that treatment is choice-constraining.

Paternalism is not necessarily a bad thing. We take a paternalistic stance toward the young, for instance, because children do not know enough to protect themselves. Their very irresponsibility is a measure of their youth, and so their will is checked for reasons rooted in affection. But children are also regarded as less than full persons in this society; as dependents, they are not adults' equals. To treat women as children, as paternalism historically did, carries the same consequence without comparable justification.

If the past treatment of women bears at all on present policy thinking, it should encourage skepticism of policies that, however benignly motivated, effectively restrict choice on the basis of gender. Certain of these policies resemble the protective legislation of the not-so-distant past: laws that make it a crime to have sex with female minors but not with male minors, for instance. But paternalism can also be detected in less benighted efforts to promote "good" gender-specific outcomes, as in deciding how many members of one sex are to be hired for jobs traditionally dominated by the other, or insisting upon identical educational experiences for adolescents of both sexes. The historical record identifies the dilemmas associated with gender preferences, whatever their motivation and whoever instigates them, and so offers support for a policy that stresses individual volition.

II

With the perspective of hindsight, the legal inferiority of women—most especially married women—through much of the nineteenth century seems plainly indefensible. Adult single women enjoyed some of the legal rights given to men, although, like their married sisters, they were barred from many professions and trades. Married women had it much worse. They were unable to sign contracts; they lacked title to the wages they earned and to property, even property inherited or owned prior to marriage; in the event of legal separation, they had no claim on their children. While the stringency of these laws was somewhat relaxed in practice, as American courts and legislatures exercised a "humane paternalism over marriage without precedent at common law,"[2] the early feminists who signed the 1848 Seneca Falls Declaration of Sentiments had it largely right: the married woman found herself "in the eye of the law, civilly dead."[3] Blackstone's classic eighteenth century account of the common law observed that "by marriage, the husband and wife are one person in law; that is, the very being or legal existence of the women is suspended during the marriage. . . ."[4]

This situation did not go uncriticized. In *The Subjection of Women,* John Stuart Mill condemned a regime which rendered married women perpetually subordinate to their husbands. "The almost unlimited power which present social institutions give a husband over his wife" enabled him to become a household tyrant.[5] Under existing laws of marriage, wives might endure lives far worse than slaves, suffering the "worst description of bondage" ever known. The wife "could be denied even Uncle Tom's privilege of having 'his own life in the cabin.' " She could not secure her own release, for divorce was usually unavailable. The wife was not even allowed to deny her husband "the least familiarity," but had to submit to "the lowest degradation of a human being, that of being made the instrument of an animal contrary to her inclinations."[6]

Although husbands theoretically had such power, reported instances of its exercise were rare. Nor did the common law treatment of women license brutality. Paternalism was instead supposed to serve the broad purposes of preserving prevailing social arrangements and protecting women. By denying an independent legal status to the married woman, this paternalism was meant to minimize family strife; in that sense, the law helped to secure a stable social order. As one senator declared during the first congressional debate over women's suffrage in 1866, "The whole theory of government and society proceeds upon the assumption that [the husband's and wife's] interests are one. . . . The woman who undertakes to put her sex in an adversary position to man . . . displays a spirit which would, if able, convert all the now harmonious elements of society into a state of war, and make any home a hell on earth."[7]

Paternalism also aimed at protecting women from the consequences of their own misjudgments. While protection has long been regarded as an appropriate rationale for public policy, problems arise in trying to contain its scope. In *On Liberty,* Mill declared the state should exercise its authority over "any member of the civilized community, against his will" only "to prevent harm to others." "This doctrine," Mill added, "is meant to apply only to human being in the maturity of their faculties. . . . Liberty, as a principle, has no application to any state of things anterior to the time when mankind have become capable of being improved by free and equal discussion."[8]

Although this exception to the principle of governmental nonintervention was supposed to refer only to children and "barbarians," it could readily be applied to other groups thought to be similarly incapable of directing their own lives. Writing a half-century before Mill, the German philosopher Johann Fichte defended husbands' dominion over their wives in much these terms. Such authority was held to embody woman's "necessary wish":

> Woman is not subject to her husband in such a manner as to give him a *right of compulsion* over her; she is subjected through her own continuous necessary wish—a wish that is the condition of her morality—to be so subjected. She has the *power* to withdraw her freedom, if she could have the *will* to do so: but that is the very point: she cannot rationally will to be free. . . . Her husband is, therefore, the

administrator of all her rights in consequence of her own necessary will; and she wishes those rights asserted only in so far as *he* wishes it. He is her natural representative in the state and in the whole society.[9]

That view underlies the common law. Women acting rationally would choose their present estate, since any other stance would be inconsistent with their "morality."

Present-day defenses of paternalism rest on criteria similar to Fichte's, justifying paternalism "only to preserve a wider range of freedom for the individual."[10] To usurp decision-making authority for the good of the collectivity or the usurper does not constitute paternalism; there may be reasons for such policies, but they are of a different sort. Because paternalism benefits another, love or affection is usually an animating factor; if paternalism is a form of enslavement, it assumes a quite special guise. Critical to the defense of paternalism is the assumption that the beneficiaries are in fact helpless, or at least less competent than the deciders to make their own life choices. Should that prove untrue, the argument for paternalism collapses, and the intervention is unmasked as an assault on the personal dignity of those whose lives have been unfairly constrained.

The common law treatment of married women in America and the exclusion of women from certain occupations was justified in just these terms. Paternalism would preserve the finest traits of womanhood—delicacy, sensitivity, innocence—by insulating women from the corrupting influence of the outside world. Women were fragile, and thus rightly dependent upon men. Doctors fretted about the impact of higher education on women's frail constitutions: the fact that women's colleges of the period extensively studied the effects of schooling on health, and deliberately mixed physical with mental labors, shows how seriously the concern was felt.[11]

This point could also be made less scientifically. As one senator noted during the 1866 suffrage debates,

> The God of our race has stamped upon [American women] a milder, gentler nature, which not only makes them shrink from, but disqualifies them for the turmoil and battle of public life. They have a higher and holier mission. . . . Their mission is at home, by their blandishments and love to assuage the passions of men as they come in from the battle of life, and not themselves by joining in the contest to add fuel to the very flames.[12]

The Supreme Court, rejecting the argument that a woman was constitutionally entitled to practice law, said much the same thing seven years later. "Man is, or should be, woman's protector and defender. The natural and proper timidity and delicacy which belongs to the female sex evidently unfits it for many of the occupations of civil life."[13]

When viewed in this light, the distinct treatment of women did not oppress them. On the contrary, as Blackstone had written in his *Commentaries on the Laws of England,* "Even the disabilities, which the woman lies under, are for the most part intended for her protection and benefit. So great a favourite is the female sex of the laws of England."[14] The source of gender paternalism was not oppression but, as Mill himself wrote, the "loving exercise of authority on one side, loving submission to it on the other."[15]

Small wonder, then, that politicians refused to take seriously the feminists' complaint of unfair treatment. In an 1856 report, the New York State Assembly's Judiciary Committee chided those who sought further rights for women:

> The ladies always have the best place and choicest tidbit at the table. They always have the best seats in the cars, carriage and sleighs; the warmest place in the winter and the coolest place in the summer. . . . A lady's dress costs three times as much as that of a gentleman; and, at the present time, with the prevailing fashion, one lady occupies three times as much space in the world as a gentleman.[16]

How could women object to this state of affairs, these legislators wondered; others treated emergent feminism as a threat to social stability. The Congregationalist Ministers of Massachusetts derided feminism as ungodly:

> The power of woman is her dependence, flowing from the consciousness of that weakness which God has given her for her protection. . . . If the vine, whose strength and beauty is to lean on the trellis-work, and half conceal its cluster, thinks to assume the independent and overshadowing nature of the elm, it will not only cease to bear fruit, but fall in shame and dishonor into the dust.[17]

Queen Victoria reacted more tartly, scolding feminists for embarking on a "wicked folly . . . forgetting every sense of womanly feeling and propriety."[18]

It is revealing that Victoria, herself hardly a hausfrau, would find feminist stirrings so disquieting, for the defense of the status quo often had little basis in reality. Arrayed against the image of frail female was the reality of the married women laboring on countless farms, and the three million single working women in America who were obliged to make their way in the world. In this disjuncture between belief and behavior resided one of the signal weaknesses of the paternalistic argument. Just who was being protected? As Jane Swisshelm, one of the first women to publish her own newspaper, pointedly commented,

> It is well known that thousands, nay, millions of women in this country are condemned to the most menial drudgery, such as men would scorn to engage in, and that for one-fourth the wages . . . and who says anything against it? But let one presume to use her mental powers . . . and take up any profession or avocation which is deemed honorable and requires talent, and O! bring cologne, get a cambric kerchief and feather fan, unloosen his corsets and take off his cravat! What a fainting fit Mr. Propriety has taken! Just to think that 'one of the deahcreathures,' the heavenly angels, should forsake the sphere—woman's sphere—to mix with the wicked strife of this wicked world![19]

John Stuart Mill identified a related irony. "Woman are declared to be better than men; an empty compliment, which must provoke a bitter smile from every woman of spirit, since there is no other situation in life in which it is . . . considered quite natural and suitable that the better should obey the worse."[20]

Although the stereotyped image of women corresponded only to the paternalistic vision and not the workaday reality, that image nonetheless affected women's lives. Paternalism sometimes became a self-fulfilling prophecy, making women as dependent as they were conventionally supposed to be. "Men do not want solely the obedience of women," Mill wrote. "They want their sentiments."[21] To the extent that they succeeded in their aspiration, men shaped the women's character.

Nineteenth century feminists understood this well. Lucretia Mott, in *Discourse on Woman*, described woman as "enervated, her mind to some extent paralyzed; and, like those still more degraded by personal bondage, she hugs her chains."[22] Protectiveness could indeed be seductive, as Sarah Grimke noted:

> I believe the laws which deprived married women of their rights and privileges, have a tendency to lessen them in their own estimation as moral and responsible beings, and that their being made by civil law inferior to their husbands, has a debasing and mischievous effect upon them, teaching them practically the fatal lesson to look unto man for protection and indulgence.[23]

The protected and indulged woman becomes, as Grimke observed, a less than whole person. Her incapacity to make choices robs her of her status as a "moral and responsible" individual, initially in the eyes of the community, eventually and more damningly in her own eyes as well. Paternalism in the economic realm, which kept most married women out of the marketplace, had a similar impact on women's personalities. As Charlotte Perkins Gilman stated at the close of the nineteenth century,

> An intense self-consciousness, born of the ceaseless contact of close personal relation; an inordinate self-interest, bred by the constant personal attention and personal service of this relation; a feverish, torturing moral sensitiveness, without the width and clarity of vision of a full-grown moral sense; a thwarted will, used to meek surrender, cunning evasion, or futile rebellion; a childish, wavering, short-range judgment, handicapped by emotion—such psychic qualities as these, born in us all, are the inevitable result of the sexuo-economic relation.[24]

The woman described by Gilman resembles all too closely Betty Friedan's cossetted housewife of the 1950s, who awakes one day with a nameless grievance against something so all-encompassing that it has long since lost its specific identity. "I have been robbed of myself"—so these women, denied the opportunity to take responsibility for their actions, might say, if only they could recognize what they had lost. For the best of reasons and the most benevolent of motives, the paternalist impulse undermined women's claim to equal treatment, rendering them "victims of protection;"[25] it also encouraged "feminine" behavior, which supported the continuing imposition of a paternalist regime.

III

The history of labor legislation, adopted early in the twentieth century especially to protect women, bears little apparent resemblance to the paternalism of eighteenth and nineteenth century American and English law. For one thing, the earlier common law denied married women the prerogatives of men, among them the right to sign a contract or own property, while labor legislation was intended to give women something that men did not have: mandated maximum hours and minimum wages, decent working conditions, proscriptions against night work: If the benefits that married women enjoyed under the common law were not self-evident, it seemed clear at the time that working women were better off than men because of the workplace protections that they enjoyed. For another thing, it was men who structured the earlier legal regime for the ostensible benefit of women. By contrast, women themselves actively sought the insulation from the harshness of the market that the new labor legislation afforded, insisting that such protections served their own best interests.

Yet the similarities between these two historical epochs turn out to be more consequential. Underlying the labor legislation was a set of presumptions about women very much like those embedded in the common law. In seeking safeguards, the supporters of protective labor legislation claimed that working women were uniquely vulnerable and so needed special treatment. Because the focus was on women's frailties rather than on the conditions under which all workers labored, this understanding enabled employers to refuse women access to physically demanding jobs, on the grounds that the weaker sex could not perform such work. Of greater moment, the demand for special sex-based protection proved hard to square with the claim that women were also entitled to equal treatment. In a non-Orwellian world, could women be at once different and the same? Full personhood and special protection turn out to be difficult if not impossible to reconcile; in this sense, the consequences of paternalism during the two periods are not incommensurate.[26]

At the outset of this century, there was considerable reason to seek special help for women workers. The conditions under which many women labored were wretched: "wages of $2.00 a week for women not living at home; hours from 7:45 A.M. till midnight, with only a few minutes off for lunch; a six-day work week, with sometimes stocktaking on Sundays at no additional pay; no seats behind the sales counters; no lockers; no vacations; and no place to eat lunch except in the toilets and stockrooms."[27] Men working at comparable jobs were likewise ill-treated, and for that reason the initial concern of labor reformers had been to improve the lot of both sexes. Maximum hours legislation covering all workers was urged by the largest labor unions and adopted in several states. In the *Lochner* decision, however, the Supreme Court undercut these efforts by striking down such laws as inconsistent with an individual's constitutionally guaranteed freedom to enter into contracts.[28]

If women were to enjoy the protection of maximum hours laws, their plight had to appear legally different from that of men. In *People v. Williams,* decided shortly after *Lochner,* New York's highest court rejected such a distinction. "An adult woman is not to be regarded . . . in any other light than the man is regarded, when the question relates to the business, pursuit or calling. . . . She is not to be made the special object of the paternal power of the state."[29] Only proof that women were uniquely in need of special protection—that, as the National Consumer League put it, women were "not identical in economic or social function or in physical capacity"[30]—might persuade the Supreme Court to see things differently.

The famous Brandeis brief, filed in the 1908 case of *Muller v. Oregon,* was designed to satisfy this need. State commission reports as well as data from European inquiries were marshalled to demonstrate that long working hours had especially bad effects on the health of women workers. An 1875 report of the Massachusetts Bureau of Labor Statistics, asserting that "girls cannot work more than eight hours, and keep it up; they know it; and they rarely will," typified the quality of evidence pulled together in the brief. Although by contemporary standards the data hardly constitute scientific proof, the Court in *Muller* relied in good part on this evidence in upholding maximum hours legislation that applied exclusively to women. That it was women, not all workers, who were the focus of the legislation was vitally important to the justices, who concluded that inherent sex-based differences justified differentiated treatment:

> Woman has always been dependent upon man. He established his control at the outset by superior physical strength, and this control in various forms, with diminishing intensity, has continued to the present. . . . Though its limitations upon personal and contractual rights may be removed by legislation, there is that in her disposition and habits of life which will operate against a full assertion of those rights. She will still be where some legislation to protect her seems necessary to secure a real equality of right. . . . Differentiated by these matters from the other sex, she is properly placed in a class by herself, and legislation designed for her protection may be sustained.[31]

This description of "dependent" woman has its obvious antecedents in rationales for earlier common law paternalism. Women won their maximum-hours laws, but only because they could be described in a way which rendered such special treatment permissible, even laudable.

The Court's decision in *Lochner* posed a Hobson's choice for advocates of protective legislation: pursue special treatment for women alone or abandon the hope of obtaining any legislative relief from the hardships of the workplace. When the Supreme Court upheld a maximum-hours law that applied to both men and women nine years later, a reconsideration of the woman-only strategy became conceivable, but this option was not pursued. In the wake of the *Muller* decision, a majority of states adopted maximum-hours legislation for women workers. The continuing push was for minimum wages and regulation of working conditions, again just for women.

In a 1923 case, *Adkins v. Children's Hospital of the District of Columbia,* the Supreme Court overturned a minimum wage law for women and children.[32] Wages were not so directly linked to women's working capacity as were hours, the Court asserted, and hence *Muller* could be distinguished. The Court also pointed to the tension between protectiveness on the one hand, the emerging liberation of women on the other:

> In view of the great—not to say revolutionary—changes which have taken place since [*Muller*], in the contractual, political, and civil status of women . . . it is not unreasonable to say that these differences have now come almost, if not quite, to the vanishing point. . . . To do otherwise would be to ignore all the implications to be drawn from the present-day trend of legislation as well as that of common thought and usage, by which woman is accorded emancipation from the old doctrine that she must be given special protection or subject to restraint in her contractual and civil relationships.[33]

The justices related these labor laws to the common law disabilities in linking special protection and special restraint. In that sense, the Court was at one with the new feminists and the Woman's Party in cheering on women's emancipation from what feminists regarded as the morass of unlovely dependence.

Some social reformers saw the matter very differently. *Adkins* had upheld an abstract principle at the expense of improvements in the concrete conditions of women's lives, ignoring the "economic fact of the exploitation of women in industry, who as a class labor under tremendous economic handicap."[34] Men were not interested in maximum hours and minimum wage laws, since they could bargain for whatever benefits they wanted through their unions. But women, many of whom worked for a pittance in nonunionized industries, had no such collective help. As Felix Frankfurter, a prime strategist in securing and defending special protective legislation, declared, "Only those who are ignorant of the law . . . or indifferent to the exacting aspects of women's life can have the naïveté, or the recklessness, to sum up women's whole position in a meaningless and mischievous phrase about 'equal rights.' "[35]

Tangible benefits properly counted for more, in Frankfurter's view, than principles. Taking a similar approach, *The Nation* editorialized that while the feminist position was "logically sound and theoretically progressive," it was in human terms "impractical and reactionary." Nor was the rightness of the equal rights principle accepted by those who would reform the working environment. The advocates of protection were offended not just by the fact that "equal rights" would deny women the benefits they achieved; they also resisted the notion inherent in an equal rights approach that, for purposes of public policy, the sexes were identical. "Nature made men and women different," Felix Frankfurter asserted. "The law must accommodate itself to the immutable differences of Nature."[36] Other reformist advocates insisted that special treatment for women in the workplace was essential if women were to be able to do what most mattered—be good mothers.

Equal rights adherents saw the matter very differently. Protection was a costly approach, they argued, for it kept women from competing for certain kinds of jobs. The woman entitled to a minimum wage, maximum hours, and freedom from night work, deemed unable to lift even fifteen pounds and needing rest periods, was handicapped in the marketplace. "It is obviously not the women who are protected," wrote Sophonsiba Breckenridge. "For them, some of this legislation may be a distinct limitation."[37] One study estimated that between 2 and 5 percent more women would have been employed without such protection, and that most would have had jobs in the "men's world."[38]

More than particular jobs were at stake in this dispute. Feminists also assailed protective statutes for dooming women to inferiority in the labor market. Court cases upholding such laws gave "a strong presumption of legitimacy to any kind of employment discrimination which could be related to permanent differences" and so encouraged discrimination.[39] Historian William Chafe concludes that "ultimately the feminists objected to special labor legislation because it symbolized the evil of a social system which set women apart as a separate class and assigned them a place less equal than that of men."[40] The implication of this separation, that women were less able than men to care for themselves, was clear and offensive. A pamphlet supporting the Equal Right Amendment, circulated in the 1930s, bluntly made the point. "Under the common law, women were 'protected' from themselves in being placed under the guardianship of father and husband. Most women do not wish protection as inferior beings."[41]

Disputes over the desirability and permissibility of laws giving special protection to women workers persist even today. Through the early 1970s, "protection" remained a concern for the National Consumers League and the AFL-CIO, which argued that, while similar treatment of the sexes was appropriate, it made sense to preserve women's benefits. If such laws constrained women's workplace opportunities, that was not a source of concern; women needed to limit their commitment to work in order to maintain a home. To the AFL-CIO, as to those who had earlier concerned themselves with the connection between motherhood and working conditions, women required protection so that they might assume a particular role. The woman worker would also be a housekeeper and mother, not because she had been coerced but because it seemed natural. The notion of womanhood that had justified the common law fetters a century earlier was heard in arguments about women's proper place in the work force. In both instances, what protection secured for women was a marginal status in the political and economic order, rendering them less than the equals of men.

A similar argument is made in the 1980s by those insisting that women should be granted maternity benefits, assuring them time off to care for their infants. To be sure, advocates of such special help do not argue that women's workplace opportunities should be correspondingly limited; instead, they demand this benefit in addition to equal help. But it is hard to view this special pleading for women as anything other than the latest version of paternalism, with all its debilitating consequences for working women.

The revelation that some jobs may be specially hazardous to women poses a related set of concerns. Women working in certain environments are exposed to toxic substances that either impair their reproductive capacities or directly reach the fetus, causing birth defects; the impact of exposure on men is less apparent. There is a plausible argument for denying women of childbearing age access to these jobs, and a clear duty to inform them of the risk. The impact of imposed constraint is, though, much the same as in the instances already canvassed. For "their own good," and without their acquiescence, women are denied an opportunity open to men.[42]

IV

The paternalism that historically characterized gender policy presumed that women needed to be kept cloistered, were properly dependent on men, were primarily devoted to the home, and were incapable of making basic life decisions. Those presumptions led to the early common law treatment of women and much protective labor legislation. When such beliefs were transformed into policy, they produced sex role stereotyping that did not always disadvantage women economically but denied women's claims to moral parity.

Traces of paternalism are discernible in policies that deny women certain rights because of pregnancy, that prevent even working women from obtaining credit in their own names, and that distinguish between men and women in determining when an individual may drive, drink, or marry. Paternalism is also apparent in rules that turn all males into workers, by denying them any possibility of alimony or support for childrearing. Underlying each of these examples are perceptions indistinguishable from those that bottomed the older common law view. As we discuss in part II, paternalism of this variety is disappearing: court decisions regularly strike down such differentiations as inequitable, and legislatures have expanded the reach of benefits to include both sexes.

Paternalism can also be identified in the special treatment aimed exclusively at one sex or the other. The similarity between protective legislation and preferences was asserted in a 1973 labor union brief, filed in support of a state law requiring premium overtime pay for female but not male workers. While the law itself had its roots in *Adkins*-era concerns for women workers, the argument advanced on its behalf was distinctly more contemporary: since the law increases women's wages, "it is similar to affirmative action programs and benign quotas. . . ."[43] Paternalism provides the intellectual connection between preference and protection. That is one good reason to treat preferences skeptically.[44]

If our historic experience with paternalism reveals anything, it is that even benignly motivated policies, which dictate to women or men in their alleged best interest, convey a sense of moral inferiority and diminish the sphere of liberty available to both sexes. As Isaiah Berlin concludes,

> Paternalism is despotic, not because it is more oppressive than naked, brutal unenlightened tyranny, nor merely because it ignores the transcendental reason embodied in me, but because it is an insult to my conception of myself as a human being, determined to make my own life in accordance with my own purposes, and, above all, entitled to be recognized as such by others. For if I am not so recognized, then I may fail to recognize . . . my own claim to be a fully independent human being.[45]

These consequences are unfortunate, significant—and largely avoidable in the crafting of gender policy.

V

Women were not, of course, the only group historically to have been subject to paternalistic treatment. As earlier noted, children have been, and remain, bound by rules adopted for what is thought to be in their own best interest, and apologists for slavery declared that slaves were better off for their enslavement. Although policies toward each of these three groups may be termed paternalistic, the differences among them are noteworthy, as too is the lesson to be gleaned from each instance.

If the lives of children, blacks, and women have all been subject to external shaping, the circumstances have varied markedly among these groups. Children represent the classic candidates for paternalism, for their very immaturity defines them as less than full members of society. Despite the claims of those who urge the liberation of children, there exists no apparent way for the young to alter this state of affairs: someone will manage their lives.

To say that does not end the inquiry, for one may well ask who should serve as the shaper of behavior, what the source of values and the extent of value-shaping should be. One concerned about liberty generally will prefer a paternalism toward children which is more, rather than less, liberty-enhancing.[46] But whether the paternalism is exercised by state, church, community, or family; whether it is, to our eyes, benignly neglectful or sternly oppressive; whether it demarcates way-stations on the road to maturity or prolongs childlike dependency, paternalism toward children is inherently time-bounded. At some point, the child becomes an adult, someone who is deemed to have the capacity for morally autonomous judgment. Whenever that transition is finally marked, the hold of paternalism ceases.

Paternalism with respect to the young is both inevitable and necessarily self-liquidating, as children grow into adulthood. Neither circumstance pertains to gender paternalism. "Two-thirds of mankind, the women and children, are everywhere the subjects of family government," wrote George Fitzhugh, in his impassioned antebellum defense of slavery. "In all countries where slavery exists, the slaves also are the subjects of this kind of government." That slaves were treated just as women and children, Fitzhugh argued, made slavery somehow more acceptable. "God has . . . provided a better check, to temper and direct the power of the family and the master than any human government has devised."[47]

Yet despite this attempt to liken the treatment of blacks to that of women and children, paternalism acquires an altogether different meaning in the racial context. Historically, the analogy seems little more than a rationale for oppression, a means by which whites could evade guilt for their otherwise intolerable conduct. Neither the beneficent motivation nor the tangible benefits that characterized gender paternalism were exemplified in the treatment of blacks by whites. However misguided their actions might seem to the contemporary observer, men sought to dignify women by elevating and protecting them; whites, by contrast, insisted upon the subservience of blacks.

In the years before the Civil War, historian Eugene Genovese writes, slavery could be thought by the slaveholders to serve a paternalistic function. "Paternalism defined the involuntary labor of slaves as a legitimate return to their masters for protection and direction." Some such rationalization was necessary in a world where master and slave needed each other. But imbedded in the idea of paternalism is the understanding of the slaves as humans—acquiescent humans, to be sure, but humans nonetheless. That revolutionary concept could not be reconciled with the very idea of slavery, which denied to the slave any will and hence any humanity. Paternalism toward blacks, somewhat illogically, was thus premised on their status as less than human. In its "flesh-peddling chivalry,"[48] it embodied all the contradictions of slavery itself. Paternalism enabled the slaveholder to defend his actions as benefiting blacks, protecting them from their own baser nature.

Gender and race paternalism diverge in other consequential ways. Gender paternalism was generally supposed to preserve the special strengths of women while race paternalism was motivated by a desire for stability and economic necessity, not concern for the goodness of blacks. A concern for social stability also informed the treatment of women, of course, and women found themselves ultimately worse off for all the protection they enjoyed, but the situation that blacks confronted was remarkably freer from ambiguity. The slave was literally, not figuratively, chattel, and Jim Crow laws passed after Reconstruction did not evidence the slightest sympathy toward blacks. Further, the separateness of blacks and whites allowed whites to vent their hostility, with limited social and economic consequences for the majority. By contrast, because women lived with their "oppressors," their fortunes could not be disentangled from those of men. Segregation of the races invited a tyranny without a parallel in relations between the sexes, who, whatever the patterns of domination, occupied the same intimate space. Racial discrimination could largely ignore the private sphere, focusing on political and economic subordination, while gender discrimination was tempered in the public sphere by the necessity of mutual affecting relationships in the private sphere.

The clear sense that gender paternalism was undertaken with the human worth of women in mind distinguishes it from race paternalism. It appears at once more subtle in application, more mixed in effect—and more likely to enlist its "victims" in the enterprise. For blacks, whether living under slavery, or later, in a society that converted racial prejudice into official policy, hostility was life-shaping. For women, the social order was neither hostile in motivation nor so all-embracing in its reach. While paternalism denied choice to women, it did so even as it celebrated women's humanity.

The paternalistic experiences of women and blacks are not happy stories. They are distinct stories, however, with equally distinct implications. It may be that, in certain instances, race consciousness is necessary today to eliminate the enduring taint of prejudice, an essential if regrettable benchmark on the path to eventual neutrality. Integration of public institutions, for example, almost inevitably blunts the capacity of whites to inflict harms on blacks. As a pragmatic matter, given the nature and degree of past racial oppression, no other approach may work.[49] The history of gender paternalism, by contrast, affords no warrant for such continuing paternalism.

3

Neither Oppression nor Naturalism: Why the Prevailing Paradigms Distort the Present

There are people who are attracted by the permanence of stone. They would like to be solid and impenetrable, they do not want change: for who knows what change might bring? . . . It is as if their own existence were perpetually in suspense. But they want to exist in all ways at once, and all in one instant. They have no wish to acquire ideas, they want them to be innate . . . they want to adopt a mode of life in which reasoning and the quest for truth play only a subordinate part, in which nothing is sought except what has already been found, in which one never becomes anything else but what one already was.

Jean-Paul Sartre, *Portrait of an Anti-Semite* (1948)

At independence the people of our region had gone mad with anger and fear—all the accumulated anger of the colonial period, and every kind of reawakened tribal fear. . . . If the movement had been more reasoned, had been less a movement of simple rejection, the people of our region might have seen that the town at the bend in the river was theirs, the capital of any state they might set up. But they had hated the town for the intruders who ruled in it and from it; and they had preferred to destroy the town rather than take it over. Having destroyed their town, they had grieved for it.

V. S. Naipaul, *A Bend in the River* (1979)

I

The past acquires clarity when contrasted with the present, for the passage of time permits one to distinguish the evanescent from the enduring. About the present, we enjoy no such purchase. The difficulty has little to do with the data bearing on gender policy—marriage, birth, divorce and employment rates, and the like—for in these respects, we know much more about ourselves than about our predecessors. But when it comes to making something of the data, deciding which comparisons are fruitful, which causal relationships plausible—in short, identifying what matters and why—cacophony reigns. Many voices are heard, offering many nostrums. Even determining what questions deserve attention becomes problematic, for we lack the perspective that distance and distancing permits. How do we make sense of the present?

With respect to most issues reached by policy, women and men are now formal equals. There are, to be sure, important exceptions, but these should not obscure a central truth about gender equality in the publicly regulated spheres of life. Women enjoy full political rights. Their employers and educators are obliged to guarantee them equal opportunities. They hold and trade property. They marry and determine whether to bear children of their own volition.

It was precisely this state of affairs that earlier generations of feminists fought to achieve, in the belief that formal equality would render inevitable equality in fact: the vote would alter the political order, which would in turn transform political and social reality. But that, we are told, has not happened. Leaders of the contemporary women's movement routinely insist that, despite this transformation of policy and law, women have remained the second sex, weak and dependent, finding their vocation in responding to the needs of men rather than satisfying their own self-generated purposes. Why might this be so?

As a perusal of the overflowing shelves of the "women's" and "men's" sections in any urban bookstore will confirm, a cottage industry has sprung up to explain one or another aspect of women's and men's estates. A closer inspection reveals how very special is this literature. It is new. Simone de Beauvoir's *The Second Sex,* published three decades ago, is already a classic, and Margaret Mead's anthropology has been consigned to prehistory. It is also tendentious. Many of the texts do not mean to persuade the uncommitted but rather to confirm the already committed in their respective points of view.

The loudest voices in the current debate are, at one end of the spectrum, those who decry present relations between the sexes and demand revolutionary change and, at the other end, those who celebrate sex differences as a biologically driven necessity. Leftist feminism, to use a single encompassing phrase for several diverse positions, is centered on woman's oppression, based variously on sex, or on women's marginal membership in a capitalist economy, or on some amalgam—some more or less "unhappy marriage"—of these two oppressions.[1] By sharp contrast, the naturalist position put forward by the Right draws on widely varied sources of data having to do with heredity and allegedly universal cultural forms, arguing for the unchanging nature of relations between the sexes.

What these theories have in common is less apparent, but for our purposes more pertinent, than what divides them. The Left and the Right both attempt, at the least, to explain contemporary society; in some instances, to comprehend all societies that ever were. Both regard policy concerns as secondary. To the naturalists, all the day care in the world won't erase the natural bonding instinct between mother and child.[2] The leftist feminists, on the other hand, dismiss "equal pay, equal work, and all of the female politicians of the world," for these "will not extirpate the roots of sexism."[3]

Most disturbingly from our perspective, both the leftist feminist and the naturalist approaches are deeply deterministic. The feminists' oppressors, whether economic or personal, seem so powerful and ubiquitous as to be impervious to attack, while the forces of biology suffused through the cultures of man that the naturalists emphasize similarly resist transformation. Flesh and blood persons vanish altogether in these treatments, to be replaced by one-dimensional figures, childbearers or maintainers of the economic order. Males and females emerge only as programmed antagonists or biologically bonded partners, not as persons with at least some common dilemmas. Those multifaceted individuals whose aspirations are so important to liberalism are much distrusted by both Left and Right. Men and women will become what the genes—or the economy—would have them be, not what they might prefer.[4]

II

Leftist feminism, as we use the term, encompasses three main groups: radical feminists, Marxists, and socialist feminists.[5] Each differs from liberal feminism in believing that women are first and foremost members of a group or class, not individuals who are female.[6] Thus, women are oppressed by men, or capitalism, or nature, or all three, *because* they are women, not because of their individual traits or accidents of birth.

Radical feminists see women's oppression deriving from male domination over women's reproductive capacity as existing in all times and places.[7] Because male oppression is universal and cannot be explained by reference to such typically political categories as production, radical feminists have made much of the idea that "the personal is political." Concentrating on ordinary political categories ignores the fact that all male power is based on "personal" institutions such as marriage, childbearing, housework, and prostitution. "Patriarchy appears to be 'everywhere,'" claims Mary Daly. "Even outer space and the future have been colonized."[8]

Women's biological nature is thus a source of women's oppression, for pregnancy and childrearing put them in a weak position in relation to men, who are seen as innately aggressive.[9] For Susan Brownmiller, the ability of men to rape women is the beginning of male oppression: "Man's discovery that his genitalia would serve as a weapon to generate fear must rank as one of the most important discoveries of prehistoric times, along with the use of fire and the first crude stone axe."[10] Women are treated as sex objects, coerced into heterosexual marriage and relegated to the hard work of child care, which they have been led to believe is their highest calling. Catherine MacKinnon sums up women's oppression this way:

> As the organizational expropriation of the work of some for the benefit of others defines a class—workers—the organized expropriation of the sexuality of some for the use of others defines the sex, woman. Heterosexuality is its structure, gender and family its congealed forms, sex roles its qualities generalized to social persona, reproduction a consequence, and control its issue.[11]

Radical feminists offer various ways of escaping omnipresent patriarchy. One often-repeated proposal is to establish separate communities of women apart from the male oppressor. More radically, the very condition that leads to male oppression—sex differences—could be abolished. The former approach is taken by those who adhere to lesbianism as a political choice. "Being a Lesbian means ending identification with, allegiance to, dependence on, and support of heterosexuality. It means ending your personal stake in the male world so that you join women, individually and collectively, in the struggle to end your oppression."[12] Others feel that lesbianism relates only to sexual, not political, preference, but argue that women-only institutions, the creation of "womanculture" or "womanspace," will allow women to discover their true needs and potentialities free of patriarchal definitions. Radical feminists have opened women's centers, health clinics, and cooperative businesses,[13] where women can celebrate these special qualities—their superiority, as some see it—that spring from their closeness to nature. The very same nurturant, life-giving qualities that allow men to oppress women under patriarchy are thus turned toward each other and used to create a new kind of society.[14]

Living apart from men is one way to escape oppression; the other is to wipe out sex differences. For Shulamith Firestone, "sex class is so deep as to be invisible," and so the necessity for abolishing sex has not been obvious. Yet the inevitability of sexism means that no other course—not even an economic or a cultural revolution—will suffice: "If there were another word more all-embracing than *revolution* we would use it." For

Firestone, the "dialectic of sex" precedes that of class. The only solution is to abolish childbearing and the family in their present forms and replace them with artificial reproduction and flexible, contractual households containing adults and children who agree to share their lives for a given period. Firestone acknowledges that production would have to change as well: "We would first have to have . . . socialism within a cybernated state, aiming first to redistribute drudgery equitably, and eventually to eliminate it altogether." Still, the important basis for the revolution is the elimination of the sex distinction itself, so that "genital differences between human beings would no longer matter culturally."[15] Technology—conventionally a male-dominated enterprise—is necessary to accomplish Firestone's revolution, which may be why it has not become part of the mainstream of radical feminist thought.[16]

Traditional Marxists see women's oppression very differently, as an element of capitalist oppression.[17] Women are relegated to secondary status in the home—cooking, cleaning, and bearing and raising children—while men do important productive work in the paid economy. Women's housework is unpaid and hence seen as unimportant, but women are available as a surplus labor pool when the money economy needs their services.[18]

By isolating adult women from one another, the family as an institution denies women the opportunity to develop class consciousness.[19] Some Marxist feminists have called for women to be paid wages for housework, so that their status as workers would be recognized and to give them a basis for organization. However, critics have charged that the change would perpetuate the present inefficient system of doing laundry, cooking, and childcare separately for each family, as well as reinforcing traditional sex-biased status lines.[20]

For Marxist feminists, capitalist men—not men generally—are the enemy. The radical feminists' focus on male oppression within the family is derided as a "pernicious ideological mask to obscure the class struggle."[21] Still, Marxists have not answered what is for many feminists the most important question: why is it women who do women's work?[22] By concentrating on economic class instead of sexual class, traditional Marxists lose sight of women's oppression that cuts across class lines.

Socialist feminists take the Marxists to task for neglecting reproduction and criticize the radicals for overlooking history. For the socialist feminists, women are an oppressed class; this oppression varies across cultures and epochs, though it derives from women's responsibility for the private sphere of procreation. Alison Jagger summarizes the basic position:

[S]ocialist feminism does not view humans as "abstract, genderless" (and ageless and colorless) individuals, with women essentially indistinguishable from men. Neither does it view women as irreducibly different from men, the same yesterday, today and forever. Instead, it views women as constituted essentially by the social relations they inhabit.[23]

The socialist feminists believe that a sexual revolution as well as an economic revolution must occur before male dominance will end. "It is necessary to transform not just education, nor simply work, nor sexuality, nor parenting. We must transform everything." The historical confluence of patriarchy and capitalism calls for multidimensional solutions corresponding to the multiple oppressors. The wage system must be eliminated; men must be included in childrearing "and, so far as possible, in childbearing." The nuclear family, that "corner-stone of women's oppression," would give way to communal living arrangements.[24]

Oppression is the common thread running through all the leftist feminist analyses, although the nature and source of oppression vary. "The Redstockings Manifesto," an early radical feminist document, asserts that "women are an oppressed class. . . . *All men* have oppressed women."[25] Zillah Eisenstein, in her analysis of why liberal feminism must turn to radicalism, calls patriarchy "a political structure . . . a system of oppression," whose "purpose is to destroy woman's consciousness about her potential power, which derives from the necessity of society to reproduce itself."[26] For socialist feminist Sheila Rowbotham, women's oppression may be peculiar, but it is oppression nonetheless: "The relationship of men to women is like no other relationship of oppressor to oppressed. It is far more delicate, far more complex. After all, very often the two love one another. . . . We are subdued at the very moment of intimacy."[27] Simone de Beauvoir treats women's biology—their "child-bearing properties"—as the source of powerlessness; nature itself oppresses women.[28]

This reliance on oppression as a comprehensive explanation of all women's ills, from lack of day care to rape to low pay for nurses, is really not an argument subject to proof or falsification. It is best understood as a paradigm, a heuristic device for perceiving and organizing the present. In the natural sciences, Thomas Kuhn argues in his pathbreaking study, the paradigm tames disorderly data by providing "a map whose details are elucidated by mature scientific research," introducing a way to comprehend an otherwise incoherent universe.[29] The usefulness of any scientific paradigm is itself subject to constant testing by the familiar methods of observation and experience. When paradigms compete for attention, the one likely to be ultimately adopted by the scientific community is better able than its competitors to solve problems that the group recognizes as acute.

Yet competition among paradigms can never wholly be settled by recourse to objective proofs. It is not any particular body of data but rather the nonempirical issue of what most requires explanation that often underlies the dispute. In such situations, Kuhn asserts, there is no way to use the tools of normal science to choose between competing paradigms, for the tools themselves are rooted in the paradigm being challenged. The role of paradigms in these grand debates about the "right" paradigm is "necessarily circular. Each group uses its own paradigm to argue in that paradigm's defense." Such an argument cannot prove anything. It serves only to persuade, since "for those who refuse to step into the circle" it isn't determinative "logically or even probabilistically. . . . The premises and values shared by the two parties in a debate over paradigms are not sufficiently extensive for that."[30]

Concerning explanations of men's and women's status, no body of evidence explains more than a fraction of perceived reality. Even the nature of data is subject to debate, since new evidence can be described as too partial to be relevant, and can be interpreted in distinct and even antagonistic ways. While these conditions hold true for anything that cannot be tested in the laboratory, the scope and complexity of this particular phenomenon renders *any* explanation an unlikely candidate for consensus. The ideological context becomes particularly significant in these circumstances, since the paradigm functions as a political and ideological construct.

The paradigm of sexual oppression, whether focused on the system of production or the system of reproduction, serves a vital purpose in feminist analysis: it explains women's present condition in a way that absolves women from any responsibility for having entered into this condition. The power of men over women is treated as "all-encompassing," the exclusion of women from power "systematic."[31] That women lack even the knowledge of their own oppression only attests to the enormity of the imposition. "Many women do not recognize themselves as discriminated against," writes Kate Millett. "No better proof could be found of the totality of their conditioning."[32] Only those who have not succumbed to "false consciousness"—the enlightened feminists—can see the true situation.

The idea of oppression thus creates a view of the world in which choice has no meaning, at least concerning present circumstance. "A free individual," says Simone de Beauvoir, "blames only himself for his failures, he assumes responsibility for them; but everything happens to women through the agency of others and therefore these others are responsible for her woes.''[33] Because there exists neither autonomy nor power for woman, there cannot consequently be any acceptance of responsibility. De Beauvoir's "mad" childwoman, or the housewife of whom Betty Friedan wrote two decades ago, a woman who harbors some enormous and unutterable grudge against her world, lacks a will of her own. Indeed, she has no self, apart from that which has been bestowed upon her by society.

III

In explaining the contemporary salience of gender, leftist feminists do not have the ideological field to themselves. While the naturalists, like the feminists, see women as weak and dependent, they offer a very different explanation.[34] Distinctions between the lives of men and women are ascribed not to oppression but instead to biological causality. Research in such specialized and rapidly evolving fields as neuroendocrinology and brain neurochemistry is appraised with an eye to identifying fundamental physical differences between men and women, which in turn are used to explain differences in political or economic status.

It cannot be denied that as biology and psychology get more sophisticated, research finds more differences between men and women. Women are, on average, more sensitive to sound and touch, more attuned to people, and more verbal than men. Men suffer more from heart attacks and less from autoimmune disease, are better at visual-spatial tasks than verbal ones, and are more sensitive to light than women.[35] Physical bases for these differences are being explored. Testosterone, the essential male hormone, appears to prime the brain to respond in a typically "male" way, whether the person is a genetic male or not. Brain structure itself seems to differ for men and women; unlike men, whose verbal abilities are confined to the left hemisphere and visual-spatial skills to the right, the functions in women's brains seem to be less clearly separated. This difference in brain structure seems to account for why men are better at doing verbal and visual-spatial tasks at the same time and why women are widely believed to have a special "intuition" that allows them to integrate many kinds of immediate impressions into a unified whole. Men seem to be more rule-bound and women more attuned to nuances of relationships.

For all that science has learned about the differences between men and women, however, the fact remains that the similarities are overwhelming. Biopsychologist Jerre Levy points out that the differences are "rather minor compared to differences between people of the same sex: of all the variations we observe among people, eighty to ninety-five percent of them are *within* men and *within* women.''[36] The differences are averages, not absolutes. They may give us insights into puzzling outcomes, such as the persistent surplus of boys turned up by national searches for mathematically gifted youngsters, but they are not givens, reasons to revise institutions.

This fact has not stopped those who would maintain the present order from relying on biological differences in crafting their argument. Males are ''hormonally equipped with a factor giving them a greater capacity for aggression, and this factor can be invoked in any domain in which it will lead to success,'' Steven Goldberg writes.[37] Lionel Tiger and Robin Fox hold that biologically determined aggression produces certain specific forms of behavior, such as the masculine tendency to bond together, and more generally to guarantee the inevitable domination of men in positions of authority and status in politics, the academy, science, and finance.[38] This domination is held to flow naturally from the sort of the primate that we are, constituting an irremediable fact of life. To the naturalists, it is fanciful to imagine a different reality; one does not displace the given order.

Those who argue that natural differences lead to social differences disagree about what is natural. Aggression, fraternal bonding, territoriality, patriarchy, and female acquiescience have all been advanced as candidates.[39] And while something is now known about the genetic and hormonal mechanisms that contribute to innate sex differences, the relationship between hereditary and environmental influences on human behavior remains imperfectly specified. None of that seems much to affect the course of argument, however, which proceeds as if answers were plain. In the politically charged world where these matters are discussed, the fact that naturalism purports to confirm traditional perceptions of women's place assures this approach a favorable reception in some quarters. Naturalism offers a rationale for the traditional that relies, not on discredited paternalism or mere convenience, but on the arcana of modern science.

The naturalistic paradigm resembles old-fashioned paternalism in another way. It regards societally sanctioned limitations on women's sphere of competence not only (or even primarily) as an imperative to be secured by coercion if necessary, but also as a form of collective kindness. Women's condition represents a desirable state of affairs, not a problem.

> No doubt some women would be aggressive enough to succeed in competitions with men and there would be considerably more women in high status positions than there are now. But most women would lose in such competitive struggles with men (because men

have the aggression advantage) and so most women would be forced to live adult lives as failures in areas in which *society had wanted them to succeed.*[40]

Worse still from the feminist perspective, the naturalists assert that women themselves realize and act on this premise, molding their children to confirm biological differentness: "It is women, far more than men, who would never allow a situation in which girls were socialized in such a way that the vast majority of them were doomed to adult lifetimes of failure to live up to their own expectations."[41]

Unsurprisingly, the naturalist denies the explanatory plausibility of oppression. Lionel Tiger and Robin Fox, who use "conspiracy" and "oppression" synonymously, declare,

> [I]t cannot be a conspiracy of men against women that once swept the world that now—so apparently securely—sets limits on the range of female options to enter the powerful macrostructures of economic life. The evidence against conspiracy comes from too heterogeneous a set of places: females are obviously able to do the tasks that men can—that is when they are given the opportunity; males are unlikely to have deliberately thought up ways of maintaining women in their homes for domestic and sexual convenience and then brainwashed them to accept such an exploitative situation—if exploitative it is. Perhaps . . . we are dealing here with a regularity of the biogrammar that has to do with ancient forms of survival that mark us still today.[42]

"Regularity of the biogrammar": that telling phrase, linchpin of the argument, is quite as fanciful as anything that feminists have conjured up in the service of oppression. It suggests a mode of discourse in which metaphor parades as proof, even as it denies its own conclusion—for if women can "obviously" perform male tasks, how "regular" can the "biogrammar" be?—and it ultimately proves nothing. It also reveals the ahistoricity of the naturalist approach, its failure to note the possibility and reality of mediating nature's impact on the lives of men and women through education, technology, and politics.

Perhaps there was good reason to distinguish between male hunters and female nurturers in primitive society; not so in a postindustrial era, when height and weight differences between the sexes count for little. In its inattention to the possibility of political choice, naturalism also fails to recognize the relationship between "civilization," not just mere survival, and limitations on brute nature.[43] The present is neither inevitable nor necessarily beneficent: this much we owe to politics and morality.

The naturalist approach offers only another partial and partisan way to make sense of what is relevant. Its purpose is less the scientific end of enlightment than the institutional aim of conserving tradition. Yet the naturalists cannot even ground their argument on solid fact, for all around them, women and men are throwing off old roles and adopting new ones. When women serve on police forces and men become nurses, it is only nostalgia to believe that hormones and brain structure will preserve the past. As a lens through which to view the world, naturalism turns out to be wholly as paradigmatic in its derivation and its implications as oppression.

IV

Neither naturalists nor leftist feminists have much use for debates about policy. Policy has little relevance to the naturalists, since tinkering with the essentially unchangeable can only work mischief; this is how Lionel Tiger reads the evidence from the history of the Israeli kibbutz. Even in that society, formally committed to minimize sex differences, men and women came to assume "traditional" roles.[44] E. O. Wilson, who has explored the evolutionary functions of sex differences, points out that those who attempt to overcome traditional male and female traits will not do so painlessly: "We believe that cultures can be rationally designed. We can teach and reward and coerce. But in so doing we must also consider the price of each culture, measured in the time and energy required for training and enforcement and in the less tangible currency of human happiness that must be spent to circumvent our innate predispositions."[45]

Sociobiology offers a kind of naturalist paradigm that can be used to justify change, but not ordinary political change. Wilson claims that biological knowledge cannot be appreciated by nonscientists, for "neurobiology cannot be learned at the feet of a guru." Like women who do not know they are oppressed, those of us who believe we can transcend our hormones are only deceiving ourselves. "Although human progress can be achieved by intuition and force of will, only hard-won empirical knowledge of our biological nature will allow us to make optimum choices among the competing criteria of progress."[46] Wilson envisions a scientist-king who will lead us out of the shadows of political choice into a world where we transform ourselves by genetic manipulation. This dismissal of intuitive understandings and ordinary knowledge is at least as arrogant as leftist feminist accusations of false consciousness, and equally scornful of the everyday world of politics and policy choice.[47] If the correct answer can be found in the laboratory, why enter the messy realm of legislatures?

Perhaps the naturalists have avoided making policy proposals because the sorts of actions that *would* be supported by evidence of biological differences between the sexes repress the kinds of choices that are now taken for granted. The naturalist paradigm suggests that men and women require different treatment, attractive to neither. If most women will not become mathematicians without special help and training, why devote public resources to educating them beyond the level needed for everyday life? If men are innately aggressive—and young men particularly so—why not subject teenage males to curfews and confinement in order to minimize everyday violence? The naturalist paradigm can offer only a paean to science, ignoring the political world where it is unlikely to enjoy a warm reception.

Leftist feminists are also unable to speak in terms of policy. They do not deal with politics, as that term is conventionally understood—for instance, they do not discuss the idea of citizenship—for oppression is not the sort of force readily addressed in familiar political terms.[48] How does one confront something as diffuse, amorphous, and ubiquitous as "the culture"? As feminist anthropologist Gayle Rubin observes, sorting through the several understandings of the sources of oppression,

> If innate male aggression and dominance are at the root of female oppression, then the feminist program would logically require either the extermination of the offending sex or else a eugenics project to modify its character. If sexism is a byproduct of capitalism's relentless appetite for profit, then sexism would wither away in the advent of a successful socialist revolution. If the world historical defeat of women occurred at the hands of an armed patriarchal revolt, then it is time for Amazon guerillas to start training in the Adirondacks.[49]

To Rubin, the world of incremental politics is hardly equal to the task of transformation. Guerilla training, eugenics, and extermination are not the stuff of ordinary political discourse; indeed, socialist revolution is the *least* radical alternative that Rubin advances.

Unlike most naturalists, the leftist feminists fervently imagine the possibility of social change. Yet the ubiquity of oppression means that only revolution will result in their own—and society's—liberation. Seemingly every arrangement that now exists must be swept away, an extremism that calls to mind Edmund Burke's jibe at the French Revolution: "You began ill because you began by despising everything that belonged to you. You set up your trade without a capital."[50] The enormity of the leftist feminists' self-imposed task leaves the particulars unspecified. "Revolutionary politics," Juliet Mitchell writes, "is linear—it must move from the individual to the small group to the whole society."[51] But just how that might happen, what the dynamic of that transformation might be, remains mysterious.

Politics is everything, the radicals argue, for "there is no private domain of a person's life that is not political. . . ."[52] But if politics is everything, it is also nothing, too huge to be intelligently discussed. Politics and policy are "to be dispensed with altogether in some future classless order."[53] Leftist feminism underestimates the difficulties of getting from here to there. Rather than presenting a program, it makes casual and sometimes troubling assertions, which carry profound implications both for family structure and for the world of work.

Shulamith Firestone, for instance, announces an extraordinary approach to the family.[54] Firestone imagines that both the family and the child are relatively recent cultural inventions that emerged in recognizable form only half a millennium ago. The proposition sounds improbable on its face, since one cannot readily conceive of seven-year-olds passing unnoticed in adult society, even in the fourteenth century. But Firestone does not really care about the historical record. She means instead to use history to show that, because families and children have only latterly oppressed women, those oppressions may readily be removed.

What is bothersome in Firestone's analysis is not that historical invention is being turned to women's apparent advantage, for such uses of history are familiar enough, but the blithe assumption that the institutions of childhood and the family can somehow be abolished with no ill effect or social strain. If an argument for such a new world is indeed going to be made, it has to be given meaning by examining its implications. Would children truly be better off if left largely to their own devices? What of the likelihood of greater drug use, psychological disturbance, teenage pregnancy, and sexual exploitation by their elders that would predictably accompany the liberation of the very young?[55]

Because there has never been a society without families, the full impact of Firestone's proposal cannot be assayed. But where the family has been subordinated to the state—ancient Sparta and Nazi Germany, for instance—women have not fared especially well.[56] To address these matters seriously and to consider alternatives less drastic than eliminating femininity and childhood, betokens either melioration (not revolution) or absorption into the concerns of something broader than radical feminism. The Left finds neither of these acceptable.[57]

Moving from analyses to remedies poses particularly acute problems for feminists whose approach emphasizes the psychodynamics of gender, for psychology is far better at identifying what makes particular behaviors desirable—indeed, necessary at the subconscious level—than it is at proposing alternatives. Consider two of the most sophisticated of these feminists, Dorothy Dinnerstein and Nancy Chodorow.[58] Both are committed to dismantling existing gender arrangements, the division of "responsibility, opportunity and privilege" between the sexes and "the patterns of psychological interdependence . . . implicit in this division."[59] All well and good: but their explorations of the roots of those differences in early child-rearing point out how basic to personality, how deeply held, these traits are. The subtle—and differing—treatments of the psychodynamic that leads women to want to mother, usefully point us away from what Chodorow labels the "functional-cum-bio-evolutionary" approach, toward the enduring power of the ties between infant and mother. Yet if mothering is not an activity imposed on women—for a woman will not mother "unless she, to some degree and on some unconscious or conscious level, has the capacity and sense of self as maternal to do so"[60]—and if mothering by women replicates patriarchy, how is the chain to be broken?

Here the analyses falter. We could have equal "mothering" by fathers and mothers now if we wanted it, Dinnerstein claims, relegating to a footnote the colossal political and social puzzles raised by this offhand remark.[61] Men must learn to be "equal" parents while women become more autonomous, Chodorow asserts, without hinting how this profound transformation might be brought about.[62]

Analytical weaknesses of a different sort characterize radical feminists' discussion of the world of work, where the problem is one of critical default. If participation on equal terms in a capitalist economy guarantees only free admission to the world of the ulcer and the coronary, and socialist economies have proved as capable of oppressing women as has capitalism, what alternative is available? Germaine Greer looks forward to a "festival of the oppressed. . . . If [women's liberation] abolishes the patriarchal family, it will abolish a necessary substructure of the authoritarian state, and once that withers away Marx will come true willy-nilly, so let's get on with it." But such analysis has little relevance to the woman on the factory assembly line—indeed, to anyone in our society.[63] Juliet Mitchell, a more serious theorist, states that women's "entry into the work-force is not enough: they must enter in their own right and with their own independent interest."[64] But what that interest might be, how it might be communicated and acted upon, is not spelled out. Short of the overthrow of capitalism, there is little discussion by leftist feminists of what policy choices in the world of work would look like.[65]

The distaste of these feminists for politics and policy stems partly from the realization that, in treating suffrage as the crucial determinant of liberation, the early suffragists exaggerated their case. At the 1848 Seneca Falls Convention, Elizabeth Cady Stanton and Frederick Douglass argued that suffrage constituted "the right by which all others could be secured."[66] The persistent refusal of men to grant that right only magnified its importance, and by the end of the century, feminists were fixated on gaining the vote:

> The effect of generations of concentration on this one issue, the narrowing of feminism itself from the wide-open early days, the compromises made, opportunities exploited, and sacrifices endured all in the name of votes for women, destroyed the balance and perspective of hard-core suffragists. They came to desire the vote not for what it actually was or for what it could do but for its own sweet sake.[67]

Suffrage itself was an anticlimax, for it brought about none of the broader social reforms that suffragists anticipated. That suffrage had such modest impact on women's status revealed the weakness of sex as a political category. A Women's Party survived little more than a decade after passage of the amendment. Until the recent emergence of a "gender gap," women have not spoken with a coherent or effective voice within the major parties,[68] and their policy preferences have been indistinguishable from those of men. The realization that sexual differences do not define political life has, in turn, nurtured the suspicion that feminism itself was never an autonomous movement but only an instrument in the hands of the politicans, an epiphenomenon of a deeper social drama. Suffragist analysis had not probed deeply enough:

> Because the approach of the suffragists avoided questioning received ideas about women's role, it invited an over-investment of emotion in the goal it offered, and in so doing imported a familiar kind of mythic ambiguity into the heart of the struggle: the ends pursued could not even when achieved produce the results that were promised. On the one hand, the reformers declared what many women truly felt: that they could no longer accept the sort of lives which were prescribed by the narrow limits of their traditional place and activities. But on the other hand, the solution they offered—the vote—was not commensurate with the problem.[69]

If suffrage did not suffice, what would? In the early 1960s, Betty Friedan wrote that feminism has to respond to "the problem with no name,"[70] but the very magnitude of the problem appears to deny the possibility of solution—or even of meaningful change.[71] The dilemma is not unique to leftist feminism; it pertains generally to radical politics in America, which has shunned reform because melioration would only lend "indirect support to the antihumanist values imposed by the American social order," and so has often wound up embracing "utopian mirages."[72] Because feminism sought to probe deeper, the concern was even more acute, the possibility of political irrelevance even more real.

The call for women to opt out of politics entirely, forming their own separate and purer society, rings familiar changes. Its echoes are distinctly utopian, as are its shortcomings. A female countersociety, as Julia Kristeva notes, "is imagined as harmonious, without prohibitions, free and fulfilling." But "as with any society, the countersociety is based on the expulsion of an excluded element, a scapegoat charged with the evil of which the community duly constituted can then purge itself. . . . Does not feminism become a kind of inverted sexism when this logic is followed to its conclusion?"[73] A single, unified feminist vision, unqualified and unquestioned—one in which "woman" melts into "women," men having wholly quit the scene—is neither likely nor appealing, for institutions peopled by men and women cannot be so painlessly or effortlessly undone. Benjamin Barber reminds us that

> families, relationships, politics are more than integral to the problem: they define the women and men whose compound identities constitute the problem. At their best they permit the sexes to join in a mutual quest for personal freedom and human equality as they continue to serve the distinctive sexual and reproductive needs of males and females. The just polity serves not neuters but women and men, adjusting the demands of equity to meet the needs of sexual differentiation.[74]

V

Paradigms can be helpful in simplifying the complex world that we observe. Both the naturalist and leftist feminist paradigms accomplish a measure of simplification, but only by distorting reality. The leftist feminist paradigm contains an important kernel of truth. It is not just that women's choices have been constrained—in any social order, people's choices are constrained—but rather than these constraints impinge more tightly on women than on men. Yet because this rendering of oppression encompasses seemingly everything, it loses its power to distinguish between the consequential and the trivial.

Oppression is best appreciated as metaphor, not literal description, and the metaphor has been much overused. When the oppression of women is contrasted with the oppression of nineteenth century slaves or Cambodians under Pol Pot, even its value as metaphor diminishes. In asserting that oppression is a universal state, leftist feminism exaggerates. Some women acknowledge themselves as badly treated because of their sex; most, we suspect, experience both happiness and unhappiness with traditional sex roles. But to identify that far-from-mythical character, the reasonably content and nonrevolutionary housewife and mother, as oppressed precisely because she fails objectively to appreciate that her condition constitutes a plight, is to assume an omniscient position better reserved for deities than social observers. To turn all relations between the sexes into sexual politics or to define American married woman as bartered objects is deliberately to blind oneself to consequential distinctions among epochs, to ignore critical differences within and among societies. "If patriarchy is everywhere," writes Janet Flammang in her examination of feminist theories of power, "then it is nowhere, in the sense that it cannot be subject to scrutiny and analysis."[75]

There is some modest truth too to be gleaned from the naturalist approach. It is highly unlikely that the full force of genetic factors is spent in apportioning reproductive responsibilities. Even if reproduction were somehow to be "liberated" from gender, sexual differences would remain—although to what extent we do not know. Yet, contrary to the naturalists' claim, it makes better sense to conceive of most differences as predispositions, not as unalterable givens. Biology does not constitute the sole or even the primary cause of observable differences between the sexes; genetic endowment does not offer a blueprint that defines future behavior. This is particularly true in advanced industrial nations, where civilized life is more dependent on exogenous factors than on biologically driven divisions of labor.

The relevance of biology depends on the social context, although the naturalists make no mention of this. They also glide over the significant behavioral variability among males and among females. These variations, familiar to all of us, hint at the power of culturally imposed and individually willed transformation, socialization and self-socialization, on the development of personality. How we as a society might choose to channel the influence of biological factors is a vital question, not one that can be dismissed with the lofty assertion that "ethical philosophy must not be left in the hands of the merely wise."[76] If traditional patriarchy is not the answer, neither is Brave New World.

Both leftist feminism and naturalism dismiss the range and variety of human experience, and ignore the enormous overlap between the life histories of men and women. As paradigms, they paint a stark world, one filled with "either/or's," but lack any tolerance for complexity and ambiguity, for the reality of "both/and." Philosopher Bernard Williams' assault on utilitarianism applies in full force to the leftist feminist and naturalist world views: each offers "a great singlemindedness," with "too few thoughts and feelings to match the world as it really is."[77] Each assumes that correct answers exist and that the purveyors of the paradigms have discovered them, while everyone else remains in ignorance. As sociologist G. Russell Carpenter has said of Marxists, "How can they be sure they are not profoundly hoodwinked by a history more cunning than that history they think they know? That is, how can they be sure they are not falsely conscious? They cannot be sure."[78] By attributing causality to genes or patriarchy, paradigms lose sight of the individuals involved.

Thus, the analytic defects of both the naturalists and the leftist feminists, while very different, reveal a common underlying weakness: the paradigms stress what happens to women, rather than attributing to them any significant part in shaping their circumstances. Each of the paradigms ignores the existence of will; neither in the world of the naturalists nor in that of the leftist feminists do there exist morally responsible individuals. Although the causes of present circumstance are treated differently, each of the models locates those causes outside the individual. Biology, economics, or culture—not the actions of individuals—are regarded as controlling.

Although the issue of free will, broached in chapter 1, has deep philosophical ramifications that lie well beyond our reach, a few points are relevant to our argument.[79] For one thing, implicit in our tendency to judge behavior, praising and blaming individuals for their acts, is the belief that there exists a sphere of activity susceptible to individual volition; to appraise someone for behavior over which he or she has no control makes no sense. Moreover, the way we understand the world includes an element of originality in which the mind functions as responsible agent, and this is at odds with a deterministic outlook. "Into every act of knowing," Michael Polanyi has written, "there enters a tacit and passionate contribution of the person knowing what is being known, and this coefficient is not mere imperfection, but a necessary component of all knowledge." Learning always entails "wide discretion of choice."[80]

Habit does not constitute proof; determinism cannot so easily be set aside. The search for an escape from the awful ambiguity of the present by hunting for some underlying key, a causal element outside ourselves that will explain all, has abiding appeal. In this way of seeing the world, as Isaiah Berlin notes, "explanation is the discovery of the underlying pattern. The ideal is now not a distant prospect beckoning all things and persons toward self-realization, but a self-consistent, eternal, ultimate structure of reality."[81] That structure of reality, Berlin adds, has nothing to do with individual choice. "Self-realization" seems merely delusory, a way of evading underlying forces in such an ordered world. Seen in this context, oppression and naturalism are just two among many candidates for explaining all:

> Race, colour, church, nation, class; climate, irrigation, technology, geo-political situation; civilization, social structure, the Human Spirit, the Collective Unconscious . . . have all played their parts . . .as the protagonists upon the stage of history. . . . What the variants . . . entail, like all forms of genuine determinism, is the elimination of the notion of individual responsibility.[82]

This denial of individual responsibility poses the most significant moral dilemma for determinism generally and for the gender paradigms specifically. In the absence of proof, it makes pragmatic sense to judge determinism by the value one places on responsibility as itself a good. The temptation to avoid responsibility by pointing to hormones or sexist society or some other external happenstance to exonerate bad behavior is properly resisted because of the conception of humanity we thereby honor. We reaffirm ourselves as human, capable of being distinguished from other species precisely in our capacity to exercise choice. By opting for our own plan of life rather than imagining it as imposed on us, we engage in a uniquely human enterprise that expresses our moral dignity. To denigrate such choice is to denigrate human worth, for as philosopher Robert Nozick points out,

> Without free will we seem diminished, merely the playthings of external causes. Our value seems undercut. The various questions [about the meaning of life] arise from, are shaped and made vivid by, a concern with our value, significance, importance, stature, and preciousness. If our lives cannot have meaning, if we are no more than puppets of causes, if our attempts at knowledge are foredoomed to

failure, if we have no worth that the actions of others ought to respect, then we are devoid of value.[83]

Acceptance of the concept of will and responsibility also reestablishes the awesome complexity of the world we inhabit. One implication of free will is that "different value consequences occur in the world than otherwise would; these were not in the cards already."[84] It is not the case, of course, that women and men now find themselves wholly free to map their own lives. And while one can readily conceive of a society tolerant of greater latitude, a world without social conventions is neither imaginable nor appealing. A person's self-conception depends on defining the self, not in isolation but in relation to others. Any social order properly and necessarily makes its own demands, forces its accommodations as a concomitant of our living together in some form of community. The society contributes to the definition of person—gives a social context for individuality—just as persons contribute to the social order and ponder the necessity for social change.[85]

If volition has a relevance that neither the feminists nor the naturalists acknowledge, the possibility of personal choice does not tell the entire story. Midge Decter makes an important point in noting that today a woman "must decide things *for herself* that only a moment ago in history life decided for her." Yet for a great many women, the further assertion that "women are for the time being caught in a transition in which they feel themselves too little shaped by society, its demands on them too indefinite, their own demands on themselves (or lack of them) far too operative," proves too much.[86] If lifestyles may now be won by personal effort to a greater extent than ever before, if adults are in some circumstances free and hence responsible agents, that condition is surely not so universal, nor so unmediated by the varying demands of the community, as to justify its elevation to the status of universal present truth. We are not as lacking in will as the naturalists and the leftist feminists would have it, but neither can choice itself be treated as a single explanatory variable, the core of yet another paradigm.

VI

What all of this—the distortions of the present, the unsatisfactory treatment of policy dilemmas, the failure to come to terms with the reality of human will, in both leftist feminism and naturalism—may reveal is that the paradigm itself is an inappropriate way of addressing the present. The place of gender is just too complicated and multifaceted to be rendered in paradigmatic fashion; or so it seems presently, at least. We may eventually look back on what Susanne Langer describes as

> an unintended, unguided, but irresistible revolution in all human relations from the marriage bonds and family controls whereby personal life has traditionally been ordered, to the religious and patriotic loyalties that were wont to rule people's wider activities. Such a change in the human scene requires and effects a change in the concepts with which we operate practically and intellectually. . . .[87]

Langer speaks of nothing less than a paradigmatic revolution in which we now find ourselves. Perhaps this is so. Yet while concurring with Langer that "basic social conceptions [concerning gender] have changed," it is impossible adequately to specify the nature of that change.[88] The society remains in transition, not ready to embrace paradigmatic truths.

The paradigmatic view of the world contemplates a static order; observed reality is altogether different. "Becoming human is becoming individual," writes Clifford Geertz, "and we become individual under the guidance of cultural patterns, historically created systems of meaning in terms of which we give form, order, point, and direction to our lives."[89] We also change those patterns even as we become individuals—each choice is constrained by what went before and constrains what choices are possible thereafter. The flux and not the stasis, the moving picture rather than the snapshot demand our closest attention. It is the process that redefines the rules of the game and thus alters our potentiality as men and women, not some single static model of the relevance of gender, that illumines the condition of both sexes.

4

Gender in the Context
of Community

That both self-interest *and* something else are satisfied by group life is the notion that is hardest for the hard-boiled—and half-baked—person to see.
  C. G. Homans, *The Human Group* (1950)

Individualism, if it can be purged of its defects and abuses, is the best safeguard of personal liberty in the sense that, compared with any other system, it greatly widens the field for the exercise of personal choice. It is also the best safeguard of the variety of life, which emerges precisely from this extended field of personal choice, and the loss of which is the greatest of all the losses of the homogeneous or totalitarian state. For this variety preserves the traditions which embody the most secure and successful choices of former generations; it colors the present with the diversification of its fancy. . . .
  John Maynard Keynes, *The General Theory* (1936)

I

Our critique of the leftist feminists and naturalists centers on their shared assumption that individuals' lives are shaped by outside forces; we object to a view of human nature that rejects the proposition, key to liberalism, that women and men can shape their own lives. On the other side, critiques of liberalism often assail that approach for treating individuals as anomic and free-floating, with no connections to others. While we believe that individuals can and do make choices, neither do we deny that they are profoundly affected by the communities in which they live. Whether this realization should modify our conception of gender justice as grounded in individual choice is the question addressed in this chapter. Communities— clusterings bound by blood, propinquity, workplace, national identity, and interest—are viewed by some as meanly parochial and celebrated by others as the repository of civic virtue.[1] In either case, do they render choice illusory? Is there a form of community in which gender justice could flourish?

An ethic of individuality, taken to its logical extreme, looks alienating and frightening, as in Michael Walzer's bleak depiction of "individualism with a vengeance . . . a human being, thoroughly divorced, freed of parents, spouse, and children, watching pornographic performances in some dark theater, joining (it may be his only membership) this or that odd cult, which he will probably leave in a month or two for another still odder."[2] If individualism sustained only this sort of life, there would be little reason to advance it as the basis of a public philosophy. But upholding individualism does not necessarily undermine the value of at least some forms of community.[3]

The fact of community cannot be denied, for it is as potent as the families we are born into, the neighborhoods where we live, the countries to which we owe allegiance. No philosophical construct labelled "the human being" or "the individual" can undo the reality that we are in good measure what our relationships make us, that we are really, and not just incidentally, Chicagoans or Catholics or Chinese, husbands or sisters or uncles. Whether or not we choose to endow these facts with public significance, they remain facts. And even in an era that celebrates individualism, we still pity the orphan, extend charity to the homeless, work to find solutions for the problems of refugees. People do not participate in the drama of life as characters in some morality play, as Citizen or Consumer. They come with names, experiences, connections.[4]

If the reality of community in its many forms endures, the appearance of community has changed. When social and physical mobility were limited, people were joined in their quest for the necessities of life, coming together in the village, the church, and the guild. Now, however, with telephones and air travel sustaining connections across long distances and the possibilities of exiting from a class or social group having become more real, groups are more likely to be voluntarily embraced, not fixed at birth. This new form of community is harder to define than the traditional kind, of course, and some would deny that this is community at all. Still, at least one study of the contemporary experience of community finds that the new form is at least as vital as the old:

> The lowering of social and spacial barriers and the consequent increase in the freedom to choose social relationships have not led to less communal social ties. And it may just have led to the opposite. The disintegration of the monolithic community has perhaps led to the proliferation of many personal communities, each more compati-

ble and more supportive to the individual than ascribed corporate groups.[5]

Although the rise of individualism undermines the traditional community, this may license individuals to embrace new types of association, new communities; these new ties may be more compelling because they are chosen. Drawing on his studies of both primitive and modern communities, anthropologist Oscar Lewis reports that "there are deeper, more mature human relations among cosmopolitan individuals who have chosen each other in friendship than are possible among . . . peasants who are thrown together because of kinship or residential proximity."[6] A network of associations, each affecting particular aspects of our lives, has largely supplemented the all-encompassing traditional communities.

To talk of freely chosen communities presumes that people *can* choose, that they are not so molded by the worlds into which they are born that choice is chimerical. Yet this assumption is open to challenge by those who advance the sociological equivalent of the determinist position discussed in earlier chapters. Evidence of the all-powerful nature of communities, on the one hand, and of the snail's pace of social evolution, on the other, is marshalled to support the claim that individuals are not agents of their own destiny but merely the summing of their social influences. Concerning gender, the contention is that men and women are programmed to assume roles in precast forms of family and community.[7]

The critics have a case. It is hard to relate the concept of autonomy to the plight of poorly educated migrant workers who can hardly see beyond the next meal, for their realistic choices are pitifully few. It is similarly difficult to know what to make of the options actually open to children growing up in an Amish village, where heterodoxy is vigorously suppressed. These hard cases pose the most severe challenges to a conception of justice that is at once liberty-centered and hospitable to the claims of community.[8] The challenge of the sociological determinists, however, is not confined to the hard cases. They perceive all of us in the way we view Amish youngsters, as subjects and not agents. To believe otherwise, they contend, is to fall into the trap of false consciousness, in which the belief in our own volition is treated as a delusion fostered by the dominant social order.[9]

It would be foolish to deny that our life choices are influenced by our upbringing or that our relationships shape our personalities. If persons are taught the values of Mormons or Jews, Democrats or Marxists, materialists or environmentalists, this will affect their future choices. Nor is that necessarily bad. The individual nurtured in a vacuum, free from the taint of social influence, is hardly the ideal. The influence of others—nurturers, guardians, role models, peers—is inevitable, because the young necessarily depend on others for their very survival. Usually it is also a benign inevitability, since without a clear starting point, a sense of who we are, it would be hard to know what we aspire to. The prospect of infinite choice unaccompanied by a compass that enables us to set a course invites only infinite confusion, not personal clarity; the metaphor of the tabula rasa ill fits human beings constructing their own identities out of materials partly given in advance.[10]

There is no Archimedean point from which an outsider can determine whether, for a given individual, a mode of community is stultifying and inescapable or supportive and freely chosen. Only the person involved can know whether his or her life decision represents mere acquiescence or thoughtful consideration. Some people may never evaluate the ways of life they grow up with; others have thought long and hard about their futures, and have consciously chosen a particular form of association.

The idea that people who live their lives in conventional communities are oppressed presumes that if people are given the chance to choose, they will necessarily do something different. Volition does not guarantee change, however; even the most self-conscious exercise of choice will not always bring on the revolution. Legal scholars John Coons and Stephen Sugarman make this point in another context:

> A large measure of institutional continuity is what one could expect; the race is not programmed for anarchy. Nevertheless freedom to select one's own way could have profound psychological significance, even if only the few employ it to alter their external experience in substantial respects. To choose what has previously been compelled is choosing nonetheless. Perhaps the difference is only a matter of human dignity and our view of one another. To us that seems enough.[11]

Psychological differences between men and women may contribute to the persistence of traditional community forms, even in an age in which choice is possible. Psychologist Carol Gilligan finds that women typically view moral dilemmas in terms of care and responsibility in relationships, rather than in the terms of rights and rules favored by men; women prefer an ethic of care to the formal logic of fairness.[12] If women are instinctively more committed to relationships than rules, they may continue to focus much of their energy on the personal and private realms, leaving the public sphere largely to men.

The plausibility of this extension of Gilligan's argument depends on the source of the psychological differences that the data reveal. Gilligan may just be reporting the impact of traditional socialization, which is itself subject to change. Or the differences may run deeper—we cannot know on the basis of the evidence at hand. In any event, Gilligan is not proferring a fixed rule. At most, she has identified a sexually linked tendency that limits the capacity of the social engineers to order our lives.

For both men and women, the fetters of community are weakening. In this society, what is held up as desirable is seldom imposed absolutely; few people are bound for the kitchen or the plow. Moreover, in a world of instantaneous communication and information overflow, ways of life unacceptable to the group cannot be hidden from view: radios are not unknown even among the Amish. Communities may bend the twig, but they seldom set identities in stone.

II

The leftist feminists read the evidence quite differently, identifying existing communities with oppression, seeing in political and economic structures a design to subordinate women by maintaining their peripheral status. For them, as the last chapter elaborates, a women's identity as a woman precedes and necessarily forms part of her identity; thus she cannot have *chosen* her role. Since existing communities do not allow choice— and, by the feminist definition cannot, lest they destroy themselves—the only solution is to throw off the present and move to a wholly new future.

The one community that radical feminism can celebrate is a solidarity of sisterhood. In its extreme forms, that entity—variously known as the Amazon Nation, Lesbian Nation, or the Hag/ocracy—assumes its shape by the very fact of its exclusivity. It promises women freedom from oppression in a world from which men have been barred: "Lesbian or woman prime is *the* factor in advance of every projected solution for our embattled world. In her realization of herself both sensually polymorphously and genitally orgasmically she experiences her original self reproductive or parthenogenetic recreation of herself apart from the intruding and disturbing and subjugating male."[13]

This imaginary vision is described in prose that is designedly disjoint, even mystical, and devoid of particulars. Yet despite the poetic expression, the radical feminist view of *communitas* remains deeply dispiriting. To turn to the nunnery as a model for the new Atlantis betokens desperation, not inspiration—and even the nunnery is animated by a devotion to a common force that the abidingly secular radical feminists scorn. The community of exclusion signals not a new social form but a suicide pact among women so estranged from the present that an end to the species is preferable to intimate association with the antagonist, man; so prideful that they have arrogated all virtue to their sex, confusing sex with virtue; so self-centered as to dismiss the possibility that a succeeding generation might imagine a different way out of this predicament. Most charitably, the depiction is advanced as a metaphor to dramatize radical feminists' felt sense of hopelessness. Yet even appreciated metaphorically, the approach misfires, for the very idea of a world peopled entirely by a single sex remains morally obtuse.

Even those feminist proposals which accept that men cannot be banished entirely still assume that communities will look very different after the revolution, and that a revolution is required to alter them. For Marxist and socialist feminists alike, the realm of production will be transformed, and the family will also be recast.[14] In this view, women cannot break out of their roles as subservient wives and mothers on their own, and so must be prevented from taking on those roles.

The durability of particular forms of community gives rise to the leftist feminist lament that women are more shaped than shaping. But it is hard to accept their claim that male power is the only guiding force behind present institutions. The college-educated housewife depicted by Betty Friedan may have felt that there were roads not taken, that her role had been over-sold, but the organization man of the same period was also subject to a socialization that, while different, nonetheless limited his options. There is nothing inherently oppressive about American families or neighborhoods or churches, nothing akin to such unambiguously imposed forms of association as slavery and apartheid. The demands of kith and kin, seen as oppressive and limiting by some, are comforting and fulfilling to others.

Leftist feminists believe that community is something that happens *to* women, not something chosen; that, as Friedan once wrote, the home is merely a "comfortable concentration camp." For this reason, nothing less than a revolution will do to bring about less oppressive forms of community. Yet while the fear of imposition may have been plausible when the revival of feminist thought began a few decades ago, it is less clear today. Our social milieu comes permeated by the values of the age, but the United States in the late twentieth century is not a totalitarian regime, nor is the conventional imposed by a state bureau. In a world where much change has already occurred, and where that change is trumpeted nightly on the evening news, can there be many women so brainwashed as to believe that only traditional roles are open? The fact that choice and change, while not universal, are upheld as possibilities and celebrated as good suggests that existing models of community are not so pervasive—or oppressive—as leftist feminism supposes.

III

At the other extreme, the naturalists described in the last chapter, as well as those who long for the stable communities of the past, believe that choice is now too much in evidence, jeopardizing the community forms that ought properly exist. For their part, the naturalists regard the existence of gender-specific identities, clear and distinct understandings of masculinity and femininity, as a biological imperative that precedes and shapes social forms. We are what nature has programmed us to be, and those instincts cannot be wished away by social arrangement.[15] In the naturalists' world view, instinct should drive institutions.

The chorus of determinism about gender roles has recently been joined by the New Right. For them, the liberal acceptance of change and choice seems to have caused the deterioration of community, especially the break-down of the conventional family. In the New Right's ideal world, men and women would live out their God-given roles, as specified in the Bible. In the form of family- and church-based community they propose, father knows best and mother and children know their places.[16] While that vision offers stability and comfort to the devout, any wife not herself a Christian Fundamentalist is unlikely to find a model for living in the injunction to treat her husband like Jesus.[17] The determinism of the New Right implies a notion of the good life as narrow as the forms imposed by the naturalist or leftist feminist paradigms.

Those who scour history rather than biology or the Bible for their conception of community have in mind an all-encompassing way of life, a secure haven against change, an island where lives are lived in preordained fashion. This backward-looking vision embraces an idea of community in its strongest sense: a congregation of the like-minded, animated by a single knowable conception of the good. Robert Nisbet describes what we would find in an earlier age: "Whether we are dealing with the family, the village, or the gild, we are in the presence of systems of authority and allegiance which were widely held to precede the individual in both origin and right. . . . The group was primary; it was the irreducible unit of the social system at large."[18] It is this strong form of community that Tönnies had in mind when contrasting *Gemeinschaft* with *Gesellschaft;* it recalls Durkheim's mechanical solidarity, Burke's organic community, the Utopian inventions of the Owenities, the subsistence society fondly contemplated in our day by Ivan Illich.[19]

The strong community does not deny the importance of individual freedom, but asserts that it can only be realized through integration into a cohesive collective force. In Rousseau's *moi commun,* for instance, there is no tension between self and society; instead, the particular pattern of social existence is assumed "to be immanent in man's reason and will, to constitute the fullest satisfaction of his true interest, and to be the guarantee of his freedom."[20] Without a stable society and unquestioned authority, the tight bonds of family, community, vocational group, and religious orders, the individual is said to feel lost; the strong community rescues people from this sorry state.

The fixed character of the social order in backward-looking communities does not always imply fixed roles for the sexes, but this is often the case. The strong community is usually based on a vision of the family which assumes that, whatever the roles that men and women take on, they will be given beforehand, not chosen by the individuals involved. This is the kind of community celebrated by Ivan Illich in *Gender.*[21] Illich regards the prevailing patterns of masculine oppression as resulting from the demise of "vernacular gender," a state of affairs that prevailed when men and women occupied complementary roles in a subsistence economy. Stability reigned when males and females had to rely on one another, when both had their proper places, with neither sex dominant over the other.

This simple household-centered society began to disappear in the twelfth century, however, and, in Illich's account, it was finished off by the industrial revolution, which separated work and family, substituting "consumption-dependent production." In the industrial era, men and women no longer consumed what they made, but became "economic neuters belonging to two biological sexes," paid a wage that allowed them to purchase what others produced. In this transformation, Illich reports, women have lost out. Where once "mutual dependence set limits to struggle, exploitation, defeat," women's responsibility for the unvalued "shadow work" of the industrial economy now dooms her to inferiority.[22]

Illich idealizes a moment in history, and would restore the values and practices of that epoch. Yet he is selective in his restoration, for he would keep innovations that are consistent with his idea of "convivial community." Concerning the many grimmer aspects of twelfth century life, Illich is silent. Nor does his harmonious vision take account of the oppressive use of political power in societies characterized by ancient family forms; feudalism was not exactly a peaceable era, nor one in which governance was especially providential. Why should women remain in a separate, "enigmatic and asymmetrical," complementary "space-time," when the functional reasons for such a separation have largely vanished with the demise of the self-sufficient household? "The oldest traditions" undergird a separation of male and female roles, Illich notes by way of justification for maintaining these patterns, but what moral claims do these traditions make? What of the emergence of individual identity, the painstaking attempts to craft a social order in which being a man or a woman does not define one's life?

It is not only male writers who would retreat from the choice-celebrating present to a more traditional past. Germaine Greer, one of the seminal figures of the modern feminist movement, has lately reconsidered her position that sexual freedom leads to liberation; we have become too materialistic, too much obsessed with recreational sex and too little concerned about producing children, she now asserts.[23] In her celebration of Third World practices, Greer implies that the modern way of life, to which her earlier work contributed, must be repudiated in the name of the collectivity. But why polygamy and natural birth control are better than freely chosen alternative arrangements goes unsaid, aside from attacks on the "consumer-oriented" Western way of life.

To retreat from the present, rather than respond to it, is the first instinct of the backward-looking communitarian, and therein lies the problem. Having glimpsed the future, there is no going back to the past, for we cannot deny what we are. Formed by the notion of individualism with which our institutions are suffused, we cannot take refuge in a vision that denies the revolution in thought that took place. The belief in the salutary effects of a distinct individual identity, determined not by economic or sexual status but largely by our own actions, is too deeply held for us to engage in some collective act of willed forgetfulness.

Whether given by God or Nature, or derived from adherence to an ideology that celebrates the past, the supposition of preordained gender roles results in forms of community where individual choice does not count for much. Even if these visions could realistically be effectuated, the strong community is fundamentally inconsistent with the idea of gender justice rooted in individual volition.

IV

One need not embrace the patterned orthodoxies of the strong community to find the idea of *communitas* attractive. Individually designed lives remain a cardinal value, but such lives are more fully lived, not in the isolation that a purist liberalism contemplates, but within a tracery of support and obligation. Not all those who have made community their subject have harkened to the past or assumed that sex roles were necessarily preordained. Philosopher Roberto Unger seeks to move beyond the constrictions of liberalism and socialism; social democrats Michael Walzer and Raymond Williams sketch a communal life that is designedly fit for our times; social scientists, among them Daniel Bell, Benjamin Barber, Philip Selznick, and Christopher Jencks, search in their very distinctive ways for a public philosophy that allows us to reconnect the individual and the society.[24] These thinkers comprehend what we term the *open community* in a range of related ways, but all look forward toward the unknown for their visions of new forms of community, and none assumes that men or women must be limited to particular roles.

In the literature of politics, the lineage of the open community is decidedly recent in vintage. Its roots can be located in Tocqueville's celebration, in *Democracy in America,* of local self-governance and voluntary associations as essential to a legitimate democratic state, as well as in Max Weber's anguished depiction of the tension between the looming world of organization and the choice-making individual, confronted with "ultimately possible attitudes towards life [that] are irreconcilable."[25]

Those who spell out the various meanings of the open community are less inclined to adopt Tocqueville's celebratory tone, instead taking as their starting point Weber's dilemma or the lament of Tocqueville's contemporary Benjamin Constant, who contrasted the citizen of the classical city, with "real influence" that gave rise to a "lively and continuous pleasure" in participation, and the denizen of the modern state, "lost in the multitude, [who] . . . rarely perceives the influence that he exercises." The modern citizen, Constant notes, occupies himself with "the peaceful enjoyment of private independence," opting out of civic life in a state where "individual existence has little embodiment in political existence."[26] How can the relationship among individual, association, and state be recast for our time, in a manner that eschews facile resolution of deep and abiding conflicts? And how does the capacity of individuals to determine for themselves the significance of gender relate to that reconceptualization?

The animating concerns of those attentive to the open community are familiar enough. They search for social forms to arrest anomie, the social disintegration that has seemed characteristic of our time, and to give intimacy and solidarity a meaning deeper than that usually evident in complex industrial society. This agenda invites the nostalgia of the naturalists and the backward-looking communitarians, but there is considerable resistance to revering or restoring the old among those who imagine new forms of association. The tendency of small groups to exclusivity of membership, parochialism in viewpoint, and destructive combativeness in relationships, does not go unacknowledged; what is envisioned is a departure from that tradition.

If the strong community locates the individual inside a defined and defining social setting, the open community is more attentive to the autonomous, choice-making individual. There is no one model to describe this new form of association; it promises no "single and exclusive truth in politics."[27] That seeming default of theory has an obvious explanation. It is easier for those anxious to give new meaning to the ancient norm of *civitas* or to reformulate an actively deliberating polity to specify why an unbounded individualism or a too-demanding communitarianism has failed than to draft a road map for the future. The lack of specificity has also to do with the fact that the open community is more a process of association than a defined social form; it is not utopia in twentieth century guise. Open community is not yet an entity, but the beginning of an idea. Thus Benjamin Barber argues that what is needed is "not a practical change in reform efforts but a change in attitude about the aims of reform"; not a program, but "a mood, a tone, an orientation, an ethos."[28]

The open community offers a complex way to think about the choosing self, a closer approximation to what we know ourselves to be than simplistic individualism. In this conception, the community itself partly constitutes a person's identity, and the desire to fulfill one's own life plan is intertwined with the claims of the group to which one belongs. This community has been variously depicted as a reinvigorated political life marked by "the rule of the people in their assemblies . . . arguing over every aspect of the common life"[29]; a "strong democracy" where individuals are transformed into a society;[30] a collectivity building on the best of the British labor movement's social inventions during the past century[31]; and an organizational form that would allow the fullest development of complementary personalities, in the shadow of a God who has yet to reveal Himself. In any of these descriptions, "to join with others in a community of understandings and purposes increases rather than diminishes one's own individuality."[32] Individuals take into account their own needs and, having once committed themselves to the community, internalize its norms, in turn taking into account others' needs in calculating their own behavior.

Members of such communities are not "self-less," but rather identify some part of themselves with the welfare of the community. The task of the collectivity, whether it be a neighborhood association or a nation, is to find a language with which to articulate these moral sentiments and a politics of participation with which to develop them.[33] The open community promises a repoliticization of the decisions that shape our lives as citizens, for it is held that only through political discourse can individuals, motivated by self-interest, come to conceive of a common good. Concord does not derive solely from the force of tradition or the submergence of the individual will, but is also generated by the polity.[34]

Proponents of open community, in their acceptance of the rough-and-tumble of politics as a governing feature of the new vision, embrace conflict and change as a necessary part of the future. In this they differ from the backward-looking communitarians who long for a stable and static world. Their inability to specify their new vision thus becomes more fully understandable, because many values compete to govern the character of each particular community. This tension among values guarantees a multiplicity of forms of community to choose from, for there is no more reason to believe that one kind of communal life is right for all than to believe that individuals will all look the same.

The open community does not assume that those born there will remain or that those not born there can never enter. On the contrary, it posits that people grow and change, and need different forms of association at different points in their lives. Like the autonomous individual, it will not remain unaltered during its institutional life. The open community will be hospitable to new ideas, new ways of functioning; it will never be finished or complete. Raymond Williams describes how these two kinds of openness are related:

> The making of a community is always an exploration, for consciousness cannot precede creation, and there is no formula for unknown experience. A good community, a living culture, will, because of this, not only make room for but actively encourage all and any who can contribute to the advance in consciousness which is the common need. Wherever we have started from, we need to listen to others who started from a different position. We need to consider every attachment, every value, with our whole attention; for we do not know the future, we can never be certain of what may enrich it; we can only, now, listen to and consider whatever may be offered and take up what we can.[35]

This is a somewhat precarious balancing point. The open community must strive to maintain itself as a coherent enterprise with institutionalized values, while at the same time it is susceptible to change, ready to give up the old in the light of new discoveries. That communities might develop the capacity to function in such a continuously evolving state demands a suspension of disbelief, for our experience with community is more likely to show us the closing of a circle of believers, ever suspicious of outsiders, tending toward militancy to maintain the apparent rightness of their position. Williams offers an image of what the open community must instead aspire to: "While the clenched fist is a necessary symbol, the clenching ought never to be such that the hand cannot open, and the fingers extend, to discover and give a shape to the newly forming reality."[36]

The hand that is both open and closed points to the intellectual paradox of the open community, the difficulty of prescribing a new synthesis when the available paradigms are opposites. Some new outlook is needed; that is why the open community is represented by an attitude rather than an agenda. But it is an appealing vision. It affirms the importance of individualism as well as the necessity for common life; it acknowledges that old forms will not work with new people, new times, new ideas. The partisans of the open community learn from history that big government and large institutions often do a worse job of giving meaning to the lives of the people within them than do small, flexible associations, which know their members' faces and lives, their triumphs and traumas.

Even in a world of open communities, central government would do more than mediate among the associations, because the complexity and heterogeneity of the contemporary world lies beyond the capacity of any single individual or group to comprehend; there remains a vital politics of the general constituency. In this sense, communities of choice necessarily depend on the larger society for survival, even as the larger society draws on small associations for shared values in mutually dependent relationships. A governance of the whole is also needed to protect the basic liberties of individuals. As philosopher John Rawls has written, "The basic liberties are not intended to keep persons in isolation from one another, or to persuade them to live private lives . . . but to secure the right of free movement between associations and smaller communities."[37]

To the proponent of liberty, the conception of the relevance of gender in the open community is far more palatable than that advanced by the partisans of the strong community. It is implicit in the various discussions of the open community that men and women are not expected to surrender their sense of themselves for the good of the whole, to prefer others' conceptions of masculinity or femininity to their own self-defined sexual identities. In the depictions of social virtue in the open community, the search for self-knowledge and the capacity to act on that knowledge are regarded as good. Men and women properly achieve their "particular good" by making choices, Roberto Unger writes, and this achievement "is one of the bases of the community of life."[38]

The strong individual has a central place in the conception of the open community, since such individuals are essential to the maintenance of political life. Yet the partisans of the open community cannot wish away the tension between the claims they advance on behalf of political association and the primacy of autonomy in making basic life choices. Although it is true that "when politics goes well, we can know a good in common that we cannot know alone,"[39] this political model carries within itself the danger of overwhelming any other value that might animate association. In certain of its versions, it assumes that all our ties are crafted in political debate; but some will be based on love or devotion, not rational discourse, for not everyone relishes a life of meetings.

The open community can thus excessively entangle the roles of person and citizen, the sphere of private and public. Jean Bethke Elshtain argues that women especially must avoid uncritically accepting the notion that only public life is worth living; instead, they should "keep alive a critical distance . . . between female self-identity and a social identity thoroughly tied to the ongoing public-political world revolving around the structures, institutions, values, and ends of the state."[40] This point of view could just as well be adopted by men, for public life is not the only sphere where men and women make important life choices. To see the domain of political discourse as prior diminishes the importance of private communities formed by families and friends, yet those enclaves encourage individuals to become more fully themselves.

While the model of the open community may overemphasize the public sphere, it offers the best alternative for those who would honor individual determinations of the social relevance of gender while still recognizing that life must be lived in common. Even if community is freely chosen, tensions between individualist and communitarian ideas of justice will endure; the demands of persons for self-realization will always war with the call of the community for solidarity. Because the open community celebrates choice and autonomy for both men and women rather than imposing some "best" form of association on individuals, it will have a better chance of successfully balancing these competing justice claims.

The open community is the form of community that will most further gender justice, but it remains true that the model will not be immediately embraced by most. Since individuals often carry on traditions, many communities will continue to look as they did in the past, and tolerance of communities of choice is important. Government cannot set out to change these private choices in the name of imposing a better kind of community. Rather, it is government's role to ensure that the public realm treats men and women as deserving of equal liberty. How law and policy can serve the ends of gender justice is the broad issue explored in part II.

II
Elaborations

The transition from a theory of gender justice to policies that carry forward that theory is neither simple nor straightforward, for a host of factors mediate the relationship. The institutions of state are constrained as to the questions they can pursue; the economic resources of the society are finite and subject to competing priorities; the pull and haul of politics shapes outcomes in ways undreamt of by most theoreticians. Yet if principle does not effortlessly translate into policy, it can nonetheless inform policy, offering guides to decision.

Part II of the book sets out to demonstrate this deceptively simple conceit by linking the idea of liberty in the sphere of decisions pertaining to gender—the idea we have most closely associated with fairness—to the concrete policy choices that government confronts. Chapter 5 focuses on the Supreme Court, the most avowedly principle-driven of the coordinate branches, as it gives meaning to the constitutional idea of equal protection of the laws. Chapter 6 sets forth a liberty-promoting approach to policy, and chapters 7 and 8 apply it to a range of illustrative—and pivotal—problems concerning work and family.

5

Gender, Justice, and the Justices

Equality is a protean word. It is one of those political symbols . . . into which men have poured the deepest urgings of their hearts. Every strongly held theory or conception of equality is at once a psychology, an ethic, a theory of social relations, and a vision of the good society.
  John Schaar, "Equality of Opportunity and Beyond,"
  in J. Roland Pennock and John Chapman, eds.,
  Equality: Nomos IX (1967)

The restraints introduced by the law should be equal to all, or as much so as the nature of things will admit.
  W. Blackstone, *Commentaries* (1765)

I

Constitutional decisions of the Supreme Court can offer both a direction and a framework for social policy. The Court settles conflicts that in other nations would be decided politically—that is, it makes policy.[1] But the Supreme Court is not a super-legislature, free to pick up and discard nostrums on expediency or whim. Because the justices, unlike legislators, are obliged to advance explanations for what they do, their decisions offer a principled approach to policy, telling us not only what government has achieved but also specifying the underlying aspirations. The very best opinions articulate a structure for analysis whose influence reaches beyond the confines of a particular dispute to affect both the conscientious legislator[2] and the good citizen.[3] Those judicial elaborations of imbedded principles provide a useful counterpoint to policy decisions reached through political compromise and the accommodation of interest groups.[4]

This process of refining—particularizing—principle has certainly occurred in the race cases, where for over a century the justices have labored to disentangle the strands of this abiding American dilemma. Concerning race, the longstanding legal aspiration has been indistinguishability, the aim a society in which race is irrelevant. "So far as the Constitution is concerned," Justice Stewart has written, "people of different races are always similarly situated,"[5] and for that reason it is never—more precisely, almost never—appropriate for government to draw racial lines. As the familiar judicial phrase has it, the Constitution is color-blind.

There are ample historical reasons for equating equality under law with indistinguishability under law in the context of race. The classic instances of racial line-drawing—the antebellum slave laws and the Jim Crow laws of the late nineteenth century—are acts of retribution visited by a hostile majority, a mob bent on the legal lynching of an identifiable and politically weak minority.[6] These are rules of caste, from which individuals cannot escape, even though they ill fit the supposed norm. And these are irrational rules, which convert stereotypes—exaggerations, distortions, misrepresentations with no bearing on individual talent—into rules of law.[7]

Small wonder, then, that a nation which fought a civil war in part to undo such dehumanizing treatment of a sizable portion of the populace should turn a classic legal norm, that of equal protection, from its more general application into an instrument aimed specifically and primarily at protecting racial minorities. Small wonder too that the Supreme Court, as a tribunal of justice, should take this new constitutional provision, the Equal Protection Clause of the Fourteenth Amendment, as its warrant for undoing racial demarcations. That is how the rights of black and white—human rights—can best be vindicated, individual potential loosed from the ties of caste.

Sex, like race, is an immutable trait, and sex has also been the basis for "gross, stereotypical distinctions"[8] in the law. These similarities offer powerful reason for the Supreme Court to define gender equality, like racial equality, as a matter of indistinguishability or sameness. Indeed, that is the path that the justices have followed in the modern gender cases. The question regularly posed in these suits is whether women and men are being treated identically and, if not, whether there is good reason for the difference. Although the justices entertain different notions of what counts as a good reason—some are noticeably more inclined to credit "natural" demarcations between the sexes—the common, if tacit, aspiration is a world in which for all purposes the law treats men and women identically.

The question of whether men and women are treated identically is the wrong question, we argue, for it relies on an incorrect assumption about what justice generally—and equal protection specifically—should imply for gender. Our conclusion rests partly on the differing historical treatment of blacks and women, discussed in chapter 2. There, we noted that blacks have been treated with unremitting antagonism by the law, while women, viewed as better—nobler—than men, were legally protected against the baseness of the society; the law took note of "frail womanhood," not "frail negritude." To be sure, the impact of legal rules was often felt similarly, as a constraint on the choices open to individual blacks or individual women. In the one case, however, the differential treatment was intended to improve the circumstances for those "frail" women being protected, while in the other case, it was the rulemakers, the whites, who explicitly sought and stood to benefit. Even today it remains debatable whether in some cases (maternity leave, for instance) special treatment does women a service or disservice. About segregated schools or back-of-the-bus rules there is not and never was room for legitimate doubt.

It is not only the historical record that gives normative warrant for a different view of equal protection in the domain of gender. Indistinguishability fits well enough as a standard in the arena of race, where "different" is almost always a euphemism for "worse." It is, however, an inadequate way of understanding gender, where differentiation and diversity retain considerable normative appeal when attributable to personal volition, and where "better," "worse," and "identical" do not exhaust the universe of alternatives.

A preferable constitutional approach, we contend, is to consider equality in terms that nourish and sustain autonomy in the society; that means treating equal protection as securing equal liberty and equal rights of public participation for men and women. This way of framing the issue promises a richer, more variegated, and more autonomy-nurturing social ordering, consistent with the aspirations of the constitutional command. Applying this perspective also yields new ways of looking at a host of issues—concerning preferential treatment, for instance, as well as rules defining women's role as nurturer and men's duties as defender—that have bedeviled the Supreme Court and the society at large.

The Equal Protection Clause focuses not on the interests of groups but on the entitlements of persons:[9] no *person* is to be denied "the equal protection of the laws." By turning the state into the helpmate of volition, the Equal Protection Clause gives individuals breathing room to define themselves, an enterprise that expresses their dignity as moral beings.

Whenever government distinguishes between categories of people—children and adults, merchants and mendicants, geniuses and dunces—their sense of self is always at risk to some extent. Yet people live happily with a host of such distinctions—indeed, they are essential if government is to function. What makes rules about gender so special is that one's capacity to define, within the limits fixed by biology, what one's own maleness or femaleness means reaches to the core of one's identity.[10]

It is precisely because gender is relied upon by the social order to settle so much about our lives that legal rules wield clout. This is plainest with rules that designate political or economic status in gender-specific terms: rules about the qualifications for suffrage or employment, for instance. Yet even when the tangible impact is modest, as with statutes that prevent women from using their maiden names after marriage, the impress of the law on identity is evident, for these rules define how one represents oneself to the world.

Much the same can be said about racial rules, for these also bear heavily on identity. But if distinctions premised on race and gender are comparable in importance—different from, say, rules about welfare recipients or red-heads—it does not follow that the meaning of neutrality is the same. Color-blindness does not have its gender analog, at least where what is at issue is how the law shapes private choices. Only the utopian contemplates a republic peopled by hermaphrodites, only the willfully academic philosopher fondly envisions a society in which gender has been made as irrelevant as eye color.[11] The right to autonomy in pursuing one's private life, the equal sharing of the obligations of public citizenship: these, rather than something called gender-blindness, are the cardinal values.[12]

The plausibility of this ideal is strengthened by an appreciation of its implications for the individual and the state. If the law pays homage to the possibility of personal sovereignty, individuals will be motivated to seize control of their own lives.[13] If the law expects individuals to assume their fair share of responsibility for the collectivity, that too enhances their sense of self, for the individual has no meaning as an isolated, free floating being detached from the frame of community. If, by contrast, the governing norms deny the claim of autonomy and shelter individuals from the responsibilities of state, then people become dependents. Whether individuals are fettered out of a paternalistic regard for their own good or from an unblinking hostility matters little: in either event, they remain childlike, unable fully to act for themselves in exercising rights and fulfilling responsibilities.

This is how legal norms become transformed into self-fulfilling prophesies: even as contemplating autonomy makes its realization that much more likely, so too a society that regularly cabins the impulse to volition will come to confuse dependent behavior with the laws of nature, how things "really" are. Eventually, and most damagingly, individuals close the circle by turning imposed dependence into "chosen" dependence, identifying with this close-ended, status-driven view of human nature and potential that such a society advances.

That law regulates the possibility of individual autonomy is not a new idea. It is what motivated John Stuart Mill, more than a century ago, to urge that women's liberties be expanded, in the belief that the reform would allow the competencies of women to expand apace.[14] It is an enduring concern, not only for women—"treated . . . in some contexts as incapable of behaving as an adult . . . reminded at every turn that they are dependents"[15]—but, less obviously, for men as well.[16] Autonomy-constricting rules burden both sexes, for the stereotypes mirror one another in the inhibitions they impose. Women have historically been regarded as marginal economic and political citizens, with devastating consequences for their development in the public sphere. For their part, men were long denied the humane workplace conditions that protective labor legislation guaranteed to women. Men were shunted to the periphery of the private sphere, expected to pay the bills but given no voice in the custody of their children—or, more recently, the claims of their potential offspring to life. Alimony and child support rules effectively kept men steadily on the job, denying them the possibility of even shared dependency, and that too has an impact on identity.

This "behavioral strait-jacket"[17] collides with our understanding of equal protection as promoting equal respect for the liberty of persons, guaranteeing "each individual the right to be treated by the organized society as a respected, responsible, and participating member."[18] The concept of equal liberty has two complementary elements. On the one side, it emphasizes individual autonomy, disapproving of laws that maintain categories from which individual men and women cannot escape. On the other side, it stresses participation in the public order, in the belief that to share the basic obligations of citizenship—political activity, jury membership, national defense—is part of full membership in the society.

At one level, these different components of the equal respect principle are in tension, for to posit an obligation to community necessarily impedes the fullest exercise of personal preference; one cannot chose not to participate in universal service to the country or to serve on a jury panel. Yet this participation gives continuing definition to the community, and so assumes an individuation that has meaning and depth. It also, importantly, defines the individual, whose personality is powerfully shaped by participating in the decision making of the body politic.[19] The Fourteenth Amendment, which secures equal protection, also specifies the rights and obligations of citizenship.

The distinction between equality as sameness and equality as liberty-securing should become clearer in the next section, as we take up the questions that have troubled the Supreme Court justices. In many cases, the two lines of thinking will point to the same decision. But even in those easy cases, the reasoning significantly differs. In the hard cases, those raising the deepest value conflicts of the society, the choice of perspective affects the outcome as well.

II

The idea of equality as demanding identical treatment expresses a readily comprehensible view of fairness and so promises a simple justice. More-over, it draws upon the modern understanding of the rule of law, which is antagonistic to claims of caste;[20] it is consistent with the treatment of race as legally irrelevant;[21] and it is responsive to feminist concerns. "To the extent that any exception to the principle of equality is made," Thomas Emerson and his colleagues argue in a pathbreaking essay on the Equal Rights Amendment,

> women as a group are thrust into subordinate status in terms of their own capacities and experience. And . . . the interrelated character of a system of legal equality for the sexes makes a rule of universal application imperative. No one exception, resulting in unequal [read: different] treatment for women, can be confined in its impact to one area alone. *Equal rights for women . . . constitute a unity.*[22]

These several considerations—the allure of simplicity, the power of the racial analog, and the link between indistinguishable treatment of the sexes and the feminist sense of justice—press strongly for a blanket ban on gen-der-based distinctions. Yet that approach miscomprehends the nature of the constitutional animus, which has more to do with constrictions on choice than with the desirability of sameness. The confused history of the Su-preme Court's modern opinions concerning gender bears witness to this root analytical weakness.

Beginning with its 1971 decision in *Reed v. Reed,*[23] the Supreme Court has insisted that government offer some substantial justification for treating men and women differently. But as to just *how* substantial that justification must be, and what counts as justification, the justices have waffled. They have scrutinized alleged inequalities with varying degrees of closeness, moving from the least demanding requirement—the non-requirement, really—that government be "rational" in its distinction making, to the most insistent requirement that government provide "compelling justification," then abandoning both extremes in a prolonged search for some middle ground. Their opinions have been further muddled because the manner in which the Court has actually reviewed a claim of gender discrimination has not always matched the standard of review it has announced, thus adding an unwelcome element of disingenuousness.

These analytic confusions have been evident from the first. In the *Reed* case, the first modern Supreme Court decision to strike down a statute because it improperly drew a distinction based on sex, the justices tossed out an Idaho rule that gave men preference, in appointments as executors of the estates of individuals who die without leaving a will, over women equally closely related to the deceased. The majority disposed of the far-from-earthshattering question of fairness imbedded in this distinction by announcing that the Idaho rule was "irrational."

In legal parlance, irrationality suggests that government has gone bonkers—or, at least, acted in a fit of absence of mind—but that was hardly the case. Idaho could have resorted to coin flips in choosing executors, but it didn't; the straightforward rationale for its choice-of-executors rule was clearly expressed, both in the lower court opinion and in the state's legal argument before the high court. Since men have greater experience managing money, the state declared, they would, other things being equal, do a better job of administering an estate than women would. This sex-based differential in business experience was fact, not fancy, at least at the time the rule was written. Although one can disagree with the implication that Idaho drew from that fact—one can say, for instance, that business experience isn't all that important, or that gender parity is more important—it will hardly do to dismiss Idaho's conclusion as irrational.

In *Reed*, the wrong standard was announced—for the "rationality" standard is, in its accepted usage, a technique for rubberstamping a political decision, hardly the appropriate degree of scrutiny to resort to in cases about gender—and that standard was dishonestly applied by the Court to boot. The very same thing occurred in *Frontiero v. Richardson*,[24] the next gender case to be heard: the wrong standard was announced, and then misapplied. This time, however, the justices came within a whisker of making sex, like race, a constitutionally "suspect" basis for all government action, and so embracing a principle that would nearly always require identical treatment of the sexes.[25] Although the justices subsequently abandoned this approach, *Frontiero* deserves a careful look, because its misconceptions about the meaning of gender equality endure even as constitutional theory has been nominally remade.

In *Frontiero,* the Court struck down a rule that made it harder for servicewomen than servicemen to obtain dependents' benefits, PX privileges and the like, for their spouses. Under that rule, a serviceman could automatically claim his wife as a dependent but a servicewoman had to prove that she was the family's chief breadwinner. Eight justices saw this distinction as unconstitutional, but for varying reasons. Four sought to follow the *Reed* approach and treated the differentiation as "irrational." The plurality opinion, however, proposed a bolder approach: "Classifications based upon sex, like classifications based upon race, alienage, or national origin, are inherently suspect."[26]

The servicemen's benefits statute was perceived by the plurality as typifying a species of legislation meant to keep women in their place, and so the case appeared ripe for applying the standard of suspectness. Yet for an opinion meant to recast the legal conception of gender, the analysis is remarkably cursory and, again, not well matched to the facts. The plurality condemns gender-based laws wholesale, as anachronisms—reflections of a most unbenevolent paternalism that "in practical effect, put women not on a pedestal, but in a cage"[27]—yet that stirring rhetoric ill fits many laws that differentiate on the basis of sex, including the rule under review.

The military had a plausible reason for the *Frontiero* rule. Since an overwhelming majority of servicemen's wives are in fact dependents, it is cheaper to offer PX benefits to all than to identify one handful of exceptions. The pattern for servicewomen is more mixed, but the exceptional servicewoman is not stopped by the Army's rule from claiming her due. She can secure dependent's benefits for her husband by showing that she earns the bigger paycheck—indeed, the rule gives her an incentive to do so. In this respect, the servicemen's benefit rule relies on but does not confirm the economically dependent status of most American women. Nor does it significantly trench upon liberty, for it does not absolutely deny to one sex a benefit conferred on the other.[28]

Although the *Frontiero* plurality opinion was meant to chart the course of gender litigation, it did not begin to comprehend the varieties of legislation it would reach. "Gross, stereotypical" distinctions have indeed flourished: most states have had laws fixing a different age of majority for men and women, for instance, or limiting alimony only to women. But while such laws create consequential inequalities by giving one sex an opportunity not open to the other, the statute struck down in *Frontiero* created no closed category, no status from which women could not escape.

Nor is *Frontiero* a uniquely hard case. A great many laws referring to gender do not fit the male chauvinist model set out in *Frontiero*. What, for instance, should the justices make of statutes *favoring* women, purportedly to compensate for earlier stereotyping? What of rules that keep *men* in their place? Must the sex-related condition of pregnancy be legally treated as synonymous with gender? Is legislation that uses gender distinctions to *expand* the life choices of both sexes acceptable? These are difficult questions, to which we will return. What matters here is that the rhetoric of ''suspect'' state actions offers an inelegant and inapt response to the dilemmas they pose.

By the time the Supreme Court decided *Craig v. Boren*[29], the third of its watershed cases, in 1976, it had acquired a fuller understanding of these complications. During the three year interval following *Frontiero,* the Court had taken up the thorny problem of preferential treatment for women.[30] The justices had also debated whether pregnancy discrimination was sex discrimination—a distinction that only constitutional exegetes could appreciate.[31] Those cases, while not deftly handled, revealed a world more complex than that imagined by the *Frontiero* plurality.

The Court's palpable difficulties in deciding these suits confirmed the need for a new constitutional framework, its third in five years. *Craig v. Boren* became the vehicle. Again, the issue to be settled was not momentous—could Oklahoma outlaw the sale of 3.2 percent ''nonintoxicating'' beer to males under age twenty-one while permitting eighteen-year-old females to purchase it?—but a larger point of principle was at stake. Oklahoma contended that its law did not merely reflect the stereotype that young men handle liquor more recklessly than young women, but rather was designed to cope with the decidedly contemporary problem of traffic safety. This claim was not without force: unlike the Army in *Frontiero,* which relied on assertions of efficiency, Oklahoma had done its homework, gathering statistical evidence that young men, for whom beer was the preferred alcoholic drink, were ten times more likely to be arrested for driving while intoxicated than young women. A sensible legislator could readily conclude, from these data, that barring beer sales to young male drivers just might have a beneficial impact on a real and serious problem.

The majority, however, was unimpressed. It announced a new standard against which gender-based distinctions were to be tested—such laws ''must serve *important* governmental objectives and must be *substantially related* to achievement of those objectives''[32]—and concluded that the Oklahoma law failed that standard. The language of the test, stronger than ''rationality'' but weaker than ''compelling,'' intimated that gender distinctions, although more questionable than the run of legislative distinctions, were constitutionally less problematic than racial line-drawing.

Craig remains the benchmark, but what it signifies is far from clear. ''Important'' and ''substantial,'' the governing terms of the *Craig* standard, are ambiguous words that necessarily acquire meaning from their use. On the particulars of *Craig,* it is hard to see how this new test differs from the insistence on a ''compelling'' reason before government can act; in fact if not in form, the standard of the race cases is being adopted. The *Craig* majority opinion meticulously inspects Oklahoma's evidence, conveying ''the impression that a legislature in enacting a new law is to be subject to the judicial equivalent of a doctoral examination in statistics.''[33] To satisfy the majority, the link between Oklahoma's laudable objective, promoting safety on the highway, and the gender-specific way it proposed to accomplish this goal had to be not just ''substantial,'' but glove-tight.

The *Craig* decision only perpetuates the analytic confusion that marks earlier decisions. The *Frontiero* plurality declared that sex was constitutionally suspect but seemed to adopt a more relaxed standard of scrutiny, one that allowed the government to argue that its disparate treatment of men and women was acceptable because it was efficient. The *Craig* majority opinion purports to find a middle ground, developing a ''substantial rationality'' test. But those are just words and, as applied in *Craig,* this test resembles the most fine-grained judicial scrutiny.

The elasticity of the *Craig* test can only work judicial mischief, Justice Rehnquist claimed in a stinging dissent. It is ''so diaphonous and elastic as to invite subjective judicial preferences or prejudices relating to particular types of legislation, masquerading as judgments whether such legislation is directed at 'important' objectives or whether the relationship to those objectives is 'substantial' enough.''[34] That prophecy has proved true, for subsequent cases have done what might have seemed impossible, further blurring the constitutional idea of gender equality. Is there a principled distinction between a father's right to sue for the wrongful death of his illegitimate child, which the Court has denied, and the right of a father to consent to the adoption of his illegitimate child, upheld by the Court on the very same day?[35] Why may a state provide widows but not widowers with property tax relief, when awarding alimony only to women is damned as part of ''the baggage of sexual stereotypes''?[36]

There are no good answers from the justices, and the proliferation of their opinions mirrors the disarray. Rare is the sex discrimination decision unaccompanied by multiple concurrences and dissents; unanimous opinions are virtually unheard of. New formulations of a governing legal standard are regularly trotted out—the Court insisting, for instance, that government offer "an exceedingly persuasive justification," when it draws lines on the basis of sex[37]—and just as regularly discarded. None of it makes for clarity.

Justice Rehnquist, who prophesied that *Craig* could be relied on to license almost any decision, has confirmed his own prophesy by stretching that opinion to its breaking point. In two notable subsequent cases, Rehnquist smuggled in yet another standard of constitutional review: are males and females "similarly situated" with respect to the purposes of the law? This new test was applied to insulate against constitutional attack both Congress's refusal to require that women as well as men register for the draft and a California law making it a crime to have sex with a minor female, but not a male minor.[38]

These two decisions, *Rostker v. Goldberg* and *Michael M. v. Superior Court of Sonoma County,* mark another watershed in the Supreme Court's approach to gender, for although Justice Rehnquist cited the *Craig* standard, he stripped it of meaning. The draft registration decision is replete with obeisances to Congress, particularly when Congress is shaping military policy. Indeed, the opinion is so deferential to the legislature's authority in military matters that there is good reason to wonder whether gender has any independent significance in the decision. The asserted inefficiency of obliging women to register for a draft designed to strengthen the all-male combat forces persuades the majority that "men and women . . . are simply not similarly situated for purposes of a draft or registration for a draft."[39] Those questioning male-only registration are asked to prove that universal registration would *not* undermine efficiency, but this approach turns on its head the *Craig* standard, which requires convincing demonstration by the *government* of the need for a gender-based distinction.

Although neither deference to Congress nor military preparedness is at issue in the statutory rape case, the majority applies the same standard, concluding that "young men and women are not similarly situated" with respect to the aim of the law.[40] The majority begins its analysis by describing the purpose of the California law as preventing teenage pregnancy. That may be an estimable aim, but California's courts had long seen the law differently, as preserving the chastity of young women "presumed too innocent and naive to understand the implications and nature of their own acts. . . ."[41] In its assumption about naive womanhood (but not naive manhood), such an objective would presumably not satisfy the *Craig* test.

Even if preventing pregnancy were actually the legislative goal, why punish only males? The majority claims that "a female is surely less likely to report violations of the statute if she herself would be subject to criminal prosecution."[42] Yet this is merely an assertion, not evidence of the sort relied on—vainly—by Oklahoma in the *Craig* case. It is also an improbable assertion. By the time *Michael M.* was decided, thirty-seven states had enacted gender-neutral statutory rape laws; it is unlikely that they would have rewritten the law if gender-neutrality foiled its purpose. On the contrary: doubling the pool of possible miscreants, by applying the law to males as well as females, is calculated to increase rather than reduce reported instances of underage sex, and so to strengthen the force of such a law.

The potentially more critical problem for the evolution of gender justice has less to do with the details of the draft and statutory rape cases than with the meaning of this newest of constitutional standards, the "similarly situated" test. Even as *Frontiero* fixed the terms of the failed revolution, this new approach reveals the beginning of a counterrevolution. The "similarly situated" test turns out to be no test at all but merely restates the underlying problem: similar in what respect and to what extent?[43] The answer of these cases is: similar according to the legislature's judgment. Yet if government has only to show that males and females differ with respect to the purpose of the law, it will prevail, for it is always possible to distinguish between males and females for some legislative aim. "Similarly situated," in short, invites judicial abdication.

Consider what would happen if this standard were applied to cases already decided by the Supreme Court. *Reed v. Reed*,[44] the first of the modern sex discrimination suits, would surely come out differently: because men have more business experience than women, the sexes are not "similarly situated" in their ability to administer an estate. *Stanton v. Stanton*[45] challenged a Utah rule requiring fathers to support their sons until age twenty-one, while terminating the financial obligation to their daughters at age eighteen. The state would win this case too: since women tend to marry younger, they are less likely to need their father's help, and because the sexes differ in this respect, Justice Rehnquist's standard is satisfied. A Louisiana law giving the husband exclusive right to dispose of property jointly owned with his wife, challenged in *Kirchberg v. Feenstra*, reflects the contention that the husband, as "head and master" of the household, has a special status[46], and while this rule embraces the most discredited and most damaging of the stereotypes, it is also a rule based on presumed differences between spouses. The vital question in each of these cases—do the asserted distinctions between men and women justify sex-specific constraints on liberty?—goes unasked in "similarly situated" analysis.

The proponents of this test would forestall such unseemly results by focusing on the "legally relevant" purposes of the statute under review. Yet legal relevance seems even more accordion-like in its manipulability, more susceptible to misapplication, than *Craig*'s insistence that a sex-specific law substantially further an important government goal. The "similarly situated" approach to analysis, although supposed to introduce an element of exactness, appears even less principled, more attentive to rationalizing predetermined good results, than the *Craig* test. Define legal relevance broadly, as in the previous examples, and any gender distinction is defensible. Narrow the definition a bit and the most obnoxious gender categories, such as dubbing the husband as "head and master," fall. Tighten still further, to encompass only "compelling" missions of state, and most gender-based differentiation becomes illegitimate.

How is the Court supposed to choose among these competing views? The debate between the majority and the dissenters in the draft and statutory rape cases shows that calibrating legal relevance entails a sleight-of-hand that would put the Wizard of Oz to shame. The Court has ignored this approach in its most recent foray into the realm of gender,[47] suggesting, perhaps, that the "similarly situated" standard too may be a short-lived way of thinking about gender.

The Supreme Court has successively imposed different constitutional frameworks for reviewing legislation that draws lines between the sexes. In *Reed*, it demanded only that the state be "rational" in its gender-based distinctions. In *Frontiero*, it came close to converting into constitutional law the idea of equality as sameness, without understanding the implications of such a straitjacketing standard. More recent cases, while sometimes tolerating gender-based distinctions, do not articulate the terms on which they may reside in the house of law. The idea of equality liberty has been regularly reshaped during the course of this litigation, in a frantic attempt to keep pace with rapidly changing understandings of the disputed terrain. The Court's lack of success is conspicuous: whether demanding sameness or accepting differentness, the decisions weaken the central idea of gender justice. It is neither equality as sameness nor equality as differentness that adequately comprehends the issue, but instead the very different concept of equal liberty under the law, rooted in the idea of individual autonomy.

III

The Supreme Court's decisions on gender have not gone uncriticized. In *Craig v. Boren,* the decision meant to settle the framework for analyzing claims of sex discrimination, seven separate opinions were filed, prompting Justice Stevens to chide his colleagues, "There is only one Equal Protection Clause."[48] Baffled and bemused lower court judges wonder out loud whether they are playing a shell game, "not absolutely sure there is a pea."[49]

The kindest of critics partially exonerate the Court because it has had to rethink all of gender law just since 1971, a breathtakingly short time to work a revolution in the annals of the law.[50] The feminists have been harsher, scolding the justices both for their inconsistencies and for their sexism.[51]

Although the feminist criticisms are trenchant, particularly of the treatment of disputes over legislation defining women as childbearers and men as defenders, the alternatives they propose are troubling. It will not do, for instance, to urge the Supreme Court to require identical treatment except in those special circumstances when women should be preferred, for that is neither more coherent nor more principled than the opinions themselves.[52] Nor is it useful to urge that the justices embark on "a broad critique of sexist practices and patterns" in the service of "a compelling vision of a new social order."[53] It is unclear that a tribunal dominated by male septuagenarians could accomplish that goal, less clear still that they should try.

The most radical alternative is to opt out of legal discourse entirely, abandoning—or slowing up—the system because the enforcement of *any* norm through "objective" law is a hopelessly male, and hence victimizing, approach. "Formally, the state is male in that objectivity is its norm. Objectivity is liberal legalism's conception of itself. It legitimizes itself by reflecting its view of existing society," ensuring "that the law will most reinforce existing distributions of power when it most closely adheres to its own highest ideal of fairness."[54]

The principle of equal liberty appears pallid when set beside such nihilism. But the principle promises an approach coherent in its method of analysis, an idea not without intuitive—as well as constitutional—appeal

in its implications for decision. We lay out the consequences of adopting
the principle of equal liberty below.

Universal applicability. Is it rule-making based on gender or, differently,
rule-making that handicaps women that offends the idea of gender justice?
The answer to that question is centrally important, for it defines our understanding of the wrong, but the Supreme Court has responded hesitantly and
inconsistently.

In *Craig v. Boren,* the 1976 case that announced what appears to be the
prevailing standard of judicial review, it is men who fare worse under an
Oklahoma statute barring only eighteen-year-old males from buying 3.2
percent beer. The majority ignores this fact, focusing instead on the apt-
ness of any gender-based distinction. Although such studious inattention to
the sex of the legal losers might well mean that the Court has adopted a
universally applicable principle—gender as the criterion, not women as
victims—contrary hints dot the case record.

Justice Stevens' concurring opinion in *Craig* insists that the Oklahoma
law is "not as obnoxious as some the Court has condemned" because
"men . . . have not been the victims of the kind of pervasive discrimination that has disadvantaged other groups."[55] In a subsequent ruling upholding a law that treats sex with a minor as a crime only if the perpetrator
is a male, Justice Rehnquist opines that discrimination against men should
not trouble his colleagues. "We find nothing to suggest that men, because
of past discrimination or peculiar disadvantages, are in need of the special
solicitude of the courts."[56]

The source of this confusion resides in the Court's flawed attempt, in
the *Frontiero* "PX benefits case," to explain why gender has constitutional relevance. The plurality opinion asserts that, like race, sex is unalterable and unrelated to ability. If that is the root of the race-sex analogy,
then *any* gender-based rule should occasion concern. But when itemizing
the debilitating impact of gender-based laws, the opinion shifts gears,
focusing exclusively on women, "relegated . . . to inferior legal status."[57] If it is just the historically dismal treatment of women that disturbs,
then Justice Rehnquist is quite right: discrimination against men should be
as legally innocuous as discrimination against left-handers.

Uncertainty about the nature of the legal wrong also warps analysis of
laws which supposedly benefit women. With racially based rules, it is clear
enough whether blacks or whites are advantaged by the law, but with gender-based laws, it is sometimes hard to decide which sex winds up better
off. A law that gives widows a tax break not available to widowers, for

instance, may with equal logic be said to favor either those widows or their former husbands, who because of this law can leave larger estates to their wives.[58] This dilemma can often arises in gender cases, even though the Court only occasionally recognizes it,[59] and, when it does, is inconsistent in how it settles the question. So long as the nature of the wrong remains unsettled, the determination of who is harmed is important—under one reading of the case law, the conclusion that men were the being badly treated would be fatal to the claim—and for that reason the inarticulateness of the justices causes trouble.

Embracing equal liberty as the governing constitutional principle resolves this confusion by making irrelevant the matter of which sex is the legal loser, since when one sex "loses," both are worse off. Gender specificity itself diminishes individuals' opportunities, and that is reason enough for judicial concern, whether it is men or women who are specifically hedged round by legal restrictions.

"Benign" discrimination. Gender specificity wears different guises. Sometimes legislation is said to benefit women, either by helping them to overcome some historic unfairness or by compensating for some gender-specific disability. The truth of such contentions may be hard to ascertain, but even if their veracity is conceded, the question remains: is benign treatment of one sex ever an appropriate, liberty-enhancing aim of government?

Laws that favor women would once have been said to reflect the abiding differences between the sexes, and so express an almost chivalrous kindness toward china doll womanhood.[60] In an era less hospitable to overtly gender-based characterizations, these rules are now defended differently, as compensation for earlier injustices. Such legislation is particularly attentive to the plight of widows, giving them special treatment in social security,[61] workmen's compensation benefits,[62] and property taxes.[63] It also favors women workers who may have suffered from past[64] or continuing[65] job discrimination.

The Supreme Court has charted a confusing path through cases challenging these sex-related benefits. It has, for instance, upheld property tax relief for widows but not special treatment with respect to workmen's compensation. It has approved treating women favorably for purposes of calculating their social security benefits upon retirement but not when what is at issue is the size of the benefits check that a widow, as opposed to a widower, receives. Sometimes, as in the suit challenging favored property tax treatment for widows, the Court has accepted the state's assertion that the statute in question was aimed at helping poor widows overcome the burdens of past discrimination with the most minimal probing of that claim. On other occasions, as with the differential calculation of social security benefits, similar assertions have been probed exhaustively before the justices have pronounced themselves satisfied.

If one defines the aim of the law as promoting indistinguishability of treatment—equality as sameness—then the issue of benignity becomes simple: all such laws, whatever their motivation and whatever their effect, are invalid. As Nancy Erickson asserts, "all laws that purport to *help* women actually encourage the same sex-stereotypical thinking that perpetuates discrimination *against* women."[66]

All laws: the principle of indistinguishability is simple, if nothing else. But what it ignores is that, in moving from a sex-conscious past to a sex-neutral future, it may make sense to take account of those whose life choices were shaped under the old legal regime. There is force and merit to the claim that making gender-blindness a universal rule is unfair to the historic victim: she (and in all the cases concerning benign treatment that have been argued, women are the alleged victims whom the law means to aid) deserves help in overcoming the legacy of the past.[67]

This argument is at once persuasive and problematic. To discount past unfairnesses may keep an entire generation from harvesting the fruits of autonomy, but to define those unfairnesses as affecting women generally risks perpetuating the past. Efforts to compensate for past disadvantage always evoke concern, for in attempting to palliate they run the danger of sustaining the old stereotypes. From the perspective of equal liberty, the critical questions to ask of a "benign" rule are: Does it serve to sustain autonomy or to reduce liberty by maintaining ancient distinctions? Is there a less gender-specific alternative at hand?

Several of the Supreme Court's opinions follow this approach. In *Weinberger v. Wiesenfeld,*[68] the Court overturned a provision of the Social Security Act that gave financial support to a woman, but not to a man, who remained home to care for the children after the spouse died. The government had insisted that the law was designed to help women, who because of economic discrimination could not help themselves, but the Court saw things differently. The rule is premised on the " 'archaic and overbroad' generalization . . . that male workers' earnings are vital to the support of their families, while the earnings of female wage-earners do not significantly contribute to their families' support," the justices concluded, noting that it discriminates against women who substantially support their families. Because the law enables "women to elect not to work and to devote themselves to the care of children"[69] but frustrates the man who would choose a similar path, it collides with the idea of equal liberty. "A father, no less than a mother, has a constitutionally protected right to the 'companionship, care, custody and management' of 'the children he has sired and raised, which undeniably warrants deference and, absent a powerful countervailing interest, protection.' "[70] Men trying to combine child care and work are in the same boat as working mothers; they merit the same treatment.[71]

Although *Wiesenfeld* stresses that this provision of the Social Security Act discriminates against women workers, who cannot bequeath the same benefits to their surviving husbands that a male worker can pass along, the opinion itself reveals that both sexes are treated badly by the rule. The law assumes that widows will remain at home to raise their children but denies widowers the same option. A nominally benign law thus keeps both women and men in their respective places; because the distinction is based on gender, they are powerless to plan their lives in ways that will avoid application of the law. That is constitutionally offensive.

The Supreme Court was even more attentive to the straitjacketing impact on sex roles of a Mississippi statute that entitled women, but not men, to collect alimony from their spouses. The state contended that the law was supposed to help needy spouses and to compensate for past discrimination, but the justices found the statute ill designed to accomplish those aims. Although needy spouses may require support, the Court declared, there was no reason to limit assistance to women, since in those marriages that "defied the stereotype and left the husband dependent on the wife," the husband might well be entitled to alimony. Permitting only women to seek alimony is a form of legal foot-binding that keeps women dependent, "part and parcel of a larger statutory scheme which invidiously discriminates against women, removing them from the world of work and property and 'compensating' them by making their designated place 'secure.' "[72]

The women-only alimony rule victimizes men who assume what has historically been the female role, becoming financially dependent on their spouses, by denying the legitimacy of their claim for support. That rule gives men and women an incentive to follow conventional careers, the husband as breadwinner and the wife as homemaker, by punishing those who stray from the fold. In so doing, it conflicts with the principle of equal liberty.

Instances of benignity toward women untainted by "the baggage of sexual stereotypes"[73] are rare—but not so rare as those who insist on indistinguishable treatment of the sexes would have us believe. In *Califano v. Webster*,[74] the justices approved a provision of the Social Security Act that allowed women to compute their pensions on a more favorable basis than that used by men. The law was designed to redress historic workplace discrimination, which had reduced women's earnings and forced them into early retirement, and was carefully tailored in both scope and duration with that concern uppermost in mind. The legislation reflected the conclusion that in the past many women had unfairly been paid less than men; although this wasn't true for everyone, it would have been impossible to determine on a case-by-case basis whether a particular person had been victimized. When Congress expanded the antidiscrimination rules in 1972, outlawing discrimination on the basis of sex in public as well as private employment, it reverted to a gender-blind standard for calculating social security entitlement. Thus, only that generation of women most victimized by past employment practices was "compensated" by an advantageous rule for determining pensions. Congress could credibly assert that sex-differentiated calibration of social security benefits was intended, not to rationalize continuing employer discrimination, but rather as recompense for inequities otherwise out of legal reach. As the justices concluded, this gender-specific law was truly ameliorative.[75]

Equal citizenship and civic obligation. The equal liberty principle does more than bestow entitlements on individuals, for the notion of citizenship, to which liberty is related both constitutionally and normatively, also incorporates the responsibilities that accompany membership in the society. If the claims of personhood are, in some measure, one's birthright as an individual potentially capable of purposiveness and choice, they also derive from belonging to a democratic order that makes this birthright secure.[76]

The United States makes relatively few demands of its citizens. Unlike other western nations, it does not insist that all adults vote, out of the belief that nonparticipation in political decision making is a legitimate choice. Payment of taxes, service on juries, and participation in the military during times of conscription: those are the only obligations that membership in the polity entails. Until a very few years ago, women were exempt from one of these obligations, namely jury duty, and women are still not required to register for military service. These distinctions make women less than full citizens, cared-for rather than responsible, but that is not how the Supreme Court has addressed these issues.

The justices did conclude, in *Taylor v. Louisiana*,[77] that a criminal defendant is constitutionally entitled to have a jury selected from a sexually representative cross section of the community. That result is sound, but the rationale is less than satisfactory. Equal inclusion of men and women on jury rolls is proper, the Court concludes, because women bring a unique perspective to courtroom deliberations. "The two sexes are not fungible," the justices observe, and for that reason "a flavor, a distinct quality is lost if either sex is excluded."[78]

Such reasoning is problematic for several reasons, not least because of how badly it matches the facts of the case. Mr. Taylor was accused of kidnapping two women and a child at gunpoint and raping one of the women: would he really have been better off with women as part of the jury hearing his case? Moreover, since the Court holds only that women must be represented on the jury rolls, not the actual jury, there is no assurance that any particular jury would include women; how does that square with the defendant's right to appeal to women's "unique perspective"?

And just what is that perspective? The justices fall back on the most hoary generalizations about how women react to evidence in reaching their decision. The "distinct quality" of women sounds like a rephrasing of "sensitive womanhood," an echo from the past rather than the premise for a principle of contemporary constitutional law. The opinion in the jury roll case turns on the very gender differences whose relevance the Court has been at pains to deny in other contexts.

The draft registration case,[79] in which the Supreme Court scuttled a claim by men that a male-only registration discriminated against them, is troubling for different reasons. Here again, both sexes are the losers, for reasons that are not apparent to the Court. The majority concludes that, since the draft is intended to muster a combat force, the exclusion of women is acceptable, because "the principle that women should not intentionally and routinely engage in combat is fundamental."[80] Fair enough: however one elevates the idea of liberty, it is apparent that this society is unwilling to be defended by a fighting force comprised equally of males and females. But the Court did not have to reach that ultimate issue, because as the Congressional record made plain, any actual draft would recruit personnel for jobs that were neither combat nor combat-ready positions. These jobs could be carried out by women draftees, just as they are now being filled in sizable numbers by female volunteers[81], and that result would have made women more than marginal actors in the defense of the society.

Feminists were divided in their reaction to the draft case. One camp insisted on parity of civic obligations, but others argued that women should not surrender their ethic of nurturance by buying into life-destroying and aggressive militarism, the very worst of the masculine ethos.[82] Although the pacifism that underlies the latter argument is not unappealing, the consequences are deeply troubling. Those feminists opposed to extending draft registration are taking the old female stereotype of caring women and converting it into a normative characterization. The implication is that women are absolved of responsibility for—and, critically, power over—life-and-death decisions; they have opted out of that contested territory entirely. The question of women's participation in the draft thus has less to do with who wages war than with who will determine whether there will be a war; participation is a way of abandoning the status of the powerless nonparticipant.

Certain advantages accompany conscription, most notably the generous benefits that the federal and state governments offer to veterans, but the calculus of advantage and disadvantage does not fully comprehend what is at issue in the draft case. Justice Stewart's belief that exclusion from the draft gives women "the best of both worlds,"[83] enabling them to share equally in entitlements while leaving to men the meaner obligations of public life, reflects an incomplete understanding of the concept of citizenship. A rule that "categorically excluded women from a fundamental civic obligation"[84] signifies that they are less than full members of the society. It also denies equal liberty to men. Both men and women should be expected to contribute to the defense of the nation and to the discourse of defense by being equally vulnerable to service in the armed forces, as an essential element of their claim to an equal measure of liberty and respect as persons.

Autonomy, diversity, and gender-specificity. The aim of the principle of equal liberty is to support men and women in their quest for autonomy, free from state-enacted restrictions from which they cannot escape. It presumes that men and women should be treated with equal respect under the law, regarded as equal in their capacity for making life choices. In most instances, that means removing gender-specific criteria, for these usually inhibit choice. But sometimes autonomy is actually furthered by gender-defined opportunities, and in these instances gender-specific rules make sense.

Claims having to do with sexual privacy offer the clearest illustration of innocuous gender-specific rules. To those who equate equality with identical treatment, privacy is the poor cousin of argument, often deprecated as the "potty problem,"[85] the crank cause of conservatives. Yet privacy deserves better than this, for it is linked to an understanding of autonomy that encompasses the right to be left alone. In this light, the demand for separate men's and women's toilets turns out to be more instructive than Phyllis Schlafly's tireless repetitions suppose.

It strains at gnats to detect any infringement on liberty caused by maintaining separate toilets for men and women. Unlike public toilets labelled "blacks only" and "whites only," rightly condemned as a vestige of Jim Crow injustice, sex-based separation is not based on notions of the inferiority of one group but on the preference of both; and the principle that justifies maintaining separate toilets is not readily applied to other situations when the result is to keep women and men in their respective places. One can imagine a society less self-conscious about such matters or a regime of enhanced autonomy that allowed each person to choose a sex-segregated or sex-integrated toilet. But the extremely modest impact on liberty of separate toilets does not call for a massive educational effort or public spending on a wider range of toilet choices.

Segregation of any sort rightly makes people suspicious when it reinforces stereotypes of inferiority and superiority. But segregation can sometimes be useful; particularly when it is self-segregation, it may promote personal preferences. Locomotive fanciers or fundamentalist Christians segregate themselves for this reason, and that kind of behavior is so commonplace that we don't label it that way. We call it choice.

Although one can imagine a world in which blacks and whites made choices as freely and as innocuously as locomotive fanciers and vintage auto fanciers, that is not the world we know. When schools or jobs or housing are segregated by race, history teaches us to be skeptical. Especially when that separation reflects the preferences of whites, the implication is that whites have chosen segregation because they want nothing to do with an "inferior" race. Even a benign racial distinction, which is supposed to help blacks, is troubling because it legitimates a principle that would, if applied more generally, do great harm.

Gender segregation falls someplace between the innocuous and the suspect. Although for most aspects of public life, integration is properly the norm, this is not universally true. Maintaining separate secondary schools for males and females, for example, is not commonly viewed as an indication of inferiority for either sex. The rationale for such schools is very different: they promise a place for teenagers to learn, undistracted by the presence of the opposite sex. For some youngsters, at least, that insulation enables them to do better academically. Restricting an institution to males may, of course, sustain "tacit assumptions of male superiority, assumptions for which women must eventually pay;"[86] and for that reason the comparability of the educational opportunities actually offered has to be taken into account in appraising the merit of separation. Yet all sex-segregated schools are not bastions of male superiority or female vulnerability. By offering males and females the chance to be apart, if only for a small portion of their lives, the best of these institutions—Boys' High and Girls' High in Philadelphia, for instance—afford a richer mix of choices to everyone, and so are compatible with the idea of equal respect.[87]

The Supreme Court took up a similar question in *Mississippi University for Women v. Hogan*.[88] Mississippi University for Women, established in 1884, had historically been limited to female students, and when the university established a school of nursing in 1971, it was also restricted to women. Joe Hogan, denied admission to the nursing school in 1979 on the basis of his sex, filed suit. Hogan alleged that the women-only policy of the nursing school denied him equal protection, for although Hogan could enroll in a Mississippi coeducational nursing program at another campus, the nearest such program was 147 miles from his home. A closely split Supreme Court upheld his claim.

The majority opinion reopens old doctrinal puzzles by asserting that sex may yet be regarded as a "suspect" classification, requiring "an 'exceedingly persuasive justification' "; it ignores post-*Frontiero* opinions that embrace a less procrustean standard of review. *Hogan* treats the single-sex nursing program as a misguided attempt at benign discrimination, which merely "perpetuates the stereotyped view of nursing as an exclusively woman's job."[89]

An equal liberty approach would inquire about the impact of the nursing school's admission policy on the life choices of males and females. For Joe Hogan, the impact of the rule was more than a trivial inconvenience; its practical consequence was to force him to choose between his home and his vocation. But the admissions policy also expanded the options open to women, who were able to select a coeducational or single-sex course of instruction. In disregarding that fact, the majority ignores "the liberating spirit of the Equal Protection Clause."[90] It is one thing to free men and women from gender-based rules premised on "archaic and overbroad generalizations," something quite different to allow women to choose between two very different educational environments.

The dissent pursues this contention, noting that what is

at stake in this case is the preservation of a small aspect of diversity. But that aspect is by no means insignificant given our heritage of available choice between single-sex and coeducational institutions of higher learning. . . . A constitutional case [of discrimination] is held to exist because one man found it inconvenient to travel to any of the other institutions made available to him by the State of Mississippi.[91]

Yet it is not clear whether diversity should be embraced in this context. Maintaining a single-sex nursing school enhances a theoretical choice for women, but the testimony in the case offered no defensible educational rationale for the separation. If no positive argument can be made for keeping the single-sex school, then the fact that the policy constricts the options open to men becomes much more important. Resolving the conflict in *Hogan* requires attention to the particulars of the competing liberty claims, not an all-or-nothing analysis.

Expanding traditional roles. The most troubling of the gender cases are those that examine the sex-role arrangements regarded as basic to the culture: those having to do with what is regarded as quintessentially feminine, such as childbearing and childrearing; and those that are quintessentially masculine, notably defending the society against external threat (as in the draft registration case, already discussed) and by maintaining internal order.[92]

Consider, in this light, the decisions having to do with pregnancy and abortion, where judicial decisions have been anything but coherent. While abortion and contraception have been hived off as implicating freedom of personal choice in matters of marriage and family life,[93] the legal treatment of pregnancy turns on the particulars of the rule. Mandatory maternity leave has been condemned for riding roughshod over the "basic constitutional liberty" of individual women, who cannot all be banished to the fainting couch but are entitled to particularized assessments of their capacity to continue working.[94]

The justices have taken an altogether different tack in response to the contention that excluding medical expenses attributable to normal pregnancies from disability and health insurance plans discriminates against women. Not so, the justices insist, because such a distinction is not based on sex, but merely "divides potential recipients into two groups—pregnant women and nonpregnant persons."[95] This logic is slippery, since it would be equally plausible to acknowledge that excluding pregnancy benefits from insurance coverage separates "persons who face a risk of pregnancy," all of whom are women, and "those who do not."[96] The Court's reasoning has a profound impact on women's lives, for it means that whether medical expenses associated with ordinary pregnancies are included in an employee health plan is a matter for the politicians or the marketplace, not the justices, to resolve.

There is an argument in support of the Court's position, even though it is not the one that the justices advanced.[97] Unlike other disabilities covered by employee health plans, pregnancy is usually voluntary and welcomed; because the medical costs associated with normal pregnancy are relatively low, the ordinary family can usually plan for them. The aggregate cost of adding ordinary pregnancy to health benefits plans is, however, quite high; an addition could not simply be absorbed into the wage and benefits package but would have to be offset by some other benefit cuts. Exceptional pregnancies are another matter—the medical expenses associated with a complicated childbirth operation can be substantial and unanticipated—but these are treated as disabilities by benefit plans.

The distinction between pregnancy and other disabilities is hardly perfect. Heart disease, for instance, can often be controlled through changes in diet and exercise; the costs of injuries associated with other voluntary acts, such as a street corner fight, are covered by medical plans. Yet to focus on the strength of the claimed distinction is analytically more sensible than to deny the reality that a gender-based distinction is at work.

Abortion poses different dilemmas, for it pits powerful liberty claims, that of the fetus and those of the prospective parents, against one another. The idea of advancing the cause of liberty does not help to resolve the core dispute, whether abortion is a permissible act. But if one takes as a starting point the Supreme Court's decision in *Roe v. Wade*—that the nonviable fetus is not entitled to protection—the equal liberty principle then comes into play, both in evaluating government subsidy policy and assessing the claims of fathers to some voice in the abortion determination.

When government funding for abortions is at issue, the question is whether the liberty of pregnant women who would choose to carry the fetus to term will be upheld over those who choose to abort. The Supreme Court has sustained legislation that denies funding to poor women who want abortions. At issue in the first of these cases was a Connecticut regulation that paid for childbirth but not abortion expenses; the Court upheld the law, reasoning that it did not constrain women's liberty because it "places no obstacles—absolute or otherwise—in the pregnant woman's path to an abortion."[98] As far as the Court was concerned, the legislature had not imposed its will on the woman because it left her free to find private funds to carry out her wish, though lack of private funds was the precise reason for the woman's application for government aid.

In the second of the abortion funding decisions, the Court refused to overturn a Congressional amendment to Medicaid legislation that withheld funding, not merely for elective abortions, but for those held to be medically necessary.[99] The majority concluded that the law gave Congress the power to determine what services would be provided under Medicaid; in this view, abortions were like eyeglasses or plastic surgery, medical services that could be granted or withheld if the legislature felt they imposed unreasonable costs. It also found that it was "indigency," not governmental action, that prevented women from actually carrying out their decision to obtain an abortion.[100]

The dissent read the record differently: by denying funding for one of the two possible outcomes of pregnancy, abortion or birth, the rule effectively removed the element of choice. A refusal to fund abortion meant that "the government literally makes an offer that the indigent woman cannot afford to refuse."[101]

What is most distressing about the ruling is that it is not just funding for elective abortions that is at stake, for that issue had already been resolved; here the question is whether the government would fund abortions when the mother's health was threatened by the pregnancy. Even if there is reason to believe that the morality of abortion is so unsettled that government should not pay for poor women's nontherapeutic abortions, such disagreement is irrelevant when what is at issue is the performance of a medically necessary procedure. When the Supreme Court upholds Congress's right to deny abortion funding to poor sick women while offering both men and women every other kind of medically essential treatment, it is constraining their liberty. The constraint arises both from the failure to vindicate the rights of the poor to an interest that the Court has identified as fundamental and from the differential treatment of women and men.

Rules limiting government-funded medical support, like restrictions on abortion generally, pit the family against the state. There may also be dissension within the family, as when one parent but not the other wants to abort the fetus, and the idea of equal liberty is also germane here. When the Court denied fathers any say in the abortion decision, it held that the father could not be given a voice without denying the mother the privacy that had been upheld in *Roe v. Wade*.[102] However, the fact of human reproduction—that two parents are needed—means that liberties will conflict.[103] Both parents' interests are derived from their sense of themselves as persons who wish to control their own lives and who may desire to perpetuate some aspect of their identities through their offspring, but giving one parent absolute liberty to decide whether to have children will necessarily mean denying any liberty to the other.

One can reasonably conclude that the mother's interest should ultimately outweigh that of the father in most instances where disputes arise, because the mother carries the physical burden of pregnancy. However, that does not necessarily settle the liberty issue, for it is biology, not moral right, which gives the mother this burden. A case can be imagined where a man becomes sterile shortly after conceiving a child that the woman does not want to bear: to deny him even the right to be informed of the mother's wish for an abortion means that he would never have the chance to argue for a different outcome.[104] While it is difficult to say how a balancing of liberty interests would work in practice, a blanket denial of any paternal input in the abortion decision can significantly affect life choices for men. To uphold women's absolute power to decide reinforces the notion that they are properly responsible for the private sphere, even as it denies that men have a place there as well.

Cases in which women seek to be defenders, either in combat positions in the military[105] or their civilian equivalent as prison guards[106], present analogous difficulties, for if pregnancy is historically a woman's world, defense is classically masculine. A challenge to that pattern is, to some, a challenge to the ultimate source of women's oppression;[107] to others it threatens the "very womanhood"[108] of those who would undermine this last and most powerful sex barrier.

The particularly high stakes help to explain why the Supreme Court's handling of these cases has been so unsatisfactory. The justices cannot say that the woman's claim is out of bounds, socially unacceptable;[109] they cannot express the source of their misgivings. What the Court has done instead is to take at face value the assertion that a woman seeking to be a defender puts herself at too great a risk because of her sex, relying on the scantiest of evidence to confirm its prejudice. This abandonment of analytic rigor denies the possibility of minimizing the asserted physical risk—for instance, by providing self-defense training for the would-be female prison guard. It honors the very stereotypes of violent, sex-crazed men and vulnerable, defenseless women that it has sought to undercut in other circumstances. Most basically, it forgets that, in the hardest cases, claims of gender liberty should lead the justices to rethink, not thoughtlessly reinstate, the deepest of beliefs about masculinity and femininity in this society.

The limits of equal liberty. The principle of equal liberty is "not a machine that, once set in motion, must run to all conceivable legal conclusions."[110] It may collide either with another claim premised on autonomy or with some other highly valued end, such as efficiency or the general welfare, and in these instances the principle must necessarily be balanced against its rivals.[111]

One person's liberty is sometimes felt by another person as a constraint, and so some way of choosing between competing liberty claims is required. It is acceptable, in classic understandings of liberty, to frustrate individual choices in order to prevent harm to others, since such activities diminish the ability of the would-be victims freely to select their own way of life.[112] Similarly, the fact that one person finds the choice-enhancing behavior of another odious is not grounds for undermining autonomy; were it otherwise, the very idea of choice would be meaningless.

Yet liberties do sometimes collide. We deny employers who prefer a sex-segregated workplace the right to have their way and so value the liberty of some more highly than that of others. Imbedded in this preference is the assertion that the harm to the employee, the constriction of personhood, is of greater importance than honoring the employer's prejudice.

A different type of liberty-based concern has to do with the distinction developed in the first part of the book between negative liberty, which gives freedom from state-imposed constraints, and positive liberty, which guarantees opportunities to achieve certain goals.[113] The line between these concepts is not hard and fast, either descriptively, for a great many rights may be phrased in both positive and negative terms, or normatively, as there is no reason to believe that freeing the individual from restraint is always preferable to providing an opportunity.[114] That is why, when framing rules with respect to gender, a legislature will adopt measures that protect liberty in both senses; indeed, the history of contemporary social welfare policy chronicles the spread of positive liberty.

The constitutional concern, by contrast, usually concentrates on liberty understood as removing constraints: antidiscrimination suits and challenges to abortion restrictions are the paradigmatic instances. Issues of positive liberty, although very much a part of the contemporary docket, strain the capacities of a court to evaluate the outcomes of social programs and carry out the institutional reforms that such issues often demand.[115] In the gender domain, such questions may be unavoidable, but positive liberty claims are generally better left to the legislature. For instance, a court should not condemn government's failure to enrich choice by not supplying free child care for working parents, since whatever the merits of this idea, failure to implement it does not instance disrespect to individual autonomy premised on sex.[116]

The liberty-enhancing idea of equal respect may also collide with the claim that some alternative promotes the general welfare.[117] Arguments couched in terms of general welfare that infringe upon gender-based volition need to be scrupulously inspected in order to calibrate the nature and degree of the infringement, the collective gain to be anticipated, and the likelihood of achieving the same end through a less liberty-constricting approach.[118] The more central to personal autonomy is the intrusion, the more absolutely convincing must the state's reasoning be, since where a person's very identity is at risk "considerations of the individual's interests and deserts are paramount."[119] In the realm of gender, most policies would fail this test, since less status-defining approaches seem capable of accomplishing the aims of government.

Indeed, leaving individuals free to pursue their own desires often serves to promote the general welfare. That is the teaching of classical liberalism, which defines general welfare as the sum of individually calculated welfares.[120] It is the premise of microeconomic theory, which teaches that exchanges made among persons who decide for themselves what they most value will make the society as a whole better off.[121] Individual views registered through the efforts of interest groups describe politics as understood by those who subscribe to a pluralist conception of democracy.[122]

Yet efficiency, intended to make the aggregate better off, can sometimes be secured only by impinging on individual liberty or relying on group characteristics such as gender. Pension and life insurance plans, with different payment and benefit schedules for men and women, are one example; the "PX benefits" case, described earlier, is another. How should these situations be analyzed?

Pension plans typically require that women make larger contributions than men because of their longer average life expectancy; for the same reason women pay lower life insurance premiums.[123] These rules treat men and women differently, but males and females *are* different in this respect. "This is in no sense a failure to treat women as 'individuals'. . . . It is to treat them as individually as it is possible to do in the face of the unknowable length of each individual life."[124]

The lack of a readily available alternative basis for pricing pensions is one way to distinguish this instance from other occasions in which statistical differences between the sexes are relied on in framing rules. A rule denying women the right to compete for jobs which demand that heavy weights be lifted cannot be sustained, even though on the whole women may well be weaker than men, because it is readily possible to make individual determinations of strength. Such an option does not exist for pensions or life insurance.

Pension pricing and life insurance pricing reflect a differentiation that does not discriminate. As a criterion for making distinctions, life expectancy carries no stigma, and in this sense too it differs from such other gender-related criteria as the ability to heft weights. It strains logic to analyze pension or life insurance differentials as affecting the capacity of an individual to form and act upon a life plan. Few of us can set the length of our lives, and fewer still would exchange shorter lives for smaller pension contributions. Such differentials merely mirror the facts of life.

Auto insurance policies are another story, since safe driving, unlike the length of one's life, is controllable by individuals. Sex-based differentials create categories from which careful men cannot escape and which benefit reckless women. Safe driving habits can be predicted by factors already in use: whether a person completed a driver's education course, or uses seatbelts, or doesn't get speeding or drunk-driving tickets. To charge males higher rates regardless of their behavior perpetuates stereotypes of hot-bloodedness even as gender-neutral alternatives, such as age, driving records, and the observable behavior mentioned above, are available.

The classic use of stereotypes in law involves reliance on some sex-based difference that is generally but not universally accurate to grant one sex a benefit denied to the other: allowing only men to apply for jobs with a strength requirement, on the theory that men are stronger than women, or denying widowers help in raising children that is available to widows, in the belief that widows but not widowers will stay home to bring up their youngsters. However efficient such stereotyping may be, it is nonetheless intolerable, because the impact on personal autonomy is too great.

Does this same objection pertain to rules relying on sex-based differences for the weaker purpose of obliging those who don't conform to the gender stereotype only to demonstrate their fitness? *Frontiero* is the classic illustration.[125] As noted earlier, that case tested the permissibility of automatically giving wives of servicemen dependents' benefits, while requiring the husbands of servicewomen to prove their dependency. This rule reflects the familiar assumption that the husband heads the household; but as this stereotype found its way into the law, it had only a modestly inhibiting effect on those who opted for nonconformism. The servicewoman's husband could enjoy the full range of benefits available to the wife of a serviceman by proving that he was the exception to the rule. Unlike, say, the husband who is legally prevented from substantiating the seriousness of his wish to stay at home with his children,[126] the truly dependent husband in *Frontiero* could claim the privileges of the PX.

There is also a plausible reason for the Army to treat servicemen and servicewomen differently. In seven out of eight American households, the husband remains the chief breadwinner.[127] That proportion is likely to be much higher in the armed services, where frequent transfers disrupt the civilian careers of spouses (and where conventional marriages are more the norm). It thus may well be much cheaper for the Army to grant dependent status to all wives, rather than insisting on family-by-family review. No such pattern can be anticipated when it is the wife who serves in the armed forces, and for that reason case-by-case review makes good sense in those instances. This argument requires more than assertion—that is why the Court in *Frontiero* was right to reject the military's unsupported claim— but if the Army established the point, it could advance an argument based on efficiency that deserved attention, particularly when arrayed against a weak autonomy-based argument.[128]

A differential decision rule of this type makes sense only as long as the stereotype on which it relies holds almost universally true. If a sizable minority of Army wives come to earn more than their husbands, the justification based on efficiency vanishes. For that reason, a *Frontiero*-type rule does not forever perpetuate assumptions about economic relationships within the family. Such a rule is no longer appropriate when the convention it mirrors has grown dated.

The equal liberty principle may also be read to reach a contrary conclusion in this case, and in analogous instances of rules that condition a husband's eligibility for social security and workman's compensation benefits on proof of his dependency.[129] Treating men and women differently in terms of who is presumed to be the dependent family member not only confirms a real present distinction; it may also reinforce the stereotype, signalling to the dependent woman that her behavior remains the norm in the eyes of the law. Demanding that the unconventional couple assume the obligation of proving its exceptionality also invades the privacy of women's families, who must reveal their income and assets to public view, while the families of comparable males are not subject to such scrutiny. In these ways, the rules are offensive to the aspiration of liberty.

Whatever one makes of a rule that requires members of one sex to prove that they do not conform to a stereotype in order to receive a benefit, that approach is impermissible when civic obligations rather than public benefits are at issue. Individuals entitled to a benefit, like PX privileges or workmen's compensation, have a stake in showing that it is rightfully theirs—that they don't fit the stereotype. But women excluded from the jury rolls or kept out of the draft because of their sex have no comparable incentive to take issue with the determination. In theory, both sexes suffer under a conception of citizenship that requires only men to serve as jurors or soldiers, but no individual woman who acts on the basis of her self-interest has any reason to volunteer. Differentiating on the basis of sex in fixing the terms of any civic duty merely preserves the stereotypes of gender.

IV

Treating the Equal Protection Clause as centrally concerned with liberty is all well and good, one might say, in its social consequences, but is it a constitutional approach or merely a *tour de force* that reads more into the vessel of "personhood" than is constitutionally imaginable? This is a fair question, especially for contemporary legal scholars immersed in analyses in which "equality" has become "sameness"; the notion of liberty seems out of place here. Yet a sharp analytic demarcation between liberty and equality turns out to be a most ahistorical approach. The preconstitutional idea of equal protection, an idea that flourished in law through the middle of the nineteenth century, was a liberty-driven idea; and in several pre-modern cases having to do with the treatment of women, the Supreme Court advanced an argument similar to that offered here.[130]

Although the Fourteenth Amendment was adopted with particular reference to the plight of newly emancipated blacks who had been denied their civil rights by Southern states in the aftermath of the Civil War,[131] the core concern of the Equal Protection Clause was imbedded in the Constitution well before the passage of that amendment.[132] That underlying principle is more general in scope: "Everyone has a right to demand that he be governed by general rules."[133]

This majestic and disarmingly simple statement has its roots in the Declaration of Independence and in the political philosophers of the Enlightenment, on whom the Founders drew for inspiration. In barring the granting of titles of nobility, prohibiting the enactment of laws that apply after the fact, and singling out particular individuals for official attention, the Constitution confirms this belief that "all are equals in government."[134] For that reason, American law had to be general and not particularized, future-looking and not retrospective. Many state constitutions insisted that the legislature proceed by way of general and not special laws.[135] Judges too picked up this theme, citing time and again John Locke's maxim that those who legislate "are to govern by promulgated, established laws, not to be varied in particular cases, but to have one rule for rich and poor, for the favorite at court and the countryman at plough."[136]

This central idea of equal protection, fair and generalized treatment by law, was widely accepted before the Fourteenth Amendment was enacted; indeed, it was one of the chief limitations placed on legislation.[137] The Equal Protection Clause, and the parallel provision of the Fourteenth Amendment extending the privileges and immunities of citizenship were intended to secure the fundamental rights of all persons, and so promote the fullest exercise of personal liberty. *Equal* was the term relied on because the protections of the law were being denied to some, notably freed slaves, but the word *full* would have conveyed the same meaning. As Jacobus ten Broek concluded in his massive study of the origins of the Fourteenth Amendment, the Equal Protection Clause obliges "each state [to] supply the protection of the laws to persons in their natural rights and the protection shall always be equal."[138]

A second noteworthy element of equal protection analysis is its relationship to the historical insistence on laws of general application. The distaste for special laws did not reflect hostility toward legal line-drawing generally: distinctions for purposes of taxation, expenditure of public funds, and health and safety regulation were routine, and routinely accepted. Instead, judicial hostility was directed specifically at rules that undermined the ability of individuals to order their own lives with respect to predictable legal consequences.

If a special law requires that only Jones shall pay a land tax at a particular rate, the law creates a class of one person; it also establishes a closed class. Jones cannot escape the reach of this rule, whatever he does; and Smith and Johnson cannot enter the class, whatever they do. By contrast, if a tax is levied on real but not on personal property—land but not jewelry— an individual may choose which type of property to hold with those tax consequences in mind. Open classifications of this type enable individuals to exercise their liberty, knowing the legal implications of their decisions. In this sense too, liberty and equality are joined.

Although every law bespeaks a denial of liberty, as Jeremy Bentham once observed, the force of those denials vary; laws that bear down on groups that can neither be joined nor avoided by individual action are the most egregious inhibitions, for they withhold from mature persons responsibility for their conduct.[139] Viewed in this light, state court decisions striking down special legislation and the elaboration of Fourteenth Amendment protections for blacks are both aimed at the same evil: closed legal categories that define individual rights in term of discredited notions of status. A black can no sooner become white than Smith can transform himself into Jones.[140]

Nor, of course, can a woman transform herself into a man or a man into a woman; for that reason, this line of analysis has obvious relevance to the gender cases. Legislative lines based on sex establish close-ended distinctions, rooted in status, which generally deny liberty to one or both sexes. Yet whether they are viewed in this manner depends on a prior conception of substantive rights. We require some less abstract notion of people, some sense of the ways in which they are and aren't alike, before we can determine what fairness means. That is why certain close-ended, status-based laws—laws differentiating between children and grownups, for instance, or between the mentally handicapped and the normal—are accepted; these are regarded as reflecting "real" differences, real inequalities.[141] If persons are to be treated with equal respect, then one must apply "anterior constitutional standards" in figuring out what traits entitle an individual to equal respect; and, to square the circle, those traits can be only derived from a substantive conception of rights.[142]

Gender was not one of the distinctions taken up by those who framed the Equal Protection Clause.[143] Indeed, some leading feminists opposed the adoption of the Fourteenth Amendment because another of its provisions added "male" to the Constitution for the first time, implying that women could be denied suffrage. Nor are the early Supreme Court cases sympathetic to the plight of women. In 1873, the Court concluded that denying Myra Bradwell a license to practice law because of her sex did not undermine the privileges and immunities of citizenship, as she had claimed;[144] the next year, the justices dismissed out of hand a similar claim made by a woman who had demanded the right to vote in national elections.[145]

Later, the Supreme Court came to examine more directly the constitutionality of denying women liberty: specifically, the liberty to contract. Throughout the late nineteenth and early twentieth centuries, the justices struck down a great many laws regulating hours and wages on the theory that they undermined the right of individuals, under the Due Process Clause of the Fourteenth Amendment, to enter into contracts. Some of those laws related only to women, thus posing the constitutional question: If *persons* were entitled to the protections of due process of law, including the liberty to contract, on what basis could women be subjected to greater restrictions than men?[146]

The Supreme Court's answer came in *Muller v. Oregon*,[147] decided in 1908. Three years earlier, a badly split Court had overturned a law prohibiting the employment of bakers for more than ten hours a day. That law interfered with the liberty to make contracts, the majority reasoned, and "there is no contention that bakers as a class are not equal in intelligence and capacity to men in other trades or manual occupations, or that they are not able to assert their rights and care for themselves."[148] Women were another story entirely, the Court concluded in *Muller*, which sustained a maximum hours law that applied only to women. Unlike bakers, women couldn't take care of themselves; since they needed the help of the state, a rule securing their welfare in the workplace robbed them of no liberty.

Fifteen years later, however, in *Adkins v. Children's Hospital*[149] the justices took a different approach—an explicitly liberty-enhancing approach—in overturning a federal act that fixed minimum wages for women in the District of Columbia. Although physical differences "must be recognized in appropriate cases," the Court acknowledged, there was no reason generally to credit the notion that women are less able than men to make contractual decisions for themselves. The trend of modern legislation—notably, the Nineteenth Amendment, extending suffrage to women—"as well as that of common thought and usage" was to emancipate women from laws that accord them special protection, limit their capacity to enter contracts, or constrict their civil responsibilities. Much had changed since the dark days of *Muller*, the justice declared: "The ancient inequality of the sexes, otherwise than physical, has continued 'with diminishing intensity.' " Indeed, the Court asserts, changes in the "contractual, political and civil status of women" of such "revolutionary" magnitude had occurred that "these differences have now come almost, if not quite, to the vanishing point."[150]

Although *Adkins* is couched in the language of due process, its analysis bears directly on equal protection reasoning. The Court recognized that women are no less capable than men of making life choices for themselves, and for that reason legislation intended to protect them in fact injures them. But *Adkins* marked only a temporary victory for gender equity, since this line of reasoning was abandoned almost as soon as the ink was dry on the Court's opinion. As Blanche Crozier, an early student of women's constitutional rights, observed shortly thereafter, "It does not appear that at any time since the adoption of the Constitution has discrimination based on sex been unconstitutional."[151]

Just a year after *Adkins*, the Court upheld a state law prohibiting women, but not men, from night restaurant work. A decade later, when the New Deal Court belatedly gave its blessing to a host of governmental regulations of the marketplace, it treated *Adkins*, not as a charter of liberation but as the last gasp of the discredited notion that the justices should secure the hypothetical liberty to contract against government intrusion. In 1937,

Adkins was unceremoniously laid to rest. The justices concluded that a state can single out women for specially solicitous treatment because they receive less pay, have less bargaining power, and "are the ready victims of those who would take advantage of their necessitous circumstances."[152] This determination made general sense in the economic sphere, but it effectively kept the Supreme Court from taking seriously the claims of women for fair treatment by law.

In *Goesart v. Cleary,* decided in 1948, the Court reviewed an equal protection challenge—the first such sex-based challenge—to a Michigan law that barred any woman from being licensed as a bartender unless she was "the wife or daughter of the male owner of the licensed liquor establishment."[153] The Court dismissed the constitutional claim in a jocular three-page opinion short on analysis but replete with references to the ale-wife in Shakespeare. Its opinion says, in effect, "we cannot rewrite the rules of social etiquette." But that reading of the law ignores how a gender-based rule undermines women's liberty and protects a male monopoly; it ignores the fact that the Equal Protection Clause secures rights to "persons"; and it ignores the reasoning of *Adkins,* a decision that could well have been given new life in equal protection garb.[154] Thus, when sex discrimination cases were heard by a more sympathetic Supreme Court in the early 1970s, the justices were so busy repudiating the line of the pre-modern decisions, restoring the rights of the would-be lawyer and the prospective barmaid, that they paid no attention to a conception of equal protection centered on claims of liberty. From *Reed v. Reed* to the present, the modern opinions embrace a doctrinal choice, not an inescapable reality of the Equal Protection Clause.

V

Gender and religion are not usually conceived in analogous constitutional terms, for they have very different histories. But the noteworthy parallels in the uses that the law makes of these concepts puts the liberty principle in clearer focus.

Both religion and gender join behavior and belief, both are central in forming individual identity, both have their orthodoxies and heterodoxies, both have implications for individuals and privately formed groups. Most of all, religion can provide an illuminating analogy for gender, because the central aspiration of the law in each instance may be stated in broadly similar language: to protect free exercise, whether of religion or life choices; and to proscribe governmental imposition of conventions, establishments of religion or sex-role stereotypes.

Religion has an honored place in our society since, as the Supreme Court has declared, "we are a religious people."[155] Broadly understood, religion calibrates the individual's moral compass, defining "whatever is central and paramount and pervasive in the individual's life,"[156] and for that reason is "essential to the projection of human personality and the opportunity for self-fulfillment."[157] Despite—or perhaps because of—its personal importance, religion is a private and personal calling, not an activity of government. We may be a religious *people,* but we are not a religious *nation.* If the metaphor of a wall of separation between church and state exaggerates the division, clouding the complexity of the interplay, it dramatizes the fact that government's mission is not to advance particular religions.[158] In this domain, unlike many others, no power lodges in the state to declare what is right; the majority rule that governs in politics has little relevance.[159] Government can neither prefer one religion to another nor favor religion over irreligion[160]—even as, in gender, orthodox masculine and feminine behavior may not be routinely preferred.

The central concern of the constitutional order, for religion as with gender, is to encourage liberty.[161] That aim mirrors a widely held conception of the good society as one in which diversity itself is worthy, or at least preferable to government regulation. Religion flourishes when based on voluntary commitment, not when government promotes it. And individual conscience, the capacity to form a moral life plan for oneself, deserves to be free from the taint of official scrutiny in both spheres.

Voluntarism and the inviolability of conscience, the values that inform the constitutional guarantees of free exercise and nonestablishment of religion, are more closely associated with freedom and personal autonomy than with equality. Often those values are phrased in terms of a required governmental neutrality with respect to religion, an egalitarian concept. Yet, like attempts to craft an indistinguishability principle for gender, religious neutrality has assumed so many different forms that it has lost much of its meaning. Government is not barred from taking religion into account:[162] accommodations by the state to the religiosity of the people and to individual claims of religious liberty are permitted and may even be required. A state may exempt from Sunday closing laws those whose religious faith specifies a different Sabbath,[163] and government must honor the beliefs of those whose religious liberties are threatened by an otherwise reasonable regulation.[164]

Liberty seems more the aspiration of these decisions than neutrality; at its best, the Supreme Court is insisting on freedom from majoritarian conceptions of the good life. Within the private sphere, religion, like gender, animates institutions—churches and families—and relationships. The state protects these voluntary associations, guaranteeing "to an individual adult maximum freedom in the determination of his religious or irreligious beliefs."[165]

The scope of religious liberty, while substantial, is not unbounded. Claims premised on religious liberty sometimes collide with concerns for peace and order, welfare,[166] public morality,[167] and civic obligation.[168] When that happens, the Court's balancing act resembles the application of the equal liberty standard. Just how important is the rule? How severely is liberty undermined? Are the means of government tailored to accomplish the goals of government? Is an alternative rule available that infringes less on personal liberty? How vital is the religious practice for which special protection is claimed?[169] Such an analysis is "in the larger sense not neutral among religions," as Marc Galanter has pointed out. In its preference for faiths that tolerate competing beliefs and are privatistic in character, it mirrors the equal liberty approach.[170]

Religious liberty has been hedged round in other ways. As with gender, the Supreme Court has sometimes been willing to subordinate the claims of the unconventional to the dominant moral position. In gender cases, war and violence seem especially problematic; liberty is regularly subordinated to national security. In religion, the society's well-being has sometimes been the source of felt, rather than analyzed, judicial opinion, with challenges to traditional attitudes toward the moral and social order viewed dimly. A century after the fact, it is hard to credit the notion that polygamy, as the Mormons historically practiced it, really jeopardized the social fabric, despite the Court's ruling on the issue.

In recent years, however, the Supreme Court has increased the reach of religious liberty. The state must exempt Seventh Day Adventists, whose Sabbath falls on Saturday, from the otherwise valid rule that those seeking unemployment compensation be available to work on Saturdays, for religious liberty cannot be made so costly.[171] Nor may the state insist that Amish youngsters receive more than an eighth grade education, which the sect regards as immoral, unless government can demonstrate that the value of those additional years of schooling justifies the imposition; the interest in religious liberty prevails over the state's wish to introduce these children to a broader span of secular knowledge.[172] Even though a pluralist order in which individuals determine their life plans only after exposure to alternative conceptions might be theoretically preferable to a world replete with private indoctrination, the Court has been unwilling to insist upon such exposure. In both religion and gender, even unthinking orthodoxy is preferable to official involvement, if that orthodoxy represents a voluntary and private commitment.

The limits on how far government may go to support the majority's religious premises are less clearly fixed. Certainly, government may offer religious groups such generally available services as police and fire protection. Although such largess undoubtedly aids religion, it does not offend individual choice and enables each religion to flourish; indeed, to deny this kind of help would manifest an unacceptable antagonism. But more than police protection and clean streets are presently at issue. As the government has furnished new welfare benefits to an ever-expanding clientele, religious groups have sought a share:[173] support for church-run schools is the most familiar example, an analog to feminists' insistence on the provision of day care.[174] The Supreme Court seems increasingly inclined to accommodate these ambitions of religious groups. Recent decisions intimate that, as long as such aid is not designed for nor primarily beneficial to religious groups, it does not offend the Establishment Clause.[175]

The analog between religion and gender is hardly perfect. In particular, the Establishment Clause imposes an absolute bar in some circumstances that have no gender-specific counterpart. For instance, no matter how beneficial an official religion might be for the *esprit* of the armed forces, its adoption would not be allowed; concern for *esprit* is decidedly relevant in assessing the appropriateness of a sexually integrated combat force.[176] But in most instances, the guiding constitutional norms seem much the same. The law is designed to safeguard individuals' capacity to give meaning to a core aspect of their identity.[177] Although the claims of freedom are in neither instance unbounded, the state must have a very good reason before it can diminish liberty. That concern for liberty, not a fixation with sameness of treatment by government, rightly shapes the role of law in matters both of religion and gender.

6

Gender in the House of Policy

A statesman differs from a professor in a university. The latter has only the general view of society; the former . . . has a number of circumstances to combine with those general ideas and to take into his consideration. Circumstances are infinite, are infinitely combined, are variable and transient: he who does not take them into consideration is not erroneous, but stark mad.

Edmund Burke, "Speech on the Petition of the Unitarians" (1792)

I hardly know which is the greater pest to society, a paternal government . . . which intrudes itself into every part of human life, and which thinks it can do everything for everybody better than anybody can do anything for himself; or a careless lounging government, which suffers grievances, such as it could at once remove, to grow and multiply, and to which all complaint and remonstrance has only one answer: "We must let things take their course; we must let things find their own level."

Thomas Babington Macaulay, "Speech" (1846)

I

What should be the substance of gender policy? It is one thing to advocate autonomy in the domain of gender, quite another to specify what the political branches of government can do to aid autonomous decision making. That is the task of this chapter, which offers a structure for analyzing policy, and the two following chapters, which center on the workplace and the family.

Some caveats are in order. The issues summed in the phrase "gender policy" are legion, the political environments that nurture them disorderly, the competing claimants many and vociferous. To deal fittingly with topics ranging from the protection of pregnant women in the toxic workplace[1] to the awarding of custody to gay would-be parents,[2] would require an encyclopedia; we mean to be illustrative and not exhaustive. We also stint on detail, leaving fine points to be elaborated within the framework. Although

124

we are not timid about urging particular policy outcomes in the name of choice, we recognize that in many instances there is no clearly best approach, for the evidence is too unclear, the results of intervention too uncertain, or the play of preference too substantial.[3] Our larger intention is not to insist upon some pet scheme but to show by example that thinking about policy issues in principled terms, as properly aimed at enhancing personal choice, is both useful and potentially consequential.

From both ends of the political spectrum, much of what passes for gender policy discussion is disappointing in its content and form. The expectation that government can decree gender justice, ushering in the future or reinstating a sanitized version of the past, is strongly held, even in the face of evidence that most Americans question the usefulness of new government interventions and doubt that officialdom will usually do what is right.[4] And conflict among the partisans over gender policy resembles less the familiar jockeying for attention among interest groups than a death-struggle to validate one or another conception of the right and true.

The platform of the 1978 National Women's Conference offers a useful introduction to the policy aspirations of politically active leftist feminists. Delegates declared that government should eliminate violence in the home and develop shelters for battered women, support women's businesses, eradicate child abuse, provide federal funding of nonsexist day care, assure full employment in order that all women who wish to work may do so, protect homemakers who would make their marriages into partnerships, end the sexist portrayal of women in the media, establish reproductive freedom and end involuntary sterilization, revise the criminal codes dealing with rape, eliminate discrimination on the basis of sexual preference, establish nonsexist education, review all welfare proposals for their specific impact on women, and so forth.

What is remarkable about this litany is the implicit expectation that anyone, let alone government, might accomplish all those things—that government might, for instance, actually end child abuse. The conference recommendations ignore priorities—everything is important—and acknowledge no limits to collective action or resources in the public and private spheres, thus linking the plausible and significant with the petty and unachievable. Naively enough, they reflect the belief that a Big Sister government which policed day care programs and the media to root out sexism would be less coercive than Big Brother, that thought control in the pursuit of benign outcomes is acceptable. It is the kind of public document that gives gender policy a bad name.[5]

Worse still in this respect are the dreams of the feminist future collected in *Woman in the Year 2000*.[6] These twenty-one fantasies manifest an extraordinary faith in the saving force of legislation. The contributors root for the passage of a Parental Responsibility Act, which limits parents to twenty-five hours a week of paid employment in order to make fathers and mothers equally responsible for child care; an Income Security Opportunity Act, assuring government support for all; and a Neighborhood Playgroup Act, which attends to the recreational needs of children. Such laws, which are supposed to unleash the creativity of individuals and to radically alter the character of the family and the workplace, evoke instead Orwellian visions of an intrusive government that oversees and regulates our most private decisions.

In fairness, this kind of fantasizing hardly exhausts feminist thinking about policy or efforts to place feminist goals on the political agenda. Beginning in 1963 with the passage of the Equal Pay Act, a great deal of federal legislation aimed at undoing one or another form of unfairness has been adopted. That roll call includes the provisions of the 1964 Civil Rights Act dealing with sex discrimination, the 1972 legislation proscribing sex discrimination in schools and universities, the 1974 law mandating equal credit opportunity, the 1978 bill assuring that employers treat pregnancy as a normal disability in calculating benefits, and the pension equity and child support enforcement measures of 1984.

These bills did not pass because of the sheer good will of legislators. Although there were some fluke victories—the 1964 Civil Rights Act included sex as one of the prohibited bases of discrimination only because Southern legislators thought that was a good joke, a way of pointing out the absurdity of the larger civil rights enterprise—these measures were, for the most part, energetically promoted by a coalition of activists who played conventional politics like maestroes. They effectively mustered pressure in aid of goals that could be depicted as unthreatening to the general scheme of things—as extending to women the rights enjoyed by men, for instance, without disturbing women's role as homemaker.[7]

Moreover, not all policy appraisals of gender-related issues are so readily caricatured as the *Year 2000* proposals. There are, for instance, treatments of child care that reckon frankly with the tension between the interest of women in freedom and the interest of children in nurturance,[8] and discussions of the need for a federal housing policy that would respond to changing family demographics by increasing options, both in the siting and character of publicly supported housing.[9] But these analyses remain the exception; even among mainstream gender policy analysts, there is a stubborn persisting preference for the costly, the centralized, and the uniform, an unwillingness to learn from the demise of the Great Society mode of governing.

Judged by the criterion of political success, feminists have fallen far short of the mark, as the possibility for action on behalf of women's causes has remained greater than the performance. The failure of the Equal Rights Amendment, a failure above all of political acumen, is the best example of this; but in Congress and the statehouses too, stamina has sometimes been in short supply.

This mixed track record is partly attributable to the view, held by some leftist feminists, that only transformational politics—the politics of the *Year 2000* essays, if not of Mary Daly's Hag/ocracy—is worth struggling for, that meliorist politics, which is what legislatures routinely traffic in, is useless.[10] There is also a tendency among radical feminists to emphasize the psychological at the expense of the political, "a preoccupation with internal processes" of personal or small group dynamics that has taken "precedence over program or effectiveness."[11] Furthermore, supporters of feminist causes, like activists in other social movements, have often confused formal victories—the passage of a bill—with real change, ignoring the grubby but vital business of policing the implementation of new laws. There have been great difficulties in enforcing the new credit restrictions, for instance, but little demand for strengthened enforcement.

This decade has been a difficult time for feminists of whatever ideological stripe. Although the attention paid to the gender gap by both parties has enabled women to preserve past gains, there have been few new triumphs to shout about, and certainly none that cost Washington any money. Meanwhile, beginning in 1980, the Right has had its chance to rewrite the rules of the game, and its proposals are more unnerving than even the woolliest fantasies of the Left.

One might imagine that conservatives would be more chary of government intervention or more respectful of past practice, but this turns out not to be the case—or, more accurately, these new activists turn out to be, not conservatives, but radical reactionaries. Radicals of the Right and Left appear equally willing to be prescriptive, differing only in the substance of the government policy being commended. For instance, in turning conventional liberal thinking on its ear, the indefatigable Phyllis Schlafly proposes to define as "discrimination" any policy concerning work that does not favor "the traditional family, and the one-paycheck family, where the father is the primary provider and the mother the primary homemaker."[12]

There is more, but not better, in this vein. Legislation designed to teach teenagers "self-discipline and chastity" has been introduced into Congress. A Family Protection Act, which has also been before Congress, urges everything from "an expansive interpretation" of the role of parents in the moral and religious upbringing of their children and a relaxation of restrictions on parental administration of the strap to a requirement that educational materials purchased with federal dollars "reflect different ways in which men and women live" and "contribute to the American way of life as it has been historically understood." It would deny federal funding, including social security and welfare benefits, to anyone who "promoted" a life style that the New Right finds distressing.[13] Advocates on the far left would lead us into the Brave New World, complete with BioLib. Their radical right antagonists would return us to the imaginary world of yesteryear, when men wore the pants, gays stayed in the closet, and children were seen but not heard.

In style as well as substance, gender politics has often been the politics of Armageddon, characterized by clashes between social movements that do not know the language of compromise. When President Nixon expressed fears for the demise of the American family and the rise of "communal approaches to child rearing," as he did in vetoing day care legislation in 1971, he set the ideological tone of debate.[14] The issues have since evolved but the element of moral crusade has only grown stronger. If the participants believe that each has a monopoly on virtue, if opponents are labelled as wrong or unvirtuous, as regularly occurs in disputes over such bitterly contested questions as homosexual rights, child care, and abortion, political civility is hard to sustain. Here the moral dilemmas are truly vexing, the stakes high, the strain in the social and constitutional fabric considerable, the winners of public debate harder to determine than the losers.

Ideological donnybrooks are not unique to gender. But the ferocity of the clashes masks a complicating truth: on a great many subjects of policy debate, the right answer is not really ascertainable, either by recourse to theory or by reliance on data. There is, for instance, no unassailable argument for the proposition that the traditional household is best—for what has been functional isn't necessarily right—or, conversely, for the view that an imposed egalitarianism in the household would be preferable. A political system that insisted on greater female participation might produce a more humane government or just more Margaret Thatchers. The increasing reliance on day care for children whose parents both work may yield more neurotic progeny, deprived of a nurturing figure—or healthier offspring, freed from ever-obsessing Mom. There is no way to know these things.

Present societal norms reflect this relativism, and mark a change from the apparently greater certainties of the past. A thousand flowers bloom in the American social garden, and the extent of variability has been increasing rapidly. Survey data reveal a growing tolerance for life choices that once would have seemed wholly out of bounds, a diminished willingness to condemn the aberrational, whether that person be a househusband, a lesbian, or an unmarried mother. This is new: a 1984 Harris survey finds that 70 percent of men and 64 percent of women report that women are regarded with greater respect as individual human beings, compared to a decade earlier.[15] Moreover, the aberrational has increasingly become the norm, with respect to the proportion of working mothers, unmarried couples living together, abortions performed, and the like. These developments have taken us ever farther from a normative societal consensus on which a detailed and prescriptive gender policy might conceivably be based.

II

Some gender policy is an inevitability, because government actions necessarily affect individual choices. In its arrangements for child care, job training, taxation, abortion, military service, education, and in myriad other instances, government broadens or narrows the sphere of individual volition. Offer subsidized state-run day care and fewer children will be raised by stay-at-home mothers; make marriage a tax haven and more individuals may be tempted to tie the knot; turn homosexuality into a crime and gay men and women will lead furtive private lives; choose a different approach and the outcome will change. As long as the government is to have some responsibility for raising and spending taxpayers' dollars and regulating the economy, it cannot avoid affecting men's and women's choices.[16]

Policy is not only inevitable; deliberate polities also make considerable sense for a great many gender issues. "End government intrusion" may be a catchy slogan, but it offers small comfort to the battered spouse or the victim of job discrimination. "Getting government off our backs" has little meaning to the poor family that hopes to raise its children decently and maintain an adequate standard of living. Government involvement becomes especially appropriate when traditional institutions such as churches, families, and local communities can no longer do their jobs, when once-private shames become public dilemmas. Although the marketplace is in many instances a valuable safeguard of individual choice, the unregulated market will not respond to many legitimate grievances of men and women, nor will it routinely furnish individuals with the information they need to make choices for themselves. In short, a "night watchman" state is not what justice entails.[17]

The question remains: is it possible to harness policy shaped by the political branches to a useful set of principles?[18] This is not a question that one poses about the judiciary, since what makes courts distinctive, what gives this unelected "least dangerous" branch[19] of government its legitimacy, is the principle-driven character of judicial decision making.[20] Judges do not just act but also explain themselves. They elaborate reasons for a decision; search for consistency with earlier cases to justify the opinion at hand; appeal variously to historical evidence, constitutional text, and inferences from the structure of the Constitution.[21] Courts deprecate short-run considerations, and treat bargaining and vote-swapping as unacceptable behavior. Most important, perhaps, they assign rights, which are absolute in nature, rather than trafficking in interests that can more readily be "satisfied."[22] Appeals to principle, of the sort advanced in the last chapter, come naturally to such an institution.

This distinction between courts and the coordinate branches of government cannot be pushed too far, of course, for the day is long past when informed commentators believed that law awaited discovery by the diligent application of logic and the scientific method, free of value judgments. Particularly in settling disputes to which the law offers no straightforward answer, judges take note of the political as well as the legal ramifications of their decisions. Accommodation and uncertainty in law are dictated by the vagueness of legal principles, the difficulty of applying principles to concrete cases, and conflicts among principles.[23] Nonetheless, judging differs in salient ways from overtly political decision-making, and those differences consistently point to the far greater status of principle in judicial argument.

Some who disparage the pragmatic nature of politics would turn elsewhere—to experts, for instance—or recast the political process in a more rationalistic mold. Such alternatives are theoretically possible, but far less attractive than more familiar incrementalist politics in their implications for gender justice. Although experts play a dominant role in many policy arenas, especially where technical knowledge is crucial, gender policy seems an unlikely domain for the ministrations of specialists.[24] Indeterminacy concerning what works and what doesn't, what policy initiatives succeed and why, is no pathological condition but appears imbedded in the subject of gender itself; because disagreements about values dominate many of the central issues, expertise offers little guidance.[25] Under such circumstances, everyone becomes an expert; what feels right may well *be* right. Expertise can, of course, be useful at the margin of decision, as in long-term evaluations of child care programs, and expertise can better inform individual decisions. But much too little is—or is likely to be—known, for a Bureau of Gender Policy or gender impact statements to be helpful.

Nor would we be better off with a system of decision that aimed at remodelling "the whole of society in accordance with a definite plan or blueprint,"[26] as rationalist politics envisions. Rationalism of this stripe quests after perfection.[27] It aims at defining and controlling the future, since "from any department of social life which is not so controlled there may lurk the dangerous forces that make for unforeseen changes."[28] But "unforeseen changes," popular subversions, give gender policy its dynamic quality; it is those changes, those acts of *private* policy, that should be encouraged, and not tamed by regulation. The prevailing political order, incrementalist in character, is preferable to rationalist government in good part because it attempts to calibrate and respond to such preferences rather than imposing policy.[29]

Incrementalism embraces a politics of limits, not of enormous official appetite, relying on "diversity, conflict, openness and improvisation," rather than expertise, as "society's main assets in problem solving."[30] Moreover, by searching for compromise rather than all-or-nothing judgments, incrementalist politics tends to diffuse the ideological passions that, unchecked, can split a society into interests that cannot be accommodated. Simply put, incrementalist politics obliges people to talk with one another.

Even in the tug and haul of incrementalist politics, where advocates shamelessly plead for special treatment and the accolade "statesman" is reserved for someone who cobbles together a serviceable compromise, principle is not irrelevant. The "conscientious legislator" or executive sometimes acts in ways reminiscent of a judge;[31] and, other things equal, politicians generally prefer to do what is right. If politics puts the claims of principle in their place, principles nonetheless can have a place in politics.

III

The basic principles of sound gender policy are readily specified. If liberty is to have meaning, individuals must have the *opportunity* to choose, the *capacity* to make choices, *information* on which to base preferences, and a climate of *tolerance* in which to explore alternatives. These elements, taken together, form the core of a choice-enhancing approach to gender policy.

Opportunity. Discrimination offends the idea of gender justice precisely because it robs individuals of the chance to make important life determinations for themselves. Rules that restrict opportunities to one or another sex—for example, by preferring mothers over fathers in child custody disputes or barring women from ostensibly hazardous work—subordinate the person to the group. They favor categories over persons, and for that reason are the enemy of claims based on personal merit, desert, or preference, the kinds of claims that a concern for liberty makes centrally important. Discrimination may in fact appear efficient from the viewpoint of the discriminating organization, because in certain situations it is cheaper to apply rules than to make case-by-case determinations; where members of a group share a prejudice, honoring that view may be the least costly course.[32] But what is efficient is not necessarily right, and the very fact that discrimination *does* sometimes pay makes government policing essential.

Opportunities must also be made widely known, especially where they are new opportunities, the result of abandoning a past pattern of discrimination. A school that opens its homemaking class to boys or its auto mechanics class to girls, for instance, should couple that action with a clear message that the new option is not mere window dressing. So too for the craft union that admits women or the airline that hires male flight attendants after years of doing otherwise; wide publicity, coupled with attempts to make the jobs appealing, are critical to creating real opportunities in the aftermath of discrimination. Promoting the opportunity for choice thus requires taking positive initiatives as well as abandoning old practices.

Government may go further, providing a range of opportunities as well as requiring that private opportunities be made well known, without skewing choice. Just as options are overly constricted if marriage is the only legally permissible relationship, so too choices are impoverished if there are no opportunities for taking care of children outside the home. As long as government does not press its alternatives over those privately generated, it may expand the marketplace of options, for "people will have more freedom if the society in which they live restructures its institutions so as to provide more and more attractive alternatives among which to choose."[33]

Markets of one form or another, not government, routinely offer these choices.[34] Communes spring up as living arrangements for those dissatisfied with marriage, employers offer day care services to satisfy the demands of workers. Yet markets are subject to failure. The cost of introducing some new service may be too great, would-be suppliers may not accurately forecast demand, or would-be demanders may ask for too little because they do not take into account the full social benefits of their actions. In such circumstances, government-managed alternatives make sense. It was on this premise that John Stuart Mill contemplated state-run schools to compete with private education,[35] and it explains why government subsidizes solar energy. In the gender realm, day care centers might need direct government aid for start-up costs, and subsidies such as scholarships to increase opportunities in fields that have historically catered to only one sex may be appropriate.

The risk of subsidizing choices is that such assistance makes the government-aided opportunity very much more attractive than its nonfavored alternatives. The line is indeed thin between expanding the range of opportunity by offering options that the market will not provide, which seems appropriate, and specifying a particular outcome that is attractive to policy makers, which we reject. An autonomy-promoting approach to gender policy will emphasize the power of government to enhance the capacity of all individuals to choose, not promote a particular end. For that reason, it will favor providing money without strings attached rather than in-kind support. Thus, for instance, children's allowances that can be used as a family wishes resolve the child care problem in a more liberty-enhancing manner than does government provision of day care.

Capacity. Removing barriers to choice frees people to make their own life plans. While such freedom is essential to the exercise of volition, it is not sufficient if individuals lack the capacity to make choices.[36] For that reason, liberty-expanding gender policy should also incorporate assurances that the basic social and economic wants of persons have been satisfied. As a political matter, this is hardly controversial. Even as the Reagan administration was busily trimming social programs, it insisted that a "safety net" be maintained; indeed, talk of this "safety net" may have been the conscience-easing rhetoric that made the cuts possible. The limits of basic state support need to be clearly delineated, however, since arguments for social minima may be all too easily transformed into demands for equal distribution of goods, a very different proposition. What constitutes one person's safety net is another's ceiling; an acceptable minimum is necessarily a function of the resources available to the society.[37]

The concern about a policy of satisfying wants is that it so expands the scope of the state's authority that it may subsume choice in the name of a rational collective will, but it is too late in the day to argue that meeting the minimum needs of persons courts this danger. Democratic nations have long been able to couple redistribution with personal liberty; as long as government support takes the form of an assured social minimum, most likely in the form of a guaranteed income, and not a more wholesale redistribution of resources, the threat to classic understandings of liberty seems insubstantial. Indeed, the two forms of liberty are intertwined. Negative liberty, freedom from arbitrary government controls over persons, constrains the state from distributing goods according to favoritism or whim. Without the positive liberty offered by a decent social minimum, choice is as illusory as Anatole France's quip about the theoretically equal right of the rich and poor to sleep under the bridges of Paris. Basic support offers individuals the wherewithal to pursue their own ends.

One trap is easy to fall into, and that is to ask of liberty what it cannot deliver. "Everything is what it is," philosopher Isaiah Berlin writes. "Liberty is liberty, not equality or fairness or justice or culture, or human happiness or a quiet conscience."[38] Guaranteeing the prerequisites of choice does not mean that people will have the identical capacity to choose, that they will automatically make agreeable choices, that they will not often regret their choices, or that they will not often be irrational. Liberty is concerned with the process of choice, not its outcomes, and those who would influence outcomes directly must look to some other tool. We believe that government's role is to ensure that the process is comparable for all, not that the outcomes conform to some predetermined plan.

Information. A choice-promoting policy requires that information be disseminated, so that individuals may learn of the opportunities that are available. Much of that knowledge will doubtless be transmitted informally, from old boys'—and, increasingly, old girls'—networks, and some will be offered by the market.[39] But government too has a place here, for society as a whole is better off if individuals can choose from the full range of alternatives available to them. Because that range is vast and potentially overwhelming, government might sensibly concentrate its attention on publicizing unconventional, option-expanding possibilities, for by definition those are least familiar. Men are likely to know, without government telling them, that they can be telephone linesmen but they need to be told that they can be telephone operators; women will be more aware of secretarial than trucking jobs.

If government is to emphasize the unfamiliar, its stance is not neutral with respect to the availability of choice, since an individual who knows of new opportunities may well decide to do something previously unimagined, such as suing her employer or raising his children at home. This suggested policy of publicizing the new makes knowledge of opportunities as widespread as possible, but still leaves government neutral with respect to the ends of choice. In the name of furthering volition, government cannot force people to act against their wills or bring about a social order, a "people's dictatorship" that the people do not want. It can only give men and women knowledge of possibilities that they might not otherwise acquire.

Some of that knowledge may derive from government-sponsored research on questions of gender policy. It makes sense for the state to take some part in filling the knowledge gaps concerning policy-relevant gender issues. This activity might not only lead to better informed choices by individuals; insofar as data affect value preferences, it could also bring us closer to the consensus that may be the warrant for future substantive gender policy.[40]

Tolerance. Finally, government should do what it can to promote tolerance of diversity, both by enforcing liberty-enhancing standards and through education, since the quest for self-definition "will be distorted if it occurs under manipulative, coercive, or silencing conditions."[41] Although one might wish for a world in which differentness was regarded as a good thing, differentness must, at the least, be accepted as necessary if personal liberty is to flourish. A liberty-enhancing policy can succeed only if there is suffused throughout the republic an acceptance of the choices that others make, even—perhaps especially—when these seem "wrong" choices. Such toleration, as philosopher R. M. Hare notes, implies "a readiness to respect other people's ideals as if they were his own." Advocates of particular alternatives are, of course, free to persuade others of the rightness of their vision, so long as persuasion does not become coercion, fanaticism about the "*content* of the ideal."[42] The ideal of tolerance does not require accepting intolerance.

Protecting against discrimination, intervening in instances of market failure, providing minimum economic support, disseminating information, promoting tolerance—these are the essential affirmative elements of a choice-enhancing policy. What government should *not* be doing deserves equal attention. Most significantly, the state should not be "fostering . . . good lives" by imposing a particular conception of virtue on the minority.[43]

Sticking to means is a hard rule to follow. For one thing, the distinction between creating the circumstances of choice and imposing particular preferences on individuals may fade in practice. For another, public officials are often tempted to believe that they know, if not best, at least better than the rest of us. Precisely because resources are scarce, lawmakers would have them spent wisely. Since wrong choices also seem to inflict unnecessary pain, legislators, like the monkeys in Thurber's fable, are inclined to liberate the bears from freedom and the dangers of choice. In the face of such temptations, it is vital to maintain the proposition that individuals, not the state, best know their own interests, and that in almost all instances where gender-based preferences are involved, collective well-being requires empowering people to follow their own inclinations.

Because this stress on choice inveighs against governmentally-set policy outcomes, it is hostile to quotas of any sort, for quotas withhold from individuals the right of self-determination that is critical for self-respect. Quota schemes impose plans on individuals, robbing them of the dignity that stems from defining themselves as persons. Moreover, quotas specify a necessarily arbitrary conception of the good life. In a world that celebrates volition, who can predict how many pilots, poets, houseparents, and presidents will be female, or how many teachers, tennis players, and TV repairpersons will be male? There is no answer to such questions, and attempts to supply one have had the unfortunate side effect of obliging men and women to embrace the unconventional. In this way, quotas embody a tyranny of the new.[44]

The choice model also resists limiting options, whether by offering child support exclusively in the form of day care, thus discouraging parents from raising their own children, or using veterans' preferences for government jobs, thus effectively restricting those jobs to men. It resists coercion, whether by the yahoos or the enlightened. Choice-promoting policy does not aim to demonstrate how well government can solve problems, but to extricate individuals from circumstances that hinder them in making their own life commitments. The care of children, the allocation of household responsibilities, opportunities for political involvement, the distribution of the work force by sex—all are matters best left to individual preference, once nondiscrimination, basic economic support, and the provision of useful information are assured. The aspiration is for "a dialectic of choice, variability, and possibility grounded in a conviction which disallows absolute certitude and the destruction it brings in its wake."[45]

IV

Will such a policy work? Were choice chimerical, we might be tempted to define the problem as one calling for a group-focused, not an individual-focused remedy, despite the high price that such an approach exacts.[46]

Because group-based solutions disregard a person's individuality in favor of categories—sex, race, and the like—over which he or she lacks any control, only where reliance on volition has failed are such costs worth paying. The most persuasive argument for a racial preference policy is that the maltreatment of blacks has been so damaging that an individualist alternative will not work, at least for now, and hence more directly and overtly redistributive measures are needed in the short term.[47]

With gender, though, the facts are otherwise. The evidence of the past decade gives cause to believe that, offered the opportunity, men and women will take more control over their own lives. New lifestyles and forms of communion have emerged. The family, though remarkably durable, looks very different than it did even ten years ago. Nearly one household in seven is now headed by a woman.[48] Women are postponing decisions to bear children well beyond what used to be customary. Even as proportionately fewer men are employed, over half of all women are working or looking for work—a change described by economist Eli Ginzberg as the "single most outstanding phenomenon of our century."[49]

The work force is more sexually integrated in particular fields. There are many more women bus drivers, bankers, and bakers, as well as more male librarians and registered nurses.[50] Change is evident, both in large corporations that have felt the effects of civil rights laws—the number of women executives in the telephone company, for instance, has increased by a third[51]—and in countless places untouched by the law. In 1984, half of the delegates at the Democratic national convention, which has a rule requiring sex parity, were women—and there were nearly as many women at the Republican convention, which has no such rule. In both reform Jewish seminaries and Lutheran seminaries, women, almost unknown fifteen years ago, now account for nearly half the students.[52] Girls now play Little League baseball, boys enroll in school cooking classes.

Attitudes as well as behaviors have changed. Americans sense "that, unlike their parents, they have the freedom to choose." While in 1957, 80 percent felt that an unmarried woman was sick, neurotic, or immoral, two decades later only 25 percent held that opinion. More than half the populace believes that husbands as well as wives should care for small children; as recently as 1970, just one-third thought so.[53] There is now overwhelming support for women who opt to work, whether out of economic necessity or for personal satisfaction.[54]

A considerable number of men and women are designing their working and personal lives in new ways.[55] As the rules and customs that once limited the options available to men and women have been overturned or discarded, changes in behavior have followed. The extent of this transformation in both private and public life seems remarkable. For an individual contemplating his or her life prospects, the stakes are high, the costs that accompany what proves to be a wrong decision sizable; nonetheless, many are deciding not to play it safe. An increasing proportion of men and women are embarked on lives that would be unimaginable to their elders.

Choice does lead to change, but what of the *pace* of change? Although we readily understand the impatience of the activists, particularly in the more benighted corners of the social universe, we do not share that impatience. Had we in mind some goal of gender parity, an ideal state in which men and women were indistinguishable in their wants and needs, we might well be displeased with the world in flux, but that is not how we comprehend social justice. Our benchmark is the reality of choice, which is generally apparent if far from perfected, and not any particular pattern of behavior.

Now that almost all the formal barriers have been removed, the tempo of change also seems likely to quicken. There are presently female tennis stars and senators, househusbands and male phone operators; there is a woman sitting on the Supreme Court and one who has run for Vice-President, and men participate in the League of Women Voters. Being a pioneer is always the most taxing responsibility. "I cannot understand any woman's wanting to be the first woman to do anything," journalist Nora Ephron writes. "I read about those who do . . . and after I get through puzzling at the strange destinies people have, awe sets in. . . . It is a devastating burden and I could not take it, could not be a pioneer, a symbol of something greater."[56] It is much easier not to be a token, to enter a field after the rough ground of expectations and hostility has been cleared. For that reason, as once-unfamiliar roles become acceptable, more individuals will be ready to assume them. When we *don't* treat househusbands or female astronauts as exotics, then these changes will have been institutionalized, and that point seems not so far off.

Available evidence suggests that many people can and will alter their own lives to suit their needs and desires. Although this evolution has something to do with such government initiatives as child care benefits, antidiscrimination efforts in the workplace, and expanded opportunities for women in the sciences and the military, it is not primarily attributable to public policy. Shifts in feelings and beliefs came first. These gave force and meaning to the new rules, for without individuals willing to challenge the old norms, government permission to do so would have meant little. Such individuals have fueled a movement, not merely a politically motivated interest group, which shows no signs of vanishing even with the failure of its most potent symbol, the Equal Rights Amendment.[57] There is every reason to believe that the movement has done its most valuable work already, that the forms of gender will continue to evolve, implacably, over time.

The idea of choice promises fairness in theory and appears to work in practice. But empowering individuals cannot settle all the problems of gender justice. Some fear the very idea of choosing, for it risks uncertainty and insecurity; hence the worry of some women that liberation may have set them adrift without the commitment of their one-time male protectors, or the concerns of some husbands that they have "lost" their wives.[58] Betty Friedan reminds us that "it is precisely the consciousness of 'choice' and of 'equal rights' and opportunities that is resisted by women, or men, whose identity rests on passivity toward authority, inequality and hierarchy, no matter the resentments and human potential suppressed."[59] For others, circumstances make choice implausible: what are the options of the Appalachian coalminer with a ninth grade education or the twenty-year-old unskilled black woman with three children to raise? Moreover, discrimination—subtle and hard to detect, but present nonetheless—will persist despite government policies. And the ties of family may be felt as constraints, particularly in the black community, where women bear enormous responsibilities.

These facts of life are a reminder that a choice-enhancing policy cannot completely realize its aim. But what policy will? Reliance on fixed quotas, it is said, forcibly overcomes recalcitrance, yet quotas tend to acquire their own justification, becoming ends in themselves rather than means. Acting in another's best interest by taking that person out of the rut of circumstance has all the appeal of a rescue mission, but who can confidently assert that the person in question would act in the same way, if truly free to choose?

Public policy designed to spark choice will leave many unreached. And although the private policies that spring up around choice-promoting government action will affect far more individuals, some will remain untouched. It seems preferable to acknowledge the remarkable if incomplete success that such an approach promises than to insist that government favor only the new orthodoxy, or the old. In judging between approaches to governance, the relevant comparison is not between an imperfect choice-enhancing policy and an idealized alternative, but between the real cost of imposition on the one side and inattention on the other. Just what a choice-enhancing policy is likely to achieve in the workplace and for the family is taken up in chapters 7 and 8.

7

Gender Policy and the Marketplace

I manifest by my acts infinitely varied examples of my powers over the world. . . .
Jean Paul Sartre, *Being and Nothingness* (1956)

If what we change does not change us we are playing with blocks.
Marge Piercy, "A Shadow Play for Guilt,"
in *To Be Of Use* (1973)

I

Work is, significantly, the measure of the man—and of the woman. On that point Adam Smith and Karl Marx, who held very different views about how the economy operates, could concur. "In my production," declares Marx, "I would have objectified my individuality, its specific character, and therefore enjoyed not only an individual manifestation of my life during the activity, but also when looking at the object I would have the individual pleasure of knowing my personality to be objective, visible to the senses and hence a power beyond all doubt." In a similar vein, Adam Smith observes that "the property which every man has in his own labor, as it is the original foundation of all other property, so it is the most sacred and inviolable. The patrimony of a poor man lies in the strength and dexterity of his hands. . . ."[1] What we do says a great deal about our individual identities. And because men and women have traditionally pursued different callings, conventional understandings of gender roles substantially define men and women in terms of the kinds of work that each performs.

As recently as the middle of this century, most women found their vocation in the private sphere, as housewives and mothers. If they held paid jobs, they did so only before marriage or in the event of family catastrophe. Men's place was equally clearly defined: they fueled the economy, sup-

porting the household financially. This differentiation was not only empirically true but was also understood to represent fitting behavior. Surveys
reported that most men and women disapproved of wives, and especially
mothers, holding jobs.[2] A prominent sociologist studying family roles observed, "There is simply something wrong with the American adult male
who doesn't have a job! American women, on the other hand, tend to hold
jobs before they are married and to quit when 'the day' comes. . . . The
cult of the warm, giving 'Mom' stands in contrast to the 'capable,' 'competent,' 'go-getting' male."[3]

Even in 1955, when this comment was made, the demographic data did
not fully sustain the observation. The participation of men in the labor
market had already begun its slight but steady decline. Of greater moment,
more than one-quarter of all wives were also employed. Ever since "Rosie
the Riveter" joined the work force during the second world war, women
had been a notable presence in the labor market; "warm, giving 'Mom' "
might very well be a secretary, nurse, or schoolteacher by day. But the
perception that the working mother or the househusband was an anomaly
faithfully reflected the mores of the times.

How different the world appears in the 1980s. The continuing change in
labor force participation rates for men and more significantly for women
portends a "subtle revolution," one that has had an impact on our personal
and public lives, on our individual fates and governmental policies.[4] Men
spend less time on the job, women more, than ever before. Norms too have
undergone a transformation. In 1945, three-fifths of Americans felt that
women should not work if their husbands could support them. Thirty years
later, those proportions had exactly reversed. Among the young, such values had almost vanished; over four-fifths of people under the age of thirty
approved of the idea of women working, whatever the family circumstances.[5]

The story of men's gradually increasing disengagement from the labor
force has gone almost untold. Although the shift has been far less dramatic
and the implications more modest than for women, the pattern is consistent. In 1950, 83 percent of all adult males held jobs; thirty years later,
that proportion had declined to 77.4 percent. Men were staying in school
longer and retiring earlier, often supported by working wives; some few
were managing the family household. Working men also cut back their
commitment to the firm, working an average of three-and-a-half hours less
a week in 1975 than 1965.[6]

Numbers, even those revealing dramatic changes, have a way of dulling
the imagination, but a few figures usefully summarize the scope of the

revolution in women's work.[7] Between 1950 and 1980, the total female labor force increased two-and-a-half times, to 45 million. Women made up 29 percent of the work force in 1950, a proportion that jumped to 43 percent three decades later.[8] Fifty percent of all women were working or actively looking for jobs in 1980, as compared with 34 percent three decades earlier. The influx of women workers has been so rapid during this period that, for the first time in American history, more women than men obtained jobs; since 1950, six out of every ten additions to the workplace have been female.[9]

This exodus of women from the home to the work force has affected women of all ages and all social classes. Work had once been primarily something that poor women did out of necessity, but working women now come from rich as well as poor households. In some families, the wife's earnings make it possible for the family to keep up with the Joneses. In others, those added dollars pay the mortgage, and in one out of every seven households, women are the sole wage earners.[10] Young and old, married as well as single, mothers and childless, women have entered the working ranks. Less than 10 percent of mothers with children under six held jobs in 1940; forty years later, almost 50 percent did, and more than four out of every ten mothers of children age three or younger were employed.[11] Women are staying on the job longer, and taking less time away from work to raise families. In short, women workers are behaving more and more like their male counterparts. They have seized the chances that have been opened to them.

What caused this revolution? For one thing, women themselves have changed. As a group, they are better educated, and thus both more attractive to employers and more anxious to do challenging work. The introduction of such labor-saving devices as washing machines, vacuum cleaners, and dishwashers have eased the burdens of housework traditionally borne by women, making more discretionary time available. (It bears recalling that less than a century ago a typical housewife made all the children's clothes, baked the family bread, even prepared its soap.)[12] The declining birth rate has freed up hours once devoted to the home and children that can now be spent on the job.

Total family income has consistently risen since 1940, and while it might be thought that new-found relative wealth would buy more free time, this has not occurred. Unlike the male worker, whom economists envision as choosing between work and leisure, the housewife faces a more complicated decision: what mix of work at home, market labor, and leisure makes most sense?[13] As rising wages and the opportunity to get out of the house have rendered market work relatively more attractive—social science surveys show that working women tend to be happier than nonworking women—the amount of time that women spend on household chores and personal pleasures has declined.[14]

The growing demand for women workers, as well as these changes in popular attitudes or women's circumstances, account for the increase in employment among women. Certain fields—among them schoolteaching, nursing, secretarial and clerical work, librarianship, and social work— have for more than three-quarters of a century been staffed largely by women. This service sector has expanded far more rapidly than the traditionally male industrial sector. Since mid-century, over half the growth of the American work force has occurred in occupations in which a majority of the workers are women, and new fields in which women predominate, such as computer programming, have also burgeoned. Long-term trends are similar. During the first six decades of this century, the secretarial field swelled by a factor of ten, the nursing profession grew fifty-fold. As sociologist Valerie Oppenheimer observes,

> The industrial and occupational changes that seem to be characteristics of a developing economy (and have clearly characterized the economy of the United States) have all favored women as much as, if indeed not more than, men. This is because increases in labor demand have been greatest in industries and occupations that have for some time been important employers of women.[15]

More women are choosing to work in a greater variety of jobs, and their work options have expanded; that is all good news. But the history of women's work is not entirely rosy—far from it. Not so long ago, social convention coupled with overt discrimination kept many women at home, and those who worked were often badly treated. Women were paid less then men who did identical jobs. In the 1940s, for example, General Motors labelled women's work as "light," and men's work "heavy," and paid men more for what was actually the same task. Whole categories of jobs were closed to women, ostensibly for their protection.[16] Unions refused to admit women members in such historically male trades as construction. Employers often segregated women into separate occupational groups, as in the auto industry and phone company.[17] In congressional hearings preceding the passage of the Equal Pay Act in 1963, employers defended the practice of paying women lower wages than men because women were willing to work for less.

Such gross discrimination has largely vanished. It is hard to think of an occupation, other than the combat forces and some professional sports, that is not sex-integrated to some extent. The Equal Pay Act and the 1964 Civil Rights Act made it illegal for employers and unions to discriminate on the basis of sex, and women have relied on these legal weapons extensively, forcing employers to treat them fairly. In recent years, women have made more use than racial minorities of the powers of the Equal Employment Opportunity Commission (EEOC) and the courts to enforce nondiscrimination,[18] collecting more than $26 million in underpayments during 1975 alone.[19] As a result, two equally qualified and experienced workers performing the same job, one male and the other female, will receive approximately the same pay. Subtler forms of discrimination persist, but would-be discriminators have been forced on the defensive.

The entry of massive numbers of women into the work force, expanded job opportunities, and the end of explicit sex-based wage differentials give women greater freedom than at any earlier time in history to combine work, leisure, and household responsibilities in ways that make sense to them. Changes wrought by private policy—shifts in the behavior of the market, the exertions of the more pragmatically oriented element of the women's movement, adjustments in the lives of individuals—together with official initiatives, notably the enforcement of antidiscrimination laws, have made these choices possible. The change in the marketplace behavior of men reveals slightly more variability in the degree of loyalty to the job. The organization man remains very much with us and the man who remains at home is a rarity, but one would no longer confidently say, as sociologists did thirty years ago, that "there is simply something wrong" with househusbands.[20] Social tolerance toward diverse life plans seems to have touched men as well as women.

Opportunity, capacity, information, tolerance—the requisites of a successful policy of choice enhancement[21]—are all immeasurably greater for women considering whether and where to work than in the past. But in several critical respects, women are not men's equals in the marketplace. Women still earn substantially less than men. They remain concentrated in a handful of fields. And they cluster in the lower levels of those fields: there are disproportionately few women managers. Do such distinctions reveal continuing discrimination, which keeps women (and, perforce, men) from realizing their full potential? Do they instead mirror the different choices that men and women are making? Or are both discrimination and choice at work?

The way these questions are answered turns out to be crucial in determining how policy can be mobilized to enhance life options. Are present antidiscrimination initiatives as misguided as critics on the Right would have it? Are sex-based job quotas or boosting the wages for women's work to match its relative worth necessary to further choice, as advocates on the Left believe? What agenda will encourage that personal autonomy vital for gender justice?

II

Men and women who undertake the same work are legally entitled to the same pay—yet in 1984, full-time women workers earned just 64 cents for every dollar earned by men. Discrimination based on sex with respect to employment opportunities violates the 1964 Civil Rights Act, but most women still work in a handful of fields and, within fields, predominate in the lower job ranks. In the face of antidiscrimination and equal pay legislation, why do these patterns persist?

Neither conservative nor radical critics find pay disparities puzzling. To conservatives like George Gilder, the wage gap shows how the market relects nature. Since men are biologically programmed to act as providers, Gilder argues, while women's natural instinct is to feather the nest, men earn more because they are more committed to working.[22] Marxist feminists such as Heidi Hartmann see the heavy hand of male oppression as causing wage disparities; they explain the earnings gap as a plot by men to retain their superiority. Men pay women relatively less, forcing them to marry and become dependent upon their husbands. Married women are assigned responsibility for running the household, and this in turn puts them at a disadvantage when competing in the marketplace, thus widening the difference in wages.[23]

These interesting stories, elaborations of the paradigms of naturalism and oppression discussed in chapter 3, lack just two things: evidence and plausibility. The data tell a more complex tale. Discrimination is at work in the creation of the wage gap, as is the exercise of choice. More significantly, employer discrimination and employee choice appear to reinforce one another, creating distinct career lines with different rewards for men and women.

Despite the law, some employers pay male and female workers differently because of their sex. The gap may be small, on the order of 5 to 10 percent, but it cannot be explained by differences in age, education, experience, or any other obvious distinguishing characteristic; one study of starting salaries found that some firms anticipated offering newly minted male college graduates 5 percent more than females for identical jobs.[24]

Employers also rely on sex to make assignments that promise different rewards: salesmen in department stores more frequently sell "big ticket" items, such as appliances and furniture, and so receive bigger commissions.[25]

Such straightforward discrimination explains only part of the wage difference story. That much is clear from a comparison of the treatment of racial minorities, who have also been historically underpaid. Even as the earnings gap between men and women has remained almost constant since the passage of equal opportunity legislation, the disparity between black and white wage-earners has narrowed substantially.[26] Discrimination cannot account for this difference between racial minorities and women. On the contrary—if discrimination were the single cause of differences in earnings, women should fare better than minorities, not worse. When white employers discriminate against blacks, they are effectively raising their own income.[27] When male employers single out women, however, they are in effect discriminating against their own wives, lowering their own family incomes, and that makes no sense.[28]

Something besides employer malevolence is influencing the wage pattern.[29] One explanation stresses the different decisions that men and women make about education, training, and career commitment. In neoclassical economic theory, workers should anticipate being paid what they are worth to the firm. Their productivity, what they contribute, is the measure of their value. Yet unless employees are producing a tangible and divisible product, digging coal or making dresses, specifying the particular contribution of an individual worker proves devilishly difficult: just how much does the actuary, the salesman, or the secretary contribute to an insurance company's income?[30] Economists conventionally use proxy measures, assuming that differences in worker's productivity result from differences in their fund of "human capital"—their education, training, experience, continuity of employment, and the like.[31] Better trained, better schooled, more senior or more stable employees are paid more, it is thought, because they contribute more to the firm.

Men do make bigger human capital investments than women. Women are less likely to finish college or complete graduate training. They typically select educational programs that have less job relevance than those selected by men, and once on the job, women are less inclined to take advantage of further training. Women also work for shorter periods of time, are more willing to accept part-time jobs, and spend fewer years as full-time workers. These factors, taken together, depress incomes considerably, explaining nearly half the reported wage gap between the sexes.[32]

This behavior is doubtless influenced by women's sense that there is a smaller payoff for them than for men in pursuing advanced education or training, and that is indeed true. Sex-based differentiation thus acquires a life of its own.[33] Employers discriminate against women, less frequently offering them the training that leads to higher incomes because of their fear that women workers will leave the job, while women decline to participate in training because they see it—correctly—as worth relatively little to them.

Women's underinvestment in themselves is also attributable to their tendency greatly to underestimate how long they will remain working. The image of the stay-at-home housewife apparently remains fixed in many women's minds, even as it is increasingly at odds with the economic realities.[34] Women who regard themselves as merely temporary employees won't do what is necessary to secure advancement and wage boosts. Many women quit work during their twenties and thirties to raise families, later returning to the job, and this in-and-out behavior has also depressed their wages. Because these years are critical for securing promotions and learning new skills, women have paid dearly for their absence in the form of lower earnings.[35]

Employer discrimination as well as economically costly decisions by women contribute to the prevailing wage gap; and at least with respect to discrimination, government action is appropriate to break the cycle of expectation and response. But much of the disparity has less to do with the wages that are paid for similar work than with the jobs that men and women hold. Women's work routinely differs from men's work, and is less well paid—about four thousand dollars less than the average salary in male-dominated fields.[36] Job segregation is also problematic in its own right if it lessens individual choices. These concerns push the inquiry one step further, leading one to ask what causes sex segregation in jobs, whether current patterns will persist, and what instruments of policy are likely to be useful.[37]

Job segregation is a familiar fact of life for female workers. Women concentrate in the clerical occupations, health, education, domestic service, and food service; they work as nurses, school-teachers, librarians, and maids. In 1980, three-quarters of all women crowded into occupations where women made up a majority of the work force.[38] Still, women have lately entered new fields in large numbers. The percentage of women doctors doubled, for instance, and the percentage of women lawyers more than tripled between 1960 and 1980.[39] During the 1960s, the number of women carpenters increased from 330 to 11,000, as twice as many women as men entered the field.[40] Despite these forays, women remain a relatively small minority in traditionally masculine fields, and patterns of job separation have been remarkably stable for the past half-century. A high proportion of women workers would have to change jobs if the occupational distribution of women were to become identical to that of men.[41]

Job segregation is also apparent within fields and firms, where women are infrequently found in positions of authority. In elementary and second-ary schools, for instance, two-thirds of the teachers but only one-third of the administrators are women.[42] This occupational separation has had mixed effects. On the one hand, the rapid expansion of the "women's work" sector enabled many of the fifteen million women who entered the labor force during the past three decades to secure jobs, but sex separation and the stereotyping of certain jobs as "women's work" may depress women's wages.

Persuasive explanations of the sources of sex separation come harder than descriptions. The conservative social critic sees this sexual division of labor as another indication of nature's visible hand, cossetting women from the full rigors of the market. The radical feminist envisions a male plot to turn women workers into a kind of ladies' auxiliary for the human race. As with theories about wage disparities, the more plausible analyses implicate both employer's behavior and the preferences of male and female workers, each reinforcing the other. Even with the passage of equal employment opportunity legislation, discrimination due to sex doubtless persists. But just what is the mechanism for discrimination? The numerous contending points of view carry varying implications for policy.

One school of thought holds that employers have a taste for discrimina-tion, which reflects either their own prejudices or those of male workers or customers. Unless the law effectively intervenes, the prejudiced employer will pay a premium, in the form of higher wages to equally able men, to satisfy his taste. Fear of other employees' or customers' reactions will lead to a segregated labor force, which keeps women out of harm's reach.[43] Feminist economists have extended this argument, positing that em-ployers' prejudices are strong enough to confine women to a small set of occupations. Labor unions collude with chauvinist employers to crowd women into less productive and lower-paid work, and government pre-serves this arrangement by enforcing protective legislation that fences women out of particular sectors. Reliance on supposedly objective stan-dards—skills, full-time employment, and the like—supplies a veneer of legitimacy for sex-segregated job markets. This approach regards discrimi-nation not as a matter of male tastes but as an act of male power.[44]

Arguments based on employers' prejudices against women strain credulity, however, since those who believe that males manage crowding have not explained how the process might work. If one sees men as "homosocial" beings—that is, interested in working with other men, not women—who have created segregated working conditions in order to associate with one another, the theory acquires a certain bite.[45] Yet this is a couple-oriented, not a "night out with the boys (or girls)," society; why should work and leisure preferences differ?[46] And doesn't the prevailing wage differential amply compensate all but the most chauvinist employer?

Other explanations for occupational segregation identify imperfections in labor markets as a key cause. One line of analysis focuses on the division of labor within large firms, where an "internal labor market" treats men and women very differently.[47] Employers channel equally qualified men and women into distinct lines of work: women become secretaries, for instance, while men are employed as salesmen. Since the possibilities for advancement hinge on one's initial position, the worker's first job in the company proves all-important. Employers typically choose women for women's jobs, men for men's jobs, either out of prejudice or in the belief that the sexes possess different capabilities. The predictable result is distinct career lines, with differential wages, for men and women within big companies.

The dual labor market approach posits similar sex-differentiated behavior at an even broader level.[48] It sees the world of work as divided into two sectors. The primary sector, including high technology fields, public utilities, public service, finance and the like, offers decent career prospects. The secondary sector, including many service-oriented industries and such highly competitive fields as textiles and food processing, has many low-paid jobs with scant possibility of advancement and minimal job security, where employees' efforts to advance themselves through training bring little payoff. Women's work—with its relatively low wages, short job ladders, limited security, and weak seniority systems—embodies many of the characteristics of the secondary labor market, even when it is located in "primary" fields.

These sophisticated theories take job segregation out of the realm of the exclusively personal, identifying the influence of market structures and organizational dynamics on job choices. They "consider as influences in the determination of wages [and positions] such factors as the structure of the product market of employers, the arrangement of jobs by employers, unionization, capital intensity, in addition to capital attributes."[49] One detailed study of a single large firm offers support for the notion that institutions treat men and women differently as a way of coping with organizational dilemmas. Managers' jobs get filled with employees whom the bosses feel can be trusted to make a diffuse and extended commitment to their superiors. It is men, not women, who more naturally fit the demands of such a position, in part because men relate more easily to their male bosses than women and in part because women are regarded as unwilling to brook interference with their private lives.

In such a world, the woman executive is encapsulated in a limited role from which escape comes hard. Male colleagues presume that she cares less about her job than about marrying and running a household, and so rely less on her. She is caught in a no-win situation, where her efforts to acquire authority are resented and any reliance on femininity merely confirms her distinct status. A preference for men in top jobs thus becomes "a preference for power, in the context of organizations where women do not have access to the same opportunities for power and efficacy through activities and alliances."[50]

Why might employers act this way? Explanations for sex segregation rooted in organizational dynamics do not depend on the overt sexism of employers, just their interest in making a profit. Employers may believe that women do less well in certain jobs on the average than men, perhaps because they have less ability or are less dependable. The differences need not be substantial—that is, the perception may be that women are only slightly less adept—to affect hiring and promotions. Nor need the belief be correct; the employer may be relying on a hunch that has never been checked. Yet even if some women belie the stereotype, that will not alter the firm's policy, since employers cannot readily determine who the able and reliable woman might be; attempting to do so would just add to the costs of recruiting. Small and unverified differences between male and female employees may thus come to have sizable consequences.[51] The resulting discrimination is "statistical," not personal, the impact so substantial precisely because it depends not on varying attitudes but on predictable institutional concerns.

Yet there is more to sex segregation in jobs than employers' discrimination in its various forms. Men and women also get the kinds of jobs that they want; in that respect, the market partially mirrors personal preferences. And, as with pay disparities, individual choice and market imperfections configure one another.

While men often place work ahead of family, many women shape work around the demands of home life; men typically have careers but women more often have jobs.[52] Woman's typical employment decisions comfortably fit this pattern. Being a nurse, school teacher, secretary, or household worker involves importing aspects of wiving and mothering into the market place, and so turning nurturance, caring, and domestic management—traits that are valued for women in the private sphere—into marketable commodities.

These occupations also demand only a limited commitment. One can readily stop working or work part-time while raising a family, returning later to the job. Relatively little investment in continuing education or training is needed; although nurses and school teachers keep up with their fields, the expectations are lower than for doctors and university professors, positions usually held by men. Women's jobs are numerous, and very similar from one place to the next. Being a secretary or a nurse means much the same thing in Atlanta or Anchorage, and so the wife who follows her husband to his new job can readily find a position similar to the one she left behind. In short, "women's work" jobs enable a woman to combine work and family with minimal strain, by making few demands for sustained and primary commitment on those who hold them.

This portrayal too offers only a partial truth, which depicts the working lives of some, but hardly all, women. Millions of women avidly pursue careers. Millions more—notably black women who head their households, the most rapidly increasing proportion of all black families—are compelled by economic necessity to support their families through working. And the number of women whose first attachment is to the job, whether through choice or necessity, is growing. More women are postponing having families or are having smaller families in order to pursue their careers. While women formerly left the job market to become full-time mothers during their twenties and thirties, in 1980 just 10 percent of the women between the ages of twenty and twenty-four who had been working quit to assume family responsibilities. More surprisingly, 20 percent more of the women aged 25 to 34, the prime childrearing years, remained on the job in 1980 than in 1970; five out of eight women in this age bracket were employed.[53] This shift in behavior will likely reduce both job segregation and the wage gap, but as long as women's work choices do not become identical to men's, some differences will remain.

To speak about "women's careers" as if a single model could encapsulate all behavior misstates the facts. The balance between career and family may weigh more heavily on women than men, but different types of women are now responding to that tension in distinct ways. This is apparent in the jobs that women elect and the degree of their attachment to those jobs.

The majority of women continue to make conventional choices, assuming "women's work" jobs in even greater numbers. Almost ten million women joined the clerical force between 1965 and 1975, for instance. And when young women are asked what they want to be doing at age thirty-five, the overwhelming majority of those who see themselves as continuing to work aspire to traditionally female occupations. Even among college graduates, three-quarters hope for jobs in stereotypically female fields.[54] One survey finds that married women devote less time to work than men—two hours less each day, on the average, in 1975—a gap which grew by an hour a day between 1965 and 1975.[55] Among part-time workers, 50 percent of the women but just 2 percent of the men cite household responsibilities as their reason for not working full-time.

Nonconventional women, who have rejected the tried-and-true women's job sphere, are also growing in number; by now, they are a significant presence in what was a man's world. Between 1968 and 1977, for instance, the proportion of women workers between the ages of 20 and 34 in professional, technical, and managerial occupations rose from one-fifth to one-quarter.[56] In particular fields the transformation is more dramatic: the proportion of female accountants more than doubled between 1950 and 1979, rising to 32.9 percent; the proportion of women lawyers and judges tripled during the same period, to 12.4 percent; almost one-third of bank officials and financial managers were women in 1979, a threefold increase in 30 years. Even in the male-dominated crafts, women nearly doubled their percentage, to 5.7 percent; more impressive perhaps is the fact that three-quarters of a million women work as printers, upholsterers, carpenters, mechanics and the like.[57]

As more women join the camp of the nonconventionals, equal opportunity should become a more fully implemented reality and the cycle of restricted career options and reduced expectations will be broken. When whole lines of work were closed to them, women lowered their sights: "I don't want to" is sometimes hard to distinguish from "You can't."[58] More women now recognize the expanded vocational possibilities open to them; they are tailoring their education and family commitments to match these opportunities.

Such shifts, like men's entry into such once female-only careers as flight attendants and telephone operators, will not cause a startling change in the job segregation statistics. Even if the proportion of women pharmacists or veterinarians or ministers or craftsworkers grows astronomically, as it has since the mid-1960s, males will continue to dominate in absolute numbers. These developments confirm that women—and men, to a lesser extent—are more able to choose between conventional and untraditional working lives, and between jobs and careers, than ever before. Opportunity, capacity, tolerance, and information do change lives, for those interested in making changes. Although strains persist, the demands of the private sphere are not so intractable an obstacle to full-scale involvement in the public sphere as many would have us believe.

III

What might be done to expand the range of options that are open to men and women, concerning both the kinds of jobs available and the possibilities for mixing work and other activities? Any policy response depends on how one diagnoses the extent to which present working arrangements retard choice and what one identifies as the sources of prevailing constraints. If it is the nine-to-five, five-day-a-week lockstep that is troubling, either because it keeps some people who would otherwise be working from getting jobs or because it makes working life hard for those balancing family and career responsibilities, various work-time options commend themselves. If, however, it is workplace discrimination rather than structural rigidity that appears most problematic, flexible time arrangements won't suffice. Hiring and promotion practices have to be confronted more directly, in ways ranging from the vigorous insistence on sex-blind employer behavior to the demand for sex quotas. Yet another view of the work issue, one which has gained currency in the 1980s, holds that economic justice for women requires raising the wages for what is conventionally regarded as women's work in recognition of its worth.

These three possibilities—encouraging employer flexibility, addressing discrimination in the workplace, and paying wages that reflect the "true" value of women's work—have very different policy implications. They contemplate different degrees of government intervention into the working of the market, bear widely varying price tags, carry different implications for the private sphere, promise different results, produce different winners and losers. Both our support for policies aimed at promoting workplace flexibility and vigorous antidiscrimination efforts, and our discomfiture with compensation formulas based on the idea of comparable worth derive from a sense of what will, in the event, be choice-enhancing.

Work-sharing, a catchall term to describe ways of providing alternatives to the usual work schedule, is an old idea. During the Great Depression, President Hoover called on firms to share jobs and rearrange working hours to cushion the economic blow. The nostrum resurfaced in the 1970s in the wake of another economic downturn, as a way to help workers in such declining fields as automobile manufacturing and public school teaching save their jobs. Work-sharing has also been promoted by those interested in giving jobs to marginal workers, many of whom would otherwise be unemployed or out of the job market entirely, and in helping people combine personal and vocational responsibilities. In that sense, it has become an issue of gender equity.

Work-sharing often makes good sense from both the worker's and the employer's viewpoint. Because it is economically sensible, much work-sharing will occur without government initiative, although public agencies may usefully share information concerning successes and pitfalls in practice. Yet while flexible working arrangements will make it easier for some men and women to match jobs and needs, as well as improving efficiency in some firms, the idea is no panacea. Certain jobs, including those to which the greatest power and prestige attach, cannot readily be calibrated to a different time clock.

For many jobs, the familiar work schedule is just a tradition, not an inevitability. One alternative, flex-time, permits employees to work the customary 40-hour week while choosing their own working hours; the total hours that the organization operates expand to accommodate the workers' preferences. Another option, the compressed work week, also requires that workers put in a full week's work, but enables them to do so in a more concentrated period, usually four 10-hour days or three 12-hour days. Both flex-time and the compressed work week help the full-time worker who seeks a block of time away from the job.

Part-time work also gives employees flexibility but at considerable cost. Part-timers are typically regarded as itinerants, the organizational equivalent of migrant labor. They are not regular members of the firm, can be laid off whenever business is slack, receive no fringe benefits, and are not considered for promotions. Because proportionately ten times more women than men work part-time, women would be the primary beneficiaries of a policy that included part-time workers as full citizens of the organization.[59] Enhancing the status of the part-time employee would also enable men who were so inclined to spend less time on the job. Job-sharing addresses this concern by splitting a full-time position between two workers, each of whom is entitled to fringe benefits as well as salary support, and is placed on a career track that contemplates advancement over time.

Work-sharing actually works—at least some of the time. A substantial number of private firms and government agencies have already put the idea into effect, and more seem inclined to so so. A 1980 survey of 600 large companies found 17 percent using flex-time in at least some departments, 7 percent with compressed work weeks. Twelve percent of California state employees have opted for flex-time and 2.4 percent have chosen part-time careers. A half dozen states permit public employees to select some form of flexible work arrangements; California lets workers in the private sector who would otherwise be laid off collect some unemployment insurance while staying on as part-time employees. Greater variation in working arrangements is in the offing. Seventy percent of the personnel officers of major firms see job-sharing being introduced into their companies in the near future, and 50 percent contemplate permanent part-time employment becoming a fixture.[60]

The idea of breaking the lockstep of the work week appeals intuitively to the proponent of choice. Such variability lets individuals combine work and domestic obligations with leisure in ways that seem personally right. (California, perhaps reflecting the state's image, refers to job-sharing as "leisure sharing.") By keeping individuals who otherwise would be out of work on the employment rolls, these arrangements also reduce unemployment.

Yet work-time options aren't cost-free. Unions instinctively resist job-sharing because they regard it as a false solution to the problem of unemployment. They oppose the notion of the part-time career worker because they want all employees, not just a selected handful, to be able to work fewer hours each week. Some employers also encounter problems with work-sharing. The firm that adopts a permanent part-time employment plan has to recruit, hire, and train more workers, and that is expensive. The costs of fringe benefits mount, as do costs mandated by law, such as social security and unemployment insurance.[61] These new expenses may make part-timers unattractive, and so may have the perverse effect of cutting down job possibilities. Introducing part-time and flex-time workers also turns work scheduling into a headache for supervisors. Deciding on promotions becomes harder as well: must the half-time worker devote twice as many years to the job as the regular employee before being considered for the promotion?

In a world of part-time workers, the flow of work has to be handled in new ways. This heightens the risk that some tasks will fall between the cracks, since with more people there is more chance for error. Work-time options thus may make life more flexible for workers but less so for their employers. Firms are likely to implement such a plan only when the benefits of having happier and more efficient employees, and being able to draw on the talents of individuals who because of other responsibilities couldn't otherwise be hired, outweigh these costs.[62] Work-sharing won't become universal.

What might government do? Mandating work-sharing makes little sense, for where it is inefficient, firms will adopt strategies that actually reduce jobs, such as eliminating part-time workers. But because many of the adjustments that firms make to part-time and flex-time arrangements will not vary much, experience acquired in one organization will be valuable elsewhere. Government can usefully offer this how-to-do-it information to interested firms, reassuring employers that it may make good business sense to rearrange their work weeks.

For some kinds of jobs, however, work-sharing does not work. Sociologist Arlie Hochschild's thoughtful analysis of careers in universities, "Inside the Clockwork of Male Careers," nicely if inadvertently illustrates the difficulty with putting flexible working arrangements in place.[63] The question that Hochschild poses is conventional: why does the proportion of academic women constantly decline from entrance to college, where women comprise 50 percent of the population, to appointment as full professors, where only 4 percent are women? Her answer is most unconventional: neither discrimination nor the early socialization of women, pointing them away from grand careers, explains the phenomenon. Instead, "the classic profile of the academic career is cut to the image of the traditional man with his traditional wife," against whom women cannot compete. As Hochschild explains,

> The academic career is founded on some peculiar assumptions about the relation between doing good work and competing with others, competing with others and getting credit for work, getting credit and building a reputation, building a reputation and doing it while you're young, doing it while you're young and hoarding scarce time, hoarding scarce time and minimizing family life, minimizing family life and leaving it to your wife. . . .[64]

In some respects, universities are ideal for individuals wanting to combine home and career. Unlike almost any other job, one's time outside classroom and office hours is one's own to budget. But because of the differentiated household responsibilities assumed by men and women, Hochschild argues, the man—or, at least, the person with a helper—can better arrange his life in order to mitigate career disruptions. Women can remain single or rely on a housekeeper, but neither alternative holds widespread appeal.

If this is not an administrative problem, Hochschild concludes, neither is it just a woman's problem. Hochschild would convert the university into "a system that would make egalitarian marriage normal," by offering all professorial jobs as half-time employment.[65] Only good is predicted to follow from this change. The institution would be more efficient, for two halves are better than one whole; and everyone would be diverted from the false god of academic success, thus becoming more human.

Unaccountably, the implications of this change for scholarship go unmentioned. Yet in universities, as in other institutions that value a particular kind of excellence, the telling contributions are usually not made by the part-timers but by those whose chief dedication is to the task at hand, whether it be as exalted as the pursuit of knowledge or as crass as the accumulation of wealth. There would, of course, be universities—and law firms and corporations and newspapers, where the same assumptions about careers hold true—in Hochschild's part-time world, but they would not resemble the most distinguished of those enterprises.

It is one thing to urge that such traditionally male-dominated outposts as universities bend the old rules, making it possible for individual men and women to make a part-time commitment, something altogether different and more troubling to assert that lesser involvement in work should become the norm. Many jobs—those that involve limited discretion, for instance, or that can be readily defined and divided by the hour or the day— are well-suited to flexible time options, while others are not. The case of the university should remind us that, even with respect to the attractive prospect of making attachments to the world of work more varied and so expanding the scope of choice, distinctions between accommodative and disruptive policy change still need to be drawn.

Varying work schedules enables workers to regulate their vocational and private lives. Expanding part-time work careers permits more would-be workers to find jobs, and so responds to the anticipated increase in the number of women who seek work and men who want more time off the job. But flexibility alone is an imperfect remedy for the ills that are held to befall the workplace. It does not speak to the low wages in female-dominated fields, to the informal segregation of men and women into different lines of work, or to the crowding of women at the bottom of the career ladder.

One who believes that the conditions under which men and women now work faithfully reflect the imperatives of a smoothly functioning market will find no cause for uneasiness in these gender-based differences. That is indeed the fashionable conservative view expounded by George Gilder, who dismisses the possibility of discrimination against women as the lament of "Yale coeds molested by their tutors, . . . assistant professors at Smith rejected for tenure, and telephone operators who discover, years later, that what they had always wanted was to climb a pole."[66]

Gilder's examples of supposed unfairness are intended to render sex discrimination a *reductio ad absurdum,* but they backfire, for Yale coeds and Smith professors are hardly the most noteworthy victims of discrimination. Gilder blithely ignores the more than 100,000 actionable charges of sex discrimination lodged with the EEOC, as well as the hundreds of court cases filed by aggrieved individuals, men and women, against firms that refuse to hire mothers of young children or male flight attendants.[67] The 165,000 AT&T telephone operators whose aspirations Gilder satirizes were indeed victims of discrimination; of course, not all of them wanted to become pole-climbing wizards, but many sought higher-paying craft jobs to which they had been denied access because of their sex.

Discrimination is no feminist fantasy. Even though discrimination only partly explains the different career paths of men and women, it does diminish the options open to both sexes. The real question is not whether any barriers exist but what might be done about those that remain.

Nondiscrimination is, of course, essential to securing choice, for it permits individuals to chart their own life plans irrespective of gender. And nondiscrimination on the basis of sex has been national policy since the passage of the Equal Pay Act and the 1964 Civil Rights Act. This policy could still be more vigorously enforced, but the government's efforts, at least through the 1970s, were not unimpressive.[68] And individuals who regard themselves as victims have taken full advantage of their legal rights.[69]

There is reason to expand the reach of antidiscrimination legislation, for the law does not proscribe all conduct that might sensibly be regarded as discriminatory. Courts have interpreted the equal employment opportunity legislation as narrowly concerned only with discrimination directly attributable to sex, upholding standards of conduct and coiffure that reinforce sexual stereotypes, such as dress codes or rules about men's hair length. Under existing law, employers may insist that workers convey an image consistent with familiar conceptions of masculinity and femininity, and may discriminate with impunity against homosexual employees. These exceptions to the principle of nondiscrimination inhibit lifestyle choices and undermine individual liberty, the cornerstone of nondiscrimination. While employers claim to be impelled by business necessity, that claim is normatively questionable and often empirically thin.[70]

The meaning of sex discrimination in employment has generated far less controversy than the ambitious efforts to remedy it. Nondiscrimination—refusing to take gender into account for any purpose—is held to be inadequate in the face of past misdeeds, because familiar patterns of occupational segregation reassert themselves. Some form of affirmative action is urged as a needed corrective.

Few phrases in the political lexicon evoke so much controversy as affirmative action; debates take on the character of pitched battles. To conservative opponents such as Senator Orrin Hatch, "affirmative action is an assault upon America, conceived in lies and fostered with an irresponsibility so extreme as to verge on the malign. If the government officials and politicans who presided over its genesis had injected heroin into the bloodstream of the nation, they could not have done more potential damage to our children and our children's children."[71] Advocates use only slightly less bombastic language. Ex-congresswoman Shirley Chisholm declares that "whether the debate is over 'affirmative action' or 'goals' or 'equality of opportunity' or 'quotas', the attempt is the same: to undo the government's commitment to protecting the civil rights of minorities and women."[72] Among scholars the quarrel has been scarcely less impassioned.[73]

Congresswoman Chisholm's perception that "affirmative action" functions as a code word is politically on the mark, but the several meanings of the phrase carry decisively different implications for the proponent of choice. Affirmative action may focus on the process by which people get jobs, emphasizing special efforts to ensure equal opportunity for victims of past discrimination. This means not merely accepting but also encouraging applications from those who in the past have been kept out of certain jobs, and not just relying on neutral standards for hiring and promoting employees but also scrutinizing the processes of decision to ensure their genuine neutrality. Outcomes are not irrelevant in this conception of affirmative action, for a pattern of hiring or promotion at odds with what might reasonably have been anticipated would trigger a reexamination of procedures.[74] But in this understanding of affirmative action, results per se do not count for anything.

Process was the initial focus of affirmative action, both in the 1960s executive orders which spelled out the requirements of all federal contracts and in the congressional debates preceding the 1964 Civil Rights Act. Understood in this way, affirmative action is critical to the effective pursuit of a policy aimed at enriching opportunities. Past discriminators justly shoulder the responsibility not only for changing their ways but also for broadcasting those reforms and for reassessing the whole range of policies tainted by earlier misdeeds. Such undertakings promise to break the log-jam, the self-reinforcing cycle of employer discrimination and employee lack of commitment that has kept individuals from pursuing particular careers because of gender.

To those anxious to bring about sexual parity in employment, process-centered affirmative action does not suffice. The benchmark of adequacy becomes results, not choices, and there is no assurance that making the rules of the game more fair will bring about the desired outcome. If quotas need to be set or preferences given to the less qualified, the need to pay that price for achieving parity is cheerfully acknowledged. "We must have more women salesworkers in wholesale trade," economist Francine Weiskopf writes, "more electricians and chefs, as well as more female doctors, lawyers, and economists. It also means that more men must move into predominantly female jobs." The key word is "must." Although some change is presently happening, occupational patterns have to be altered even beyond what men and women might prefer if free from the deadening hand of discrimination, in order to bring about "economic equality for women."[75]

The ultimate aim of affirmative action, in this result-oriented sense, is to equalize the distribution of male and female workers throughout the workforce. "Economic equality," economist Estelle James argues, means "the sexual integration of jobs, so that men and women would be represented in each occupation in proportion of their participation in the labor force."[76] Those favoring this view of affirmative action believe that, if 40 percent of workers are women, then 40 percent of the butchers, bakers, and candlestickmakers should some day be women. In the meantime, "standards" for the measurement of "progress" have to be imposed.[77]

The result-oriented view of affirmative action became official policy during the 1970s.[78] The employer who "underutilized" one sex or the other had to survey the "pool" of available workers and set goals to remedy the situation. Government officials were at pains to distinguish goals, which were wanted, from quotas, which were supposedly unnecessary. "If it appears that the cause for failure [to meet goals] was not a lack of defined effort or adherence to fair procedures," wrote Stanley Pottinger, head of the Office of Civil Rights in the Department of Health, Education and Welfare, "then we regard compliance to have taken place."[79] When government put on its negotiating hat, however, it assumed a different attitude. Results were what counted; quotas were wielded as a "blunt instrument of intimidation."[80] The manager who hired the "right" number of women and other minorities got promoted; his less successful counterpart got into trouble. Small wonder, then, that in meeting these goals, less qualified and sometimes less interested individuals of the sought-after sex were regularly hired.

Result-oriented affirmative action, often agreed to under duress, shaped the practices of the leading firms of the country during the 1970s. General Motors agreed to fill at least 20 percent of all new assembly line jobs at its St. Louis plant with women. Merrill Lynch, the nation's largest brokerage house, accepted specific targets for recruiting women as brokers. The Prudential Insurance Company promised to more than triple the number of women on its sales force within two years. Consolidated Coal Company committed itself to filling 20 percent of its miner trainee jobs with women. The *New York Times* agreed that women would hold one-quarter of the editorial jobs and three of the company's top 22 executive posts within four years.[81]

No affirmative action program has had a bigger impact than the 1973 plan negotiated by the government and the American Telephone and Telegraph Company (AT&T). The judge who presided over the case termed this agreement "the largest and most impressive civil rights settlement in the history of this nation."[82] As AT&T was the nation's biggest private employer, with more than 800,000 workers, altering the composition of its work force was significant in its own right. The AT&T settlement also revealed government's intentions concerning affirmative action to other major companies, which quickly acquiesced rather than fight costly and protracted lawsuits. Within a year, comparable agreements had been reached with such industrial giants as General Electric, United Airlines, the Bank of America, and the nine largest steel companies. It exaggerates, but only slightly, to say that the AT&T case charted the course of national policy. The case is worth looking at in some detail because it says a great deal about how an affirmative action policy that is both process- and result-oriented influences personal choice.[83]

The AT&T work force was largely segregated on the basis of sex prior to the 1973 settlement. Women worked as telephone operators, clerks, and on inside sales jobs, while craft and outside sales jobs were reserved for men. Although more than half of the company's employees were women, females comprised only 1 percent of the company's administrators. This did not come about by accident. Managers were either recruited directly into management training programs from which women were largely excluded or from the "male" crafts jobs within the system.

The company's insistence that differences between the sexes, not discrimination, explained patterns of employment was belied by the facts.[84]

AT&T claimed that women were not suited for crafts positions, for instance, but because the firm gave different entry tests to male and female candidates for employment, it had no way to compare the qualifications of men and women. The same craft job that, elsewhere in the Bell system, was performed only by men was an all-female (and lower-paid) position at Michigan Bell. The company's assertion that women weren't interested in managerial posts discounted the impact of AT&Ts own policies on management-minded women.

The AT&T consent agreement embraced elements of a process-oriented affirmative action effort, including the redesign of recruiting, transfer, and promotion policies. It spoke in terms of procedures to "insure equal opportunity" and committed the company to treat employees and applicants without regard to sex. But the agreement also indiscriminately mixed gender preferences with neutrality, process reforms with attention to specified outcomes. It detailed ultimate goals and yearly targets, which required the company to hire and promote the underutilized gender "at a pace beyond that which would occur normally"[85] in order to bring about sexual parity.

The eventual aim was proportional representation of men and women in all Bell system jobs; that meant increasing the number of female craft workers and executives as well as male clerks and operators. Though hiring and promotion was theoretically supposed to be based on merit, the company was obliged to favor any "basically qualified" candidate of the "right" sex over his or her more able counterpart if it could not otherwise meet its goals. AT&T frequently resorted to this "affirmative action override"; during the six years that the consent decree was in effect, between 50,000 and 100,000 jobs were filled on the basis of preferential treatment.

Several categories of jobs became substantially more sex-integrated as a consequence of implementing the affirmative action plan. The proportion of female officers and managers grew from 24.5 to 29.1 percent, and the percentage of women working at inside crafts jobs, largely electronic assembling, jumped from 10.1 percent to 17.9 percent. More men entered the company as clerks and operators: males filled about 5 percent of those jobs in 1973, and between 8 and 11 percent of them in 1979.[86] Because of the large number of men and women already on the job, these seemingly small changes in percentages required tremendous changes in hiring practices to bring about. Just one out of six men hired in 1973 went to work as a clerk or operator, the rest being assigned to the crafts jobs. Six years later, nearly half the men hired started work in the traditionally female jobs.[87]

Women lost clerical jobs, as the agreement contemplated, but did very well elsewhere in the company. Although the affirmative action plan set goals for minorities as well as for women, the women fared much better. As one company official observed, "It is easier for us to recruit females to fill job openings than it is to find black and other minorities. Almost all the employment gains at my company since the consent decree have gone to white females."[88] Women, unlike minorities, came from the same social mainstream as white males, and were thus more readily hired and placed.

The impact on the company of the change in sexual composition of its workforce varied with the job. Women who had long agitated for inside crafts jobs were readily recruited into those positions and adjusted easily to their new assignments. The experience of newly recruited women executives seems to have been similarly happy. With respect to both inside crafts and management jobs, AT&T's old prejudices had denied the company access to a sizeable number of willing and able workers. Once the firm abandoned its restrictive ways, women made good use of the opportunity.

The record with respect to the outside crafts jobs, which demand strenuous physical effort, has been less happy. Although AT&T diligently recruited women, it found it hard to interest them in the work. The nearly seven-fold increase in the proportion of women employed in outside crafts between 1973 and 1979, from 0.7 percent to 4.7 percent, demanded all the salesmanship Madison Avenue could muster. Once on the job, women continued to experience difficulties. Despite a self-paced training program, as many as half quit before going to work, and the female dropout rate when on the job was close to 60 percent. Those who stuck it out proved twice as accident-prone as the men, and modifications in their equipment seem not to have improved matters much.

The men hired as typists confronted analogous, although less severe, problems. Because nearly half the entry-level positions that AT&T offered to men were as operators or typists, the company had to train men without typing or telephone-answering experience, even as they denied jobs to already skilled women. A sizable fraction of the male typists and operators sought transfers to crafts jobs during their first year with the company.[89] They had taken posts as clerical workers, not because they liked the work but because, under the affirmative action regime, those were the only entry-level jobs available to them.

Reports on employee morale since the consent agreement have been mixed. The women have generally been more pleased, but ambitious men who hoped to climb the AT&T hierarchy were frustrated by a policy that seemed aimed at keeping them back. In one year, fully two-thirds of the company's promotions went to women. One-quarter of the nonmanagement male employees felt that "the best and brightest while males" would leave the firm, a disturbing portent in an unusually stable organization.[90] Traditionally oriented females also regarded themselves as victims. A woman named Bertha Biel went to court when she was denied a promotion so that a man could be chosen for the job. The company had set male hiring goals for the post of operations clerk, and although no men then working for AT&T wanted the job, Ms. Biel was passed over in favor of an outsider. Her lament was echoed by a 25-year-old male craft worker with meagre promotion prospects. "This is not fair," he complained. "I work for the company but my chances are less than someone on the street."[91]

What is one to make of this record? AT&T, best situated to decide what is good for the firm, kept most elements of the affirmative action plan in place after the consent agreement expired in 1979. There were, however, two important exceptions: the affirmative action override, a source of considerable unhappiness, was dropped, and the ultimate goal for the proportion of women in outside crafts jobs was halved. The company has essentially embraced a process-oriented affirmative action, specially recruiting and training employees to ease their entry while appraising them on a sex-blind basis.

This approach seems in most respects a wise one to proponents of policies intended to enrich individual choice. Yet one wonders why AT&T has retained any of its numerical goals. Goals can usefully prompt regular review of hiring and promotion practices; but goals too easily become ends in themselves, and there is no apparent reason to make proportional representation the aim.

The inside crafts and management jobs from which women had been excluded were easily filled with capable workers, as women took advantage of an opportunity once it was offered to them. Sex-neutrality similarly proved a boon for those men who wanted to be phone operators. In both instances, a process-centered affirmative action sufficed; goals were superfluous. Yet if no qualified men are interested in advancement as a clerk, does it make sense—and is it fair—for the company to pass up an able and available woman worker, hiring an outsider to fill the post because of his sex? The effort to attract and retain sizable numbers of women for the outside crafts jobs also seems problematic. In light of the dispiriting history of that campaign, "to push sex quotas for such work . . . places governmental equal employment opportunity philosophy in direct conflict with government support of safety in the work place."[92]

The point is not that men shouldn't be hired as operators or that women shouldn't work on the phone company's high wires—indeed they should— but only that there shouldn't be sexual quotas for these jobs. Where full equality of opportunity has a significant impact on job choices, quotas necessarily distort people's preferences. Quotas have the perverse effect of denying opportunities to those whose desires for more conventional careers are frustrated and to those pushed unwillingly into the brave new world of male operators and female linespersons.

Opening all lines of work at AT&T to applicants of both sexes benefited everyone: women, men, and the firm. The firm recruited from among a wider range of able candidates and more individuals were able to do the kind of work they wanted. Whom did quotas benefit? A women whom the phone company wants to turn into a pole climber "may not be qualified, may fear such work, or may come from a cultural background that makes such a job unthinkable. Why should she be denied opportunity in order to expand the number of males as clericals or operators?" [93]

The AT&T case refocuses the broader debate over affirmative action in a helpful way, for it indicates that a process-oriented affirmative action policy may make more of a difference than is conventionally supposed. Employment discrimination may, paradoxically, be at once deeply entrenched and quite susceptible to change. The recruitment, training, and promotion practices that effectively discriminate against both men and women with unconventional career goals are likely to be firmly in place, part of those folkways of a company that are rarely reviewed. Because of their venerability, these company customs will not be regarded as discrimination but as rational responses to natural differences. The availability of able workers of the "wrong" gender won't come to the attention of the organization, since it won't be looking for them. And even if the firm contemplates altering the sexual mix of its workforce, the benefits to the organization way well seem too speculative, the short-run costs too high, to justify action.

Something more is needed to induce gender-neutral policies. Government intervention that brings to light hidden forms of sexism can catalyze this process. "Laws that prohibit or make costly the use of [sexual stereotypes] can completely destroy the motivation for such discriminatory behavior. One may not have to change hearts and minds; one need only appeal to economic self-interest." [94] There is little evidence that firms feel passionately about the need to separate the sexes; thoughtlessness, more than chauvinism, is at work here. For that reason, governmental insistence on an aggressive, process-centered affirmative action program has made a difference.

Genuine equal opportunity policies seem to succeed, and not just at AT&T. One study of corporate behavior reports that between 1970 and

1975, the proportion of women administrators in such industries as banking, communications, and insurance rose from 19 to 23 percent—an increase almost as large as as that reported by AT&T. Because women have entered growing fields, even limited increases in the female proportion of the work force translate into many new jobs for women. In all industries except transportation, the number of women officials and managers more than doubled during this period; the comparable increase in the number of women in sales varied between 118 percent and 310 percent.[95] National figures tell a similar story. The proportion of women in professional, technical, and managerial fields grew from 20 percent to 24.5 percent, the proportion of women in the crafts tripled between 1968 and 1977.[96]

As more women are trained for these occupations, the rate of change will predictably quicken, and that training is occurring in all fields. Six percent of all entering engineering students in 1974 were women, up from just 1 percent in 1967, and the proportion of women architecture students tripled, to 12 percent, between 1965 and 1974.[97] Awareness of equal opportunity legislation and support from company executives has spurred these developments. Such cases as the AT&T suit made a difference that the numbers do not fully reflect. "Those class action suits proved very effective teachers," one personnel executive noted.[98]

There is a second lesson to be gleaned from this history: unless one is terribly sure of the "right" distribution of men and women in all jobs and terribly impatient at the tempo of change, insisting on a result-centered, quota-based view of affirmative action seems unwise. Quotas are a troubling policy to the defender of choice because they substitute an unconvincing understanding of what the social good requires for a commitment to the claims of individuals.

Rights belong to persons, not aggregates. "It is the individual person who is the carrier of human rights," philosopher Sidney Hook reminds us, "and not the ethnic, national, sexual, or racial group."[99] Quotas deny the primacy of individuals, undermining the claim to equal consideration as a person that is the cornerstone of autonomy; it isn't persons but "batches" of the desired gender that get hired.[100] In deciding that some fixed percent of all machinists should be men, personal desert plays no part.

Treating individuals as they merit being treated enables them to assume responsibility for their own conduct, to determine what they want to make of themselves. Treating individuals as members of a class, by contrast, leaves their future in the hands of others, robbing them of responsibility.[101] The loser in this social lottery feels abused, since he or she has done nothing to merit ill treatment. Even winners cannot tell whether desert or luck of the draw produced the happy outcome, and so their self-esteem suffers. Discord and dissatisfaction, not the social harmony promised by advocates of quotas, are the likely result. "If one claims that it is reference to . . . sexual lines which have split societies into oppressors and oppressed," notes philosopher Barry Gross, "it is scarcely reasonable to heal the split and redress the wrongs by further reference to these things."[102]

This is not to suggest that numbers are irrelevant in appraising employment practices. A firm might compare its prediction of the number of women or men who would be attracted to a previously sex-segregated job with its actual experience, and use that information in reviewing its affirmative action efforts. When one firm is far more sex-segregated than its competitors, an explanation couched in terms of the processes of recruitment and promotion is warranted. But these uses of numbers are a far cry from reliance on quotas as ends in themselves.

"Affirmative action [replete with quotas] must be heading in the right direction," political scientists Nijole Benokratis and Joe Feagin insist, "because this is the first time a policy has elicited so much fear, hostility, antagonism, and virulent rhetoric."[103] This sadomasochistic view of policy, which holds that if it hurts it must be good, ignores the possibility that persisting complaints reveal not what's right but rather what's wrong with the approach. Moreover, those hostile companies are also the very enterprises that have to implement nondiscrimination; they are unlikely to make a brilliant success with rules they regard as misguided. Whatever government does, employers will not choose workers as if they were blindfolded.

The happiest remedy for discrimination is a commitment to equal opportunity rather than to proportional outcomes, so that individuals can be selected according to their ability to perform and not for other reasons. The nation has been moving in that direction, imperfectly to be sure, but with perceptible results. To do less, as has the Reagan administration, is to risk returning to a more gender-driven past once government oversight of employment practices ends. To do more in the name of gender justice is to risk perverting the enterprise by undermining individual initiative. The society will fare better in the long run if people are encouraged to develop their potentials, and are not accorded status because of some ascribed characteristic such as gender.[104]

It will take years, even decades, before the distribution of men and women in the work force is markedly different. Most people now embarked on careers won't switch fields and many who are just starting to work have decidedly orthodox job expectations. Meanwhile, women will continue to earn substantially less than men, because the jobs that they hold typically pay less. In one Maryland county, for instance, a liquor clerk earns the same salary as a school teacher;[105] secretaries at the University of Iowa earn less money than the institution's truck drivers or painters;[106] in Philadelphia, nurses earn less than wall-washers, while in Chicago, starting librarians are paid less than unskilled laborers.[107] Paying people equally who do the same work won't change these facts—for that is both the law and, by and large, the present reality.[108] Only by changing the wage structure, so that jobs of supposedly equal value receive equal pay, will this wage gap be closed. That approach is promoted by advocates of "comparable worth."

Advocates hope that comparable worth will be "the civil rights issue of the 1980s."[109] Its impact is already beginning to be felt in the courtroom and the political arena. Although one judge declared that Congress, when proscribing sex discrimination, did not mean to overturn the laws of supply and demand,[110] suits challenging unequal pay for comparable work have enjoyed modest success. A 1981 Supreme Court opinion, while explicitly disclaiming reliance on the theory of comparable worth, left the door ajar for further legal challenges to supposedly unfair pay formulas,[111] and subsequent decisions—most significantly, a federal district court ruling that Washington owes 5,500 female state employees over four years' back pay and raises—have gone further in upholding comparable worth.[112] Organized labor has been an uneasy ally since the AFL-CIO gingerly endorsed the concept at its 1979 convention; during the Carter administration, the Equal Employment Opportunity Commission lent its support. City workers in San Jose, California, successfully struck for a reshuffling of the city's wage structure.

It is easy enough to appreciate the appeal of comparable worth. Wage disparities undeniably exist, and correlate with occupational segregation. Advocates of comparable worth insist that this is not mere coincidence, that jobs held predominantly by women are paid less *because* women do them; if this is true, it seems manifestly unfair. Recalculating wages for such jobs promises to undo that unfairness in breathtakingly simple fashion. When comparable worth advocates contrast the earnings of librarians and lumberjacks, they have in mind some notion of how these jobs should be valued in relation to one another: that is why it seems wrong that the lumberjack is better paid. Yet on closer inspection comparable worth cannot be coherently implemented, for the comparisons it insists on cannot be made. Attempts to correct the wage structure may well hurt most the least well-off women, whose interests comparable worth proponents have at heart. Reliance on a market rid of its discriminatory elements enhances individual choice and equity for men and women more effectively than manipulating the wage structure.

It is not by accident that we customarily rely on the market to set prices and wages, since the market offers a common metric for valuing apples and oranges, nurses and night watchmen. Simply put, the economic value of a job depends on the supply of individuals with the wanted skills at the offered working conditions. Nor is there an obvious alternative, a "logical, economic, or practical basis for determining the values of jobs" aside from the labor market.[113] As Adam Smith wrote two centuries ago,

> There may be more labour in an hour's hard work than in two hours' easy business, or in an hour's application to a trade which cost ten years' labour to learn, than in a month's industry at an ordinary and obvious employment. But it is not easy to find any accurate measure either of hardship or ingenuity. . . . It is adjusted . . . by the higgling and bargaining of the market, according to that sort of rough equality which though not exact, is yet sufficient for carrying on the business of common life.[114]

This argument does not satisfy advocates of comparable worth, who regard the market as so tainted by bias as to justify ignoring the prevailing wage rates and starting anew with more objective calculations. But even granting the imperfections of the market, which are legion, such objectivity is not readily achieved. How does one disentangle the effects of job segregation, attributable either to individual choice or discrimination by employers, from wage discrimination? "Wage discrimination" does not imply deliberate action but refers only to differential wages, declares the National Academy of Sciences in its inquiry into comparable worth. This won't do, though, since discrimination defined in this way becomes tautological: the very fact that women earn less than men bespeaks discrimination.[115]

Though job evaluations promise an objective assessment of the value of a job, using job evaluations unsullied by the market to fix wages only builds in more biases. "It is not a scientific device like a fine caliper, but it is an objective system," insists a partner in a firm that markets such plans.[116] But the promise is illusory. Subjective preferences determine how jobs are described by the evaluator, the criteria against which they are evaluated, and the weight attached to those criteria. Job evaluations cannot reflect the "true" worth of a job but can only incorporate the beliefs of the evaluator, and one evaluator's beliefs are not necessarily the same as another's. Why, for instance, should a job appraisal assign a maximum of

3904 points to knowledge and skill while attaching no more than 3 points to working conditions, as is the case in the Washington State plan? Perhaps the evaluator has it exactly backwards; perhaps the demands of a job should be their own reward, as Adam Smith once proposed, with wages compensating for drudgery.[117]

Wage setting is a complicated undertaking. Most large companies presently use job evaluations, but not in the manner proposed by comparable worth advocates. Wages for key jobs, which vary little across industries, are market-oriented, and these establish a baseline against which salaries for other similar positions can be calculated. Employers also seek to pay workers for what they contribute to getting a job done most efficiently, and in that respect something akin to comparable worth criteria are already in place. Considerations of internal equity are kept in tight check by employers' concern, on the one hand, for employee equity that is responsive to seniority and performance and is aimed at motivating individual workers, and, on the other, by attention to external equity that takes into account wages offered elsewhere. As economist George Hildebrand notes, "no system of job evaluation can be compatible with the survival and profitability of a private enterprise if the wage structure derived from it is not closely adapted to conditions prevailing in the external labor and product markets."[118]

Workers may well seek comparable worth adjustments through bargaining. Nurses in Denver, denied judicial help, went on strike to press their point and won; comparable worth has also been on the bargaining table for California state employees. Bargaining leaves the fine calibrations of merit and cost to the parties at interest, which is where they belong. But it makes less sense to mandate comparable worth, either through legislation or—more troubling yet—through judicial decision.

Implementation of externally imposed comparable worth policies will be very difficult, since market realities have a way of intruding on even the most "objective" appraisals. Domestic firms still have to compete with one another, and increasingly with foreign producers, when setting their wages. If pushed, they will escape from comparable worth requirements by assigning contracts to firms not affected by comparable wage policies, creating new job categories, moving to a more hospitable working environment, relying on migrant labor, or sending work abroad. As the president of the International Ladies' Garment Workers Union commented ruefully, "I'll be damned if I know a way to get the women more money. The value of their work isn't set by theoretical principle but on the value of the work in the marketplace, and in the face of competition from overseas, where garment workers make 30 cents an hour.''[119]

Paradoxically, comparable worth could hurt poor workers the most. Because instituting a comparable worth scheme would substantially raise the wages of the least well-paid workers, many of whom are women, without making them any more productive, this group is most likely to be laid off by employers who substitute machines for low-level workers, hire workers unaffected by comparable worth requirements, or hire fewer and better-trained workers. Such responses would reduce the number of jobs for marginal workers, who are disproportionately female.[120]

Of even greater concern is the impact of comparable worth on those who, during the past two decades, have scaled gender barriers in occupations. A wage scheme premised on principles of comparable worth would most likely boost the salaries of those in traditionally female jobs. Though that might make it more attractive for men to become secretaries and nurses, its most significant effect would be to perpetuate widespread job segregation. Increasing numbers of women have launched careers as doctors rather than nurses, technicians rather than secretaries, in part because of the wage disparities. Comparable worth would alter these calculations. Women could carry on at their familiar jobs as librarians and teachers and secretaries, at pleasantly unfamiliar wages, the system driven by an administrative apparatus which paid them according to their "true" worth. That does not seem an especially salutary outcome.

IV

About the data there are few disputes. More women are working than ever before, even as slightly fewer men are working, and men who are employed spend fewer hours on the job. With respect to both sexes, there is some evidence of movement into nonconventional jobs. The percentage of women in jobs as varied as bankers, bakers, engineers, and carpenters has tripled since 1960, and among lawyers and bus drivers has quadrupled; the proportion of male secretaries and telephone operators has shifted similarly.[121] Yet the work force remains substantially segregated and women are still paid less for their labor than men.

The policy debate centers on the implications of these facts for the role of government, with different positions reflecting differing understandings of the lessons of the past two decades. Conservatives worry that the massive entry of women into the work force has upset the social foundations of the nation, particularly the family. Those who would insist upon job quotas or, differently, comparable worth policies, read in this history signs of a failed revolution. Whereas conservatives have been tempted to use government as a vehicle for restoring the past by shrinking antidiscrimination efforts, their adversaries see policy as the instrument of a braver future.

We read the present more positively. The drive for equal employment opportunity has been sustained, even as the number of headlines has diminished. Change is evident, particularly with respect to the kinds of jobs men and women are holding, and the pace of change is picking up. The sexual integration of once male- and female-only job preserves proceeds apace. Women rabbis and male secretaries are less of an oddity; before long, they may not even be newsworthy.[122] As for the wage gap, one recent study, using data from the 1970s, finds that personal characteristics such as training, experience, and family-induced limitations explain most of the disparity, even without taking an individual's occupation into account. Wage discrimination isn't disappearing but it may well be less significant than in the past.[123]

It has taken a sustained government effort, powerfully abetted by individual initiative and by the women's liberation movement, to bring about this transformation. Government should continue monitoring employment practices and offering information about new career opportunities for another generation, in order to institutionalize this transformation, for such official involvement will aid men and women in ascertaining for themselves what work they might do. To a lesser extent, government may also help them in puzzling out the equally difficult and personally significant task of balancing work in the public sphere against their interests and responsibilities in the private sphere. Chapter 8 takes up one primary set of responsibilities—obligations to the family, at once the helpmate and the competitor of the marketplace.

8

Gender Policy and the Forms of Family

The rules break like a thermometer,
quicksliver spills across the charted systems,
we're out in a country that has no language
no laws, we're chasing the raven and the wren
through gorges unexplored since dawn
whatever we do together is pure invention
the maps they gave us were out of date
by years. . . .
Adrienne Rich, "Twenty One Love Poems," XIII,
in *The Dream of a Common Language* (1978)

I

The American family is at once a publicly important and an importantly private institution. The family is where personalities take shape and where the most intimate of relationships are experienced, and outwardly it seems little influenced by government.

For the most part, that is a salutary state of affairs. Americans have long regarded families as essentially private institutions whose inner workings should be determined by their members. As Walter Lippmann commented three-quarters of a century ago, "We do almost no single sensible and deliberate thing to make family life a success. And still the family survives. It has survived all manner of stupidity. It will survive the application of intelligence."[1] There is no reason to think things are different today. If by "family policy" what is meant is a significant and nosey governmental presence, with an agency to manage family affairs and bureaucrats calibrating the quality of family life, the effort should remain a "futility."[2]

It exaggerates matters, however, to claim that there is no family policy,[3] for a set of rules—consistent, if disorderly—subtly shapes the form and fact of personal relationships, affecting almost every aspect of family life.[4] The state legitimates family unions, specifying who can wed and under what circumstances. It presides over family dissolutions, fixing the terms of divorce. It allocates property rights among family members, bestows entitlements to inheritance, and assures dependents of support. The rules not only define a family but also favor state-defined families over nonfamilies: married couples benefit from a special tax rate, social security payments are made to wage-earners' legal dependents, and food stamps go to related household members. There is a bewildering array of 268 family-related programs, administered by a host of state and local bureaus as well as by 17 different federal departments and agencies, according to one tabulation dating from the Carter administration.[5]

What is wrong with this regime is that, all too often, people's lives have been changing faster than the rules, which thus operate to pinch off choices.[6] Much of family law and family policy is based on a domestic unit that envisions a working father, a nonworking mother, and children at home, but only a minority of contemporary living arrangements conform to that model. The divorce rate has shot up—between 1970 and 1980, the ratio of divorced to married persons more than doubled, from 47 to 100 divorced persons per 1000 persons in intact marriages—indicating that spouses are being selected, not endured.[7] And more people are opting out of marriage entirely. In 1980, half the women between the ages of 20 and 24 were unmarried, an increase of 40 percent during the decade, and there has been a marked rise in the proportion of unmarried men. All sorts of other arrangements undreamt of by the old rules are also flourishing. Adults are living together without being married, many more individuals are living alone, and gay couples are openly acknowledging their relationships.[8]

Policies built on the assumption that adults are either housewives or breadwinners in a two-parent household with children not only fly in the face of reality; they also create disadvantages for the people who do not fit the model. Those policies can cause economic hardship, as when divorced wives lose retirement benefits that have been calculated on their ex-spouses' earnings. They can also undermine equal choice, as when rules determine where a family is legally domiciled on the basis of the husband's residence, for no defensible reason.

What is called for is an approach to family policy attentive to present circumstances. That means tolerance for a broad range of personal life choices, and something more than tolerance—support—for those who do society the service of providing nurturing environments for children and caring for dependents generally. In this context, that is what opportunity-providing and capacity-building mean.

Opportunity can generally be enhanced by government acting circum-spectly, assuming that people are usually best left to structure their own relationships. Making family rules as gender-neutral as possible—provid-ing benefits to parents, for instance, rather than singling out mothers or fathers—expands the potential range of choice; so too does decriminaliz-ing nontraditional forms of coupling and upholding agreements between spouses after a marriage has dissolved.

While the state's role in creating opportunities is largely an exercise in negative liberty, capacity-building entails affirmative assistance to those who care for children or dependents. Here too public help should be de-signed to strengthen private decision-making. This implies that unob-trusive support, in the form of cash transfers or tax credits, is better than support that threatens family privacy. It also suggests that efforts to aid families in trouble—when children are susceptible to abuse, for instance—are preferable to undermining those families by taking children from their natural homes.

It is easier to specify the form of capacity-building than to decide which kinds of families merit this support. The crucial policy distinction to bear in mind when parcelling out benefits is between those family forms that offer long-term benefits to the society and those that promise only immedi-ate benefits to their present participants; in the language of economics, only the former generate public goods and so deserve affirmative as-sistance. This distinction would assure support for the conventional fami-ly—for as sociologists have urged for a century, integration in families both encourages intimate relationships and diminishes the possibility that a member will be socially estranged—as well as for stable and nurturing forms quite different from the family.[9] More controversially, perhaps, it offers a rationale for withholding special support, such as tax benefits, from couples—heterosexual or homosexual—whose unions, while doubt-less nurturing to the partners, further no strong societal goal.

The balance of the chapter elaborates this argument: that a family policy responsive to personal liberty[10] should speak of individuals in relationships and not fixed family forms, should accept all forms of relationship not harmful to the participants,[11] and should assist those relationships that of-fer stable environments to children and other dependents. The particular policy reforms that we urge will not assure that people make wiser choices in relationships or guarantee that children grow up happy and well cared for. They are only—and importantly—the best that government can do in a domain whose contours are shaped by private decision, a domain whose most intimate workings are no business of the state.

II

Rules define many aspects of family formation and dissolution, but what occurs within the ongoing family falls mostly outside the purview of policy. Men and women are free to shape the intimate details of their lives; only when intimacy deteriorates into abuse, as with battered spouses, does the government regularly intervene. The society does assume a more activist stance toward children than adults because of its greater concern for children's welfare, its greater interest in children's development as autonomous individuals, and its need to intervene in interfamily disputes over the legitimacy of children's claims to autonomy (as with the underage married minor who wants an abortion).[12] But with children too, the tendency is to rely on parents to make the critical decisions.

This laissez-faire approach to families has much to commend it. It permits individuals to define the terms of their commitment to one another without fear that the state will punish them for their preferences, it nurtures a tolerance for varied family forms that matches contemporary reality, and it minimizes the real pain that comes from being officially labelled as deviant. The approach is a relatively recent development, the successor to policies that treated departures from prescribed norms as immoral, hence ripe for punishment, and later as unhealthy, hence fit candidates for therapy. It is a development of uneven pace, whose untidy implementation leaves pockets of unwarranted paternalism; in specific instances, the law still intrudes too much into family life.

But as the preceding section suggests, laissez-faire is not the single driving aim of policy toward families, for family members are at once aggregations of individuals charting their own life courses and members of a larger whole who have willingly, even gladly, surrendered aspects of their individuality. This dual nature of family life is properly acknowledged by a public policy that does not turn the aspiration of individualism into a too-simple slogan.

The easiest policy issues to settle have to do with rules about family life. Present day efforts to impose conventional assumptions of masculinity and femininity on family members concerning such matters as domicile are about as sensible as the injunction that real men don't eat quiche. These are old rules, many of which date to an era when the husband and wife were regarded by the law as one person. Others, such as those concerning alimony and child custody, were inserted in the statute books somewhat later, after the wife's claim to preeminence in the household had been widely recognized.[13]

Such petty restrictions need to be swept away, for they work mischiefs in particular instances and turn government into a scold. Within the past decade, many have been undone. Married women in almost all states can retain their maiden names, for instance, and the federal government has outlawed credit restrictions aimed at wives. The simplest instances of restrictions that survive—standards relating to choice of domicile and obligations of support for marriage—merit brief discussion, to make clear how the law should generally stand clear of individual preferences. Harder cases, concerning alimony for instance, pose puzzles of equity during an era of transition: what standard is fair both to those who have made hard-to-change commitments based on the old rules and to their more independent-minded counterparts? The aim of policy in these situations ought to be to encourage family members to make their own life decisions, enforcing neither the old morality nor the new. The hardest cases of all have to do with the positive treatment of certain kinds of families, where government is not proscribing behavior but rather encouraging particular family arrangements. These types of policy problems are taken up in turn.

Domicile. Domicile, the law's technical way of talking about where people live, represents a private decision for most people. Legally, however, some states still decree that the married woman acquires her husband's domicile, wherever she resides or intends to live permanently. This is a silly rule, supported by equally silly arguments. Although officially it was once believed that the wife's personality merged into the husband's, that extreme chauvinism is now safely interred. Some judges, applying an economic twist to this old argument, reason that, because marriage is a contract to live together that obliges the husband to furnish financial support, he should also be able to determine where the family lives.[14] Yet this proposition builds on the highly problematic assertion of dependency to reach the unprincipled conclusion of legally enforceable subordination. It also regards all families as permanently settled in one place; but what of soldiers' and politicians' and professional athletes' families?

Because the law of domicile rarely affects people's lives, it might be dismissed as practically irrelevant. For some women, though, that is not the case. Access to the courts in probate and guardianship cases, the right to vote and hold office, and the claim to the lower tuition available to state residents all depend upon domicile. The symbolic insult, coupled with these real injuries, offers ample reason to favor gender-neutral domicile rules.

Support. The law of support reflects the stereotype of the husband as breadwinner, requiring him to secure the "necessaries" of life for his wife. The symbolic consequences of such a one-sided obligation are plain: the wife who dutifully serves her husband may insist upon support from him, resorting to the law to reinforce her dependency. Support rules are offensive because they give a kind of reality to a myth of woman's proper place.[15] They are superfluous in most instances, unenforceable on the rare occasions that they are relied upon. Husbands and wives usually settle their responsibilities to each other, not because the law makes them but because they want to. By the time a wife turns to a judge, hoping for an order that will persuade her husband to treat her decently, there isn't much left of the marriage; in such circumstances, it is better to award a divorce than encourage such special pleading.

Government has had less to say about the content of the ongoing relationship in recent years. The rules of domicile and support are on their way out. Other restrictions, mostly pertaining to sexual conduct, remain on the books in some states, but these are infrequently enforced: sodomy laws and rules concerning cohabition have largely been abolished in fact. Such developments are all to the good. Unless what transpires between individuals is demonstrably harmful, like incest or rape, and not merely upsetting to the sensibilities of the delicate, the state has no good reason to set standards of family life. It should leave people alone to plan their own lives, neither fixing rules nor resolving disputes that arise within the union.[16]

Marriage Contracts. Most private agreements between husband and wife, which seek to regulate behavior within the marriage, are not legally enforceable, for marriages are regarded as very different from the garden variety commercial agreements regularly and competently reviewed by judges. That position has been sharply criticized by those who argue that a hands-off approach prevents individuals from fully realizing their desires, and so undermines the capacity to shape their futures.[17] If John and Mary want their marriage to terminate automatically after three years or seek guarantees that their union will be an open one, the state should enforce their preferences, the critics argue, by granting them a public forum and lending them the apparatus of official sanction.

The idea of enchancing choice through publicly enforcing private bargains holds a certain appeal. Yet the notion proves more problematic than promising, for marriage isn't like other contractual relationships. More than romanticism bottoms the observation that intimate relationships possess a subtlety and diffuseness not readily captured in fine print. A marriage or other abiding commitment embraces entire lives, not goods and services; it is hard to see how "love and law, intimacy and economics" can be merged in the language of contract.[18]

The marriage contract speaks ultimately of personal attachment and affection, not external threats of pains and punishments. To characterize marriage as just a legal document would reconfigure the public and private spheres, introducing the competitive norms of public relationships into a far more private world where trust and cooperation reign paramount. It would substitute the values of the marketplace, with their explicit valuations of exchange and reliance on promises, for the altruism that informs successful relationships. "Tit for tat" is no fit substitute for "love, honor, and cherish."

The claim that public nonenforcement of the marriage contract deprives individuals of liberty confuses the right to be left alone, or negative liberty, which a hands-off official posture assures, and the right to get what one wants, the claim of positive liberty effectuated through official enforcement.[19] Sometimes it makes sense for government to do more than formally assure opportunities—for example, in securing a social minimum—but this is not such a circumstance. Although the state should not be able to impose its favored mode of relationship on unwilling individuals, neither should government be obliged to remain agnostic about the forms of relationship. An interest in stable relationships might well lead society to favor the nominal permanency of marriage to a commitment for some shorter period of time. A belief that monogamous couples will sustain a richer environment for children would make it rational for society to support this conventional commitment. It is one thing to propose that government tolerate a wide range of personal choice, something altogether different and more troubling to demand an absolute indifference concerning the types of intimate union that people select.

Marriage contracts pose another sort of dilemma: how are courts to enforce them? The law is a remarkably unsubtle tool, ill attuned to the nuances of personal interactions, not a humane and restorative agent.[20] That is why judges are reluctant to enforce contracts calling for personal services: Luciano Pavarotti can be ordered to sing at the Met, but he can't be made to sing divinely. It would be infinitely harder for lawgivers to superintend the daily lives of the Marys and Johns who seek their help. It is hard to contemplate a court passing on a dispute between the Shulmans, whose marriage contract, featured in the first issue of *Ms.* magazine, stipulated that Ms. Shulman would do the laundry and care for the children on Saturdays (but never on Sundays); the conceivable claims and counterarguments would rival the surreal maneuverings of *The Trial*. Private bargaining, carried out for reasons undreamt of by a most unromantic positive law, makes far more sense than public enforcement. Policy concerning marriage should treat the institution as a union of equals for all public purposes, letting husbands and wives divide up responsibilities as they please within the private confines of the marriage.

Were individuals locked into wedlock by the state, unable readily to acknowledge their errors and begin anew, it would make better sense for government to enforce marriage contracts. But in the past two decades, most states have removed the element of fault or blame as necessary for divorce, reflecting the fact that divorce has become a social, not a clinical, phenomenon. "The exits are clearly marked" for those who want to get out.[21]

These changes in the law do not celebrate the social reality of divorce. Instead, it was the "festering problem" of divorce that led California to reexamine its laws, and unhappiness that rich New Yorkers were getting no-fault divorces in Mexico while their poorer neighbors could not escape from insupportable relationships that fueled liberalization in that state.[22] As more people sought divorces, states determined to stop punishing unhappy individuals by forcing them to stay married or encouraging courtroom deceit to satisfy public moralisms.

Policy in most states now acknowledges "the social undesirability of permitting a court to continue a legal relationship after the human relationship on which it was based has ended."[23] The hope is that freeing people from present mistakes makes them more responsible in the future. The government's ambition, manifested in mandated marriage and divorce counselling as part of the process of separation, is to use the unhappy circumstance of marital breakdown to promote durability of future marriages. It may be wishful thinking, but support for marriage and liberalization of divorce laws are meant to go hand in hand.

That the exits from marriage are now lighted by neon makes critical the rules governing life *after* marriage. State enforcement of child custody and property sales is essential, since only the government offers an officially sanctioned out. The problems of enforcing the marriage contract during marriage are largely irrelevant here, for there is no longer a union into which the state is insinuating itself, and for that reason private bargains deserve the support of the state.[24] If Mary has put John through law school, understanding that John will in turn aid her while Mary becomes a doctor, the courts should oblige John to carry through his part of the bargain in the event of a divorce.

The most common issues of gender justice incident to divorce concern alimony and custody. About one marriage in three entered into by individuals now in their thirties will end in divorce, a three-fold increase in forty years.[25] As more marriages dissolve, rules governing the fair treatment of the partners after marriage in matters of alimony and child custody assume greater importance.

Alimony. The instinct of someone committed to advancing the aspirations of individuals is to treat alimony and custody in gender-neutral terms, rather than routinely assuring wives of support and custody, as has been traditional. Current policy in most states is to award alimony on the basis of need and to assign children on the basis of parental fitness.[26] This approach treats the dissolving couple as independent agents. It is less bluenosed than the old rules, which premised financial obligations after marriage on immoral behavior during marriage, and is unsympathetic to claims arising from wife's dependent status. Dependency is now something to be overcome, not reinforced by lifelong alimony.

This approach makes good sense for couples who married within the past decade or so, at a time when autonomy had become increasingly the norm. Yet many marriages that are now ending were entered into on a very different understanding. In these conventional unions, the wife anticipated a lifelong commitment to home and family, even as she supported her husband in his career; imposing new rules on old marriages creates considerable hardship and apparent unfairness for the woman who has devoted herself to being a housewife and mother. Thus, the goal is to shape standards for alimony that both minimize dependency and acknowledge the concerns of a transitional generation.

Alimony embarrasses proponents of a choice-enhancing view of gender policy. The very idea pays homage to adult dependency, and so collides with the belief that individuals should be treated as capable of making and carrying forward decisions about their own life plans. Partly for that reason, the rationales for granting alimony have changed considerably in recent years. Such awards, which once represented the spoils of courtroom victory and a financial affirmation of wifely virtue, are now based on need.[27] Support, which used to be routinely ordered until the ex-wife remarried or died, is conceived of today as transitional help for dependent spouses, tiding them over until they become self-sufficient. In appropriate instances, support can now be claimed by the dependent ex-husband, since alimony is not exclusively a female prerogative.[28]

The theory behind the current approach matches prevailing perceptions of what is fair. It is generally thought that alimony should "provide support for the long-married housewife with impaired earning capacity, provide transitional support for education and retraining, provide support for the mothers of young children, and provide compensation for the wife as a partner in her husband's work." But in operation the new regime only partly reflects these beliefs. As one would anticipate, alimony awards vary with the length of marriage, the presumption being that wives who have not worked for many years cannot readily get jobs. More awards are now short-term, and employed wives are only half as likely as housewives to get alimony.[29]

Yet the present system contains unexpected pitfalls, especially for the poor and for mothers of young children. Indigent divorcees not only get small awards, as would be expected, but are also frequently denied any help. Even women who have been homemakers for many years don't usually obtain alimony unless their husbands are well off. In a California survey, just 15 percent of the women whose husbands earned less that $20,000 a year received alimony, as compared with about 60 percent of the women whose husbands made more than $30,000. Mothers of young children who get divorced after brief marriages fare worst of all. Only one woman in six with preschool-age youngsters is awarded alimony, for judges typically believe that such women should reassert their independence by working.[30] The financial picture is further clouded by the fact that many husbands haven't paid the alimony they are obliged to, and enforcement has been so serendipitous that alimony itself has sometimes seemed a voluntary gesture, not a legal obligation.[31]

The fairness of this approach depends upon one's view of the legitimate expectations of marriage. If the conventional marriage is seen as an exchange in which the wife manages the home while her husband contributes support and status, then its dissolution should be treated as the ending of a partnership, with neither spouse assuming continuing obligations. But such depiction of the marital relationship sometimes has little to do with reality.[32]

A housewife for thirty years who suddenly confronts divorce and the prospect of little alimony may consider herself punished for making a choice she didn't realize she was making. Her understanding was that this partnership, unlike a commercial agreement, was to be lifelong. Moreover, whatever marketable human skills the marriage has generated benefit the husband in traditional marriages. Alimony may be seen as recasting the bargain in light of the unanticipated circumstances of divorce, bringing the private value of a wife's contribution up to its market worth. Yet this perspective on alimony saddles the husband with a burden he neither anticipated nor now regards as fair. From his viewpoint, support accompanied a loving relationship that has now ended. Moreover, if help for the stay-at-home wife becomes the general rule, the state is making this way of life particularly attractive, and that is not the message a liberty-enhancing government wants to send.[33]

Arrangements for spousal support after marriage should ideally be worked out by those involved, not by the government. The calculations of benefits and burdens, the allocations of social costs in which policy indulges, do not suit a relationship as intimate, nuanced, and various as marriage.[34] Were there a widely recognized moral duty to support someone who has supported you, the policy issue would not arise, but the absence of a social consensus leads inevitably to the need for rules. For the future, it would be wisest to adopt procedures aimed at encouraging individuals to bargain over the terms of financial support after marriage.[35] This leaves determinations about support largely in the hands of those affected, and so enhances their liberty.

Two caveats need to be entered. For one thing, urging couples to plan for divorce may, perversely, encourage divorce, by making the possibility seem less terrifying; in light of present divorce rates, though, the horror of divorce seems largely to have dissipated. For another thing, as the thirty-year marriage just described indicates, this emphasis on personal preferences needs to be modified in order to take account of past expectations. As one California judge writes,

> In those cases in which it is the decision of the parties that the woman becomes the homemaker, the marriage is of substantial duration, and at separation the wife is to all intents and purposes unemployable, the husband simply has to face up to the fact that his support responsibilities are going to be of extended duration—perhaps for life. This has nothing to do with feminism, sexism, male chauvinism, or any other trendy social ideology. It is ordinary common sense, basic decency and simple justice.[36]

No single alimony rule, no encomium to choice or to marriage, will do justice to all marriages.

Custody. The legal presumption that the mother receives custody of their children when a couple divorces offends the idea of enchancing individual choice. Just as alimony confirms the social fact of women's dependency,

the maternal preference rule makes policy rest on mothers' presumed affinity for parenting. Such a policy reinforces the idea that biological inevitability rather than social reality leads a woman to become the primary
parent, and that consequently her chief ambition should be to raise her
offspring.[37]

Yet more men are opting to take on responsibility for parenting. They
sometimes do a better job of it—for maternal affinity isn't an iron law—
and that is reason enough to abandon the maternal preference rule.[38] Custody disputes, like disagreements over support, should be delegalized to
the greatest extent possible, and the state's interest confined to the welfare
of the children, who by definition are not yet autonomous. The ideal is an
agreement that makes sense to the parents and is responsive to the children's needs.

Child custody policy has varied considerably over the years. Until the
early nineteenth century, fathers automatically received custody, for children were regarded as their father's property. This rule was reversed as
wives assumed dominance in the household and the need for good child
care became widely recognized. Lately, as explicit sex-based preferences
of all kinds have fallen from favor, the maternal preference rule has in turn
been superseded by official emphasis on the best interests of the child.
Almost half the states specify that mothers and fathers have equal rights in
custody disputes, and courts in those states are now supposed to figure out
who is the "better fit" parent.[39]

That approach sounds sensible in theory but, like the rules governing
alimony, it works differently in practice, for the father who seeks custody
has a hard time overcoming the prevailing understanding that a mother
should raise her children. Some courts apply their own version of maternal
preference, even in the face of state laws directing them to be gender-
neutral. For example, 80 percent of Los Angeles judges report that, despite
official neutrality, they unofficially regard the mother as the appropriate
parent unless she is proved unfit.[40] The Utah Supreme Court went further,
rejecting a father's claim for equal consideration in a custody fight because
he was not "equally gifted in lactation as is the mother," thus imposing a
burden that remains insurmountable even in this technologically wondrous
age.[41]

Most children live with their mothers after the breakup of a marriage
because the parents prefer it that way. But as the conventions concerning
who is supposed to take on parental responsibilities erode, the proportion
of single parent families headed by males—up 50 percent, from 1.1 percent to 1.7 percent of all families over the past decade—will continue to

rise.[42] The tenacity of an unofficial but real maternal preference policy has slowed this natural transition, since whatever the law says, a father hoping to obtain custody against his wife's wishes has in practice to prove that she is an incompetent mother, and men usually lose such fights. More important, an estimated 20 percent of all fathers who would like to raise their children are dissuaded from making the attempt, for few husbands have the stomach to reenact *Kramer vs. Kramer*.[43] Although there is no way to calculate the number of fathers who deserve custody of their children, ending judicial discrimination against fathers and making men aware that they might realistically hope to secure custody would lead to outcomes more consistent with the wishes and capabilities of parents.

From the standpoint of concern for individual autonomy, the ideal system of allocating custody is one that respects the rights of both parents without losing sight of the child's paramount claim to be raised in a safe, stable—and autonomy-enhancing—environment. The system should reflect evolving norms concerning what constitutes a suitable home. Blanket proscriptions against awarding a child to a lesbian mother or to an unmarried couple are outmoded, for such settings are not necessarily bad for the child.[44] These cases—indeed, all custody cases—need to be considered on their merits, for what is right depends not on rules but on the particulars. "Happy families are all alike," as Tolstoy writes in *Anna Karenina*. "Every unhappy family in unhappy in its own way."

An individualized approach to custody theoretically promises to balance parents' preferences and children's needs. But the kinds of determinations a judge is asked to make in these hearings would strain the capacities of a Solomon—and few judges can claim to be Solomon. There are almost as many competing theories about what children need as there are child psychologists, and no ready ways of relating children's needs to the capacities of their parents.[45]

For these reasons, it makes even more sense in custody than in alimony cases to rely primarily on private arrangements rather than official decree. Doing good, on the part of the government, implies doing little. Parents can bargain more equally if they understand that judges will actually discard the old maternal preference rule, should matters reach the court, focusing instead on who is the primary child nurturer.[46] Negotiations about custody not only enable the spouse to obtain what they think is best for them and their children; negotiations also facilitate arrangements, like joint custody, that can only succeed if everyone favors the idea. Bargaining enlarges the range of solutions and the play of preferences, and that makes everybody better off.

III

Policies about domicile, custody, and the like regulate the internal workings of marriage and the standards government applies when marriages
dissolve. Such rules, rather than assigning fixed, sex-specific roles, should
enable individuals to decide for themselves the detailed terms of the relationship. Although constraints on volition are needed to defend the liberties
of other family members—the more vulnerable spouse, children, and on
occasion parents—and to further other vital aims of policy—laws against
incest, for instance—such state intrusions should be kept to a minimum if
gender policy is to promote autonomy.

Family policy also includes granting benefits to those who enter certain
kinds of relationships, with government regularly conditioning its largesse
on family status and expressing its preference for particular modes of family life. Although neither the provision of day care and child care tax credits
nor the tax treatment of married and single individuals carries with it the
insistence that anyone do anything, the carrot of public money may be as
powerful as the stick of sanctions in affecting one's decision to marry and
have children. Government aid may also have the inadvertent effect of
influencing the internal allocation of household responsibilities. Can we
shape policy that both enables individuals to choose among the forms of
family and encourages stable and intimate unions?

Income Tax. Feminist critics argue that the tax law accomplishes through
indirection what the laws of marriage mean to bring about directly, the
endorsement of conventional relationships. By setting higher rates for single individuals than for couples, it is said, the Internal Revenue Code
favors marriage; effectively requiring that married couples aggregate their
income for tax purposes assertedly dissuades wives from working. Taken
together, these provisions are held to fuel "the expectation [that women
will marry and become housewives] by giving preferred tax treatment to
women who are homebodies and penalizing those women who wish to
work. . . . [T]he tax law tends to put women in their place in the home and
keep them there."[47]

Unlike the rules of marriage, which still reflect shopworn nineteenth
century understandings of men's and women's separate spheres, the tax
code provisions are both more recent in lineage and more respectable in
rationale. To deride the tax code as simplistically sexist misses the mark.
Yet reform is warranted, for a simple, fair, and efficient code should not
take a person's marital status into account when taxing earned income. An

individual tax on income would enhance choice while not doing violence to the other aims of the law.

Income taxes should ideally be progressive, so that the rich pay proportionately more than the poor; neutral with respect to marital status; and even-handed in the treatment of married couples with similar incomes. Yet it is logically impossible for a tax code to accomplish all three aims. With a progressive tax code, advocacy of a marriage-neutral tax system collides with a belief that ownership within families is irrelevant and, as a practical matter, hard to assign.[48] One or the other objective has to give way: the code must either favor or penalize marriages, or subject couples with equal incomes to unequal taxes. The debate over the appropriate tax treatment of individuals and families has been waged for a long time; the differing resolutions embody different views of what fairness requires.

Forty years ago, the tax law was premised on a firmly individualistic bias.[49] Marriage was irrelevant to the tax collector, and each family member was taxed on his or her income. Yet under this system it was hard to determine who to tax for unearned income garnered from investments or who was entitled to particular deductions, such as mortgage interest payments. The tax advantages of togetherness led husbands to transfer investment property to their wives in order to reduce the couple's collective tax liability. Federal tax treatment of married couples also varied with the happenstance of where the couple lived. States that treated marital property as community property required that income be split between the spouses, thus giving their residents a significant tax advantage.

Congress put an end to such disparities in 1948. The revised formula encouraged all couples to file joint returns, pooling their incomes and paying a tax equal to twice what a single individual earning half the couple's income would pay.[50] This system was hailed at the time as fairer, because it recognized real differences between the income of a married person and the same income earned by a single person—differences that, it was thought, the tax law should reflect. In equalizing the tax burden among equal income couples, however, Congress inadvertently created a new unfairness: a single person now paid as much as 40 percent more tax on the same income as a married couple. Even if the marriage merited recognition in the tax code, it was not that special—or so Congress concluded. In 1969, Congress limited the maximum tax liability of single individuals to 120 percent of married couples earning the same amount.

Singles now had less cause for complaint. But a new inequity had accidently been spawned—a penalty against husbands and wives with approximately equal earnings—for the 1969 tax reform made it costly for two individuals earning roughly identical incomes to wed. As if to demonstrate that rational individuals do flourish outside the economics textbooks, some working couples actually announced their intention to divorce and happily cohabit in order to get this tax break. In the latest installment of this saga, the 1981 tax law eases this disparity, giving two-earner couples a new deduction of their own.[51]

Congress has been discovering and righting wrongs for almost four decades, first concerning married couples, then singles, and most recently two-earner families. Such tinkering will doubtless continue as different groups convince the lawmakers that they are being victimized by the tax code. But the basic question remains: is it efficient—and is it fair—to have one rate for married, another for single taxpayers? These provisions do not affect personal choice very much, and hence are not inefficient; despite the news stories, few people marry or divorce because of the tax laws. Yet the law still imposes a penalty on single taxpayers. Is that right?

Some analysts have concluded that there should be a lower family tax rate, since families but not individuals maintain dependents. Yet in a great many nonfamily relationships, one individual supports others without benefit of a tax break: if dependency is the concern, these ties too deserve recognition in the tax codes. Many families are also economically better off than single persons earning the same income. A childless couple with only one working spouse enjoys considerable advantages, including economies of scale (although two can't live as cheaply as one, they can live about as cheaply as one-and-a-half) and the untaxed services of the stay-at-home spouse.[52] If that couple's income comes from clipping bond coupons, then both husband and wife are free to produce untaxed benefits for the family.

Distinguishing among taxpayers solely on the basis of marital status may have been wise in 1948, when most households consisted of an employed husband, housewife, and children. Today, however, only one in four taxpaying units resembles the traditional one-worker family for whom the joint rate structure was designed; the rest are either two-worker families or single persons.[53] This demographic sea change calls for a different approach. It is possible to take dependency into account when planning a tax system without fixing different tax rates for families and individuals. To set a uniform individual tax rate on earned income, and then devise a system of deductions for such costs as childrearing and care of dependents, would be fairer and more supportive of personal choice. Unearned income should still be assigned to the family unit, though, for while such a rule ignores nominal ownership claims within the family, it acknowledges the reality that the family as a whole, not a single person, has an indivisible stake in its collective goods.[54]

The impact of the family tax rate on spouses with lower wages—secondary wage-earners, in the language of economics—is both inefficient and unfair; it offers yet another reason to treat the individual, not the family, as the tax unit for purposes of income.[55] By aggregating family income, as the tax law now does, the secondary worker's contribution is worth less to the household: that worker's first dollar of earnings is taxed at the same rate as the primary breadwinner's *last* dollar of earnings. If, for instance, the tax rate on the primary worker's highest $1000 of earnings is 30 percent, the secondary worker's initial earnings will be taxed at that rate, not at the 12 percent minimum rate that applies to a single worker.

The language of primary and secondary workers is wonderfully gender-neutral, but in nearly nine out of ten families the secondary worker is the wife, so her decision to work or stay at home is most seriously affected by the tax code. This impact is real, not theoretical, for women's decisions about how much to work are influenced by the real wage they receive, and income aggregation lowers these wages considerably. The added expenses incurred by the working wife—on-the-job lunches, clothing, transportation—also nibble at the salary check, and those cannot be deducted. Moreover, when the wife works the family may spend more by buying services that the wife could provide herself when she remained at home: frequenting restaurants, hiring housecleaning help, and obtaining child care. Among these costs, only child care is deductible, and this deduction, unlike business deductions, is limited.[56]

Congress addressed one aspect of this problem in 1981 by giving the two-earner family a fixed deduction, and although this expedient helps working wives it ignores the plight of other workers. Everyone who earns an income from working, not just the working wife, has work-related expenses. Why should only those of the two-earner family be deductible? Singling out the working wife's income as deserving a special deduction makes life comparatively harder for those who cannot follow suit—women who head households, for instance. Furthermore, this new deduction actually increases the marriage bonus for couples whose division of earnings is relatively equal, an unintended and unnecessary boon.[57]

Such unjustified penalties and unearned windfalls will plague any tax system that focuses on the family. An individual tax on earned income, coupled with a standard deduction for all full-time workers (scaled down for part-time workers), would acknowledge the expenses of working even as it preserved the principle of individualism in the tax code. A code that aspired to neutrality towards marriage would help men and women make decisions about home and work without having to take into account the tax consequences of their decisions. This is the efficient and choice-enhancing approach.

Child Care. Child care policy centrally concerns the welfare of children, not grownups. Yet from the outset of the modern women's movement, subsidizing child care has been valued as a way of enhancing the autonomy of women.[58] In her pioneering 1964 essay, "Equality Between the Sexes: An Immodest Proposal," Alice Rossi placed the issue at the very top of the new feminist agenda, urging the creation of a "reserve of trained practical mothers" and the "establishment of a network of child-care centers." It was the needs of working women, not their children, that most interested Rossi. Her support for child care was premised on the belief that institutionalizing these arrangements would allow women to pursue their careers, with only a brief interruption to attend to the obligations of full-time motherhood. Child care meant independence for women, enabling them "to enter and remain in the professional, technical, and administrative occupations in which they are presently so underrepresented."[59]

The argument for child care has grown stronger with the increasing entry of mothers into the work place. Since 1970, the biggest proportionate increase in labor force participation has been recorded among women with young children. More women between the ages of 20 and 24 are working—73 percent in 1980, as compared with 58 percent ten years earlier—and many more women in the prime childbearing years between 25 and 34 are remaining on the job.[60] With more parents of young children employed more of the time, there has been a predictable demand for government child care support.

The clamor for state-funded child care has not only come from those interested in women's liberty. The rapid rise, especially in the black community, of female-headed households, many of which receive welfare benefits has led conservatives to urge that these mothers be required to place their children in day care centers and go to work. The reality of high unemployment and diminishing public resources—in constant dollar terms, direct federal aid for child care was nearly halved between 1976 and 1984—has not dimmed the ardor of the advocates, who continue to press for new federal funding.

Most families have found their own solutions to the child care problem.

They have relied primarily on informal arrangements, especially for very young children. A 1975 Census Bureau survey reports that 65 percent of preschool children whose mothers work are cared for in their own homes, either by a parent or a relative; 29 percent spend their days with relatives or neighbors, often retired women or grandmothers who receive very low wages for their work. Just 4 percent are enrolled in day care centers.[61]

The pattern has been a bit different for three- to five-year-olds. Enrollment in nursery schools among three- and four-year-olds more than doubled between 1967 and 1977. Almost one-third of these children now attend nursery school, as do four-fifths of all five-year-olds.[62] By joining informal arrangements with nursery education and juggling their own work schedules, the new two-worker families have been able to deal with child care on an ad hoc basis.

Government has assumed some responsibility for child care. While comprehensive day care legislation was vetoed by Presidents Nixon and Ford, Washington supports some child care programs through general social services grants to the states—cut back substantially under President Reagan—and gives billions of dollars in tax relief for day care-related expenses.[63] Washington has helped to pay the child care expenses of welfare mothers who hold jobs or are in training programs, and has supported the Head Start program for preschool-age children, two initiatives aimed at the poor.[64] Families in which both parents work have been aided by a tax credit, currently 20 percent of all child care expenses up to $2000. Should government do something more—or something else?

Any child care policy that aims at promoting personal liberty should accomplish three things: expand the opportunities for interested fathers to take an active role in child care, enable families to decide whether to raise their youngsters at home or rely on day care, and assure a supportive setting that takes the needs of the children into account. Those criteria suggest that some form of children's allowance is sensible, because it allows families to raise their children as they think wisest and to allocate responsibility for childrearing; the size of that allowance will necessarily vary with the condition of the public fisc.

Existing arrangements work fairly well for middle class families whose child-minding costs are subsidized by the tax credit. Parenting leave, with job security and seniority protected for whichever parent chooses to stay at home with the child during the months after birth, would be a sensible and not prohibitively costly supplement. Such a policy would ease the conflict between job and home responsibilities and provide an incentive for equalizing child care responsibilities within the household. Converting the tax credit into a children's allowance would afford even greater flexibility, for those dollars could partly offset the income lost when one parent remains home to care for the children.

For poor parents, usually mothers, the choice between finding a job and staying home is illusory. The formula for support in the Aid to Families with Dependent Children (AFDC) program encourages such parents to work, leaving their children in others' hands; indeed, the willingness of welfare mothers to work has been a condition of eligibility. Such policies are supposed to be economical but all too often child care costs more than an uneducated mother can earn. Moreover, they are ineffective—since jobs are scarce—and unfair. A widow dependent on Social Security who remains home to raise her children attracts only sympathy and respect. Why should poor parents be treated differently?

Poor families need a form of family support that, unlike AFDC, neither stigmatizes recipients nor penalizes intact families by helping only female-headed households. A general family allowance constitutes part of that help, but only part. Indeed, if a universal family grant seems too costly to be politically feasible, an allowance for poor families and single-parent families with young children would acknowledge the greater real needs of these households. That support should be as unobtrusive as possible and come with few strings attached, permitting families either to purchase child care or to mind their children at home, using government aid in lieu of income during the first years of childhood.

Elsewhere, such arrangements are common; only the United States among the major western nations does not offer some form of children's allowance.[65] Hungary gives mothers a child care grant to remain home until her child reaches age three. Sweden has made ''parent insurance'' sex-neutral, so that fathers as well as mothers receive almost full salary for the nine months after birth if they stay home with the child. France provides cash grants and publicly supported creches. A host of other benefits, among them a birth grant (cash or clothing and supplies), paid leave to take care of one's sick child, and special assistance to single parents, are also widely available. This assistance is regarded as a basic part of a social welfare scheme that protects members of the society from undue risk.

Not all these programs represent models to emulate. Some subsidize only the stay-at-home parent or effectively force both parents to work; others clearly reinforce the traditional allocation of family duties. In general, however, these initiatives mark the emergence of an effort to ease the private strains of bearing and raising children without intruding on family decisions.

Child support is one thing, government-subsidized day care quite another. Debate over the value of day care programs is vigorous, venomous, and unceasing. Much of it focuses on the effects of day care on children, who bear the immediate impact of child care policy. Proponents insist that day care services are better for the children and their parents than less formal arrangements.[66] They cite psychological literature to conclude that whether a mother works has no effect on the emotional bond between mother and child or on the subsequent emergence of childhood difficulties.[67] Opponents worry that the family will be supplanted by "communal approaches to child rearing."[68] They stress the powerful biologically based tie between mother and young child, insisting that babies need physical contact with a mother who attends to them, responds to their attempts at communication, and fulfills their need for food, care, emotional and physical security.[69]

Such fears are unsupported by solid empirical evidence; moreover, policy must contend with the reality that many children now receive care outside the home. What policy most benefits children and their parents at the least cost is the open and vital question. The counterclaim that day care helps children is also unsupported by the research. Reports of gains in cognition are generally based on experience with experimental nursery schools housed in university settings, and these small successes are not easily translated into widespread practice. Such gains seem also to dissipate over time, for "children's lives are subject to too many complicated influences to expect an early experience to immunize them from later difficulties."[70]

Like so many other social experiments, organized day care is neither a disaster nor a panacea for children. As with most child-related policy choices—decisions about who should have custody of children, for instance, and how to provide effective education for them—the impact is uncertain. Beyond an intuitive understanding that certain minimum amounts of food, shelter, and caring in a stable environment are essential if children are to have a chance of becoming autonomous adults, very little is reliably known about what shapes their lives.

Day care means different things when provided by a grandfather, neighbor, or community center. What actually happens to a child presumably affects how he or she responds to the experience, and what transpires depends less on the professional credentials of the provider than on the quality of caring, attention, and nurturance offered in day care and at home. Advocates of day care are fond of contrasting grumpy grandpas or ill-trained, tired mothers with well-staffed, richly equipped day care centers. Opponents cite the specter of impersonal institutions that resemble orphanages, or speak of character-molding infant factories and Kentucky

Fried Children franchises, comparing these with devoted, competent, and caring moms. Both sides are merely selecting extreme cases to make a rhetorical point, an accepted tactic in debate that offers little basis for making policy.

How then does one decide whether substantial federal involvement in the provision of day care makes sense? Cost certainly matters. Organized day care turns out to be far more expensive than reliance on kith and kin. Estimates vary widely, but $4000 (in mid-1980s dollars) per child is about the lowest figure for a year of full-day quality day care reported in the studies. Expenses of that magnitude would effectively preclude government from reaching more than a small fraction of the population; by contrast, fewer additional dollars would produce a generous family allowance for those needing government help.[71] The quality of day care also seems to have surprisingly little effect on whether women work: very few of the women participating in national income maintenance experiments cited inadequate child care as a reason for not finding a job.

From the perspective of autonomy, one deficiency of government-managed day care is that it offers parents less choice than a children's allowance. State-subsidized day care also does little to expand the range of parenting options open to men and women. Even if day care liberates some mothers from the home, it effectively confirms that men will be marginal parents by permitting both parents to take on traditionally male working roles. By contrast, a child allowance encourages interested men to assume greater family responsibilities. And this interest apparently exists. In Sweden, one of few countries to adopt a gender-neutral policy, the proportion of fathers requesting child care leave rose from 2 percent in 1974, when the program was introduced, to 14 percent just four years later.[72]

A children's allowance also buys greater flexibility for the family than day care. Parents can select the mix of work, care by neighbors and family, developmentally oriented care, and parental attention that fits their needs and those of their children. An allowance enables parents to purchase help that is close at hand, inexpensive, and enriching to the child—the things parents say they care most about.[73] Parents have been ingenious in managing child care until now, and what they select on their own is likely to be as good as what government offers. Government may usefully assist day care centers with their initial costs, so that they can get off the ground, and in publicizing their availability. Beyond that, however, the state should not promote day care. By distributing dollars and not services, government can best serve the needs of the children by honoring the preferences of their parents.[74]

IV

These reforms in family policy, an individually based income tax and a family allowance, are intended to enhance individual opportunities. They aim at equalizing options for men and women and undoing the sanctions that attach to nontraditional relationships, even as they encourage stable and supportive personal ties. More aggressive government intervention in the private sphere would create inordinate risks to liberty in intimate associations, infusing that sphere with values more fit for the public domain and undermining the ideals of choice and community.[75] Consider the proposals advanced by the radical left. The notion of abolishing the role of mother and housewife is too fanciful to consider seriously; such changes are not brought about by decree.[76] More attention has been devoted to paying wages for housework, giving that job greater dignity and enticing men into taking on more household responsibilities.[77] Women do most of the home chores, even when they also work. Housewives are an anomaly, the only workers operating under a status-based system in our otherwise monetized economy.[78] For that reason, it is argued, housewives are locked into positions of powerlessness and denied real options.

In reducing the family to a system of economic exchanges, however, the argument for housework wages misconstrues the basis of family solidarity, treating families as small markets. Nor does the proposal seem workable, since those who advocate wages for housework have no good answer to the obvious question of who pays. A government subsidy is unwarranted, for outsiders could anticipate too few benefits to justify such a massive income redistribution. Nor should employers pay a family wage, as was done two centuries ago, or send a portion of the employee's salary directly home; the employer is only hiring someone to do a job and has no reason to be concerned with the employee's lifestyle.

The most common suggestion, that husbands pay their wives for the housework they do, exposes the root weakness of the wage idea. This practice would only reinforce the notion that women are destined to be housewives, introducing a new and very good reason for wives to remain home. Although advanced in the name of making women more autonomous, housewives' wages would entrap them far more securely than present arrangements. The one analogous existing scheme—parents giving allowances to children in exchange for their performing certain chores—has not brought about children's liberation, and there is no reason to anticipate that housewives' wages would operate differently. Even those who promote housewives' wages as a transitional policy fail to recognize that the direction of such a transition is toward more, not less, dependency.

One policy reform concerning housewives would make sense: the retirement portion of the social security system should be altered to better take into account women's dual responsibilities at home and in the market. Under the present system, a woman who retires must choose between two benefits: her own, or a derivative benefit based on her husband's account, whichever is greater. Since the derivative benefit is often the larger of the two, she will receive no return on the taxes paid during her work life. On the other hand, when a woman is not eligible for a derivative benefit and must rely on her own intermittent work record, she will often receive only the minimum payment. Both kinds of inequities could be addressed by pooling the earnings of the husband and wife for the purpose of calculating contributions to the social security system, while paying benefits to individuals.

The social security system presently focuses on the worker; it tacitly assumes that workers are males in stable family relationships that will end in death, not divorce. Workers make social security contributions based on their wages, and receive benefits based on average wages. It is not a strict insurance scheme, however. Vertical equity—that those who contribute more, receive more—has been tempered by the need for adequacy, assuring that those who contribute only a little do not fall below a legislatively fixed minimum. Even before the first social security payments were made, concerns about the adequacy of payments were advanced, and four years after the original 1935 Social Security Act passed, it was amended to provide extra benefits to retired workers with dependents. The many adequacy-based changes added since, such as assuring minimum payments, have moved the system far from the notion of an insurance policy for a worker with a specific wage history.[79]

Many of the provisions grafted onto the original insurance concept have to do with wives, although in the gender-neutral terms now required by law, they are referred to as "spouses." A retired worker with a dependent spouse is entitled to 150 percent of the payment he would have received if he lived alone. Under the survivor's program, widows or widowers of workers may collect their deceased spouses' benefits when they reach age 65; if they are younger than 65 and caring for the minor children of the deceased worker, they and the children are eligible for added benefits until the youngest child reaches age 18.

When most families were comprised of a working husband and a non-working wife, as was the case in 1935, paying the married worker a larger retirement benefit than the single worker seemed to make sense. However, the practice gave rise to horizontal inequity: two men with the same wage history are paid different amounts, merely due to the presence of a wife in one household.[80] Calculating benefits based on marital situation at the time of retirement ignores the past history of the two workers and places a hypothetical need above a fair return on taxes. The married worker receives 50 percent more retirement income, despite the fact that he and his wife presumably lived on the same income as the single worker before they retired. (The inequity is compounded when the services provided by the homemaker spouse are taken into account.) This practice was instituted in an era that had not yet conceived of minimum payments, so it is possible that the retirement check was usually so small in relation to preretirement income that one person could hardly survive on it, let alone two. Subsequent adequacy-based changes, however, have never repealed this basic equity between single and married workers.

The derivative benefit paid to homemaker spouses also causes inequities between one- and two-earner couples. A single-earner couple with the same average wage as a two-earner couple will usually receive a larger total benefit check. For instance, 150 percent of a benefit based on an average monthly wage of $600 will be bigger than the sum of two benefits, each based on a $300 average wage, and this happens despite the fact that the system now replaces a larger proportion of wages at low income levels.

The dependent benefit works in favor of the nonworking wife in a life-long marriage, but she is a vanishing breed. Women are now more likely to move in and out of the labor force, and to be married more than once. Women are unfairly penalized by the practice of calculating benefits based on the worker's marital situation at the moment of retirement. A dependent spouse may receive a derivative benefit on her husband's account, 50 percent of his benefits, or a payment based on her own account, whichever is greater. Because the benefit calculation averages wages over a "normal" work life, and the norm is a full-time, lifelong commitment to the workplace, calculating childbearing years as zero-wage years drastically lowers women's average wages.[81] Working women in long-term marriages will often find that benefits based on their own sporadic work records are less than 50 percent of their husband's benefits, and thus, despite their work histories, will receive a dependent benefit. For these women, social security taxes are a sunk cost; as far as retirement benefits are concerned, they might just as well have never worked.

For the divorced spouse, the effects of the present system can be even more grave. A divorced woman will be eligible to collect derivative benefits based on her spouse's wage record only if the marriage lasted at least ten years and she has not remarried; this entitlement holds no matter how many years have passed between the divorce and retirement. A woman who has had several short-term marriages and an erratic work history attributable to childrearing during those marriages will find herself with no derivative benefits and an extremely low average wage when retirement comes. Even if her last marriage endured for ten years, she will only collect a benefit equal to 50 percent of her divorced spouse's benefit, just as though she were still living with him.

As the divorce rate has increased and a far greater percentage of women have entered the labor force, the inequities latent in the assumption of the "normal" marriage have become apparent. They stem from the fact that the social security system only considers marital status when the time comes to award benefits. The system asks how many people are dependent on the worker when death or retirement occurs, and makes no inquiry about how long the dependent relationship lasted, except in the case of the divorced spouse.[82]

Women are penalized by the assumptions about expected duration of work life because they will usually be the ones who interrupt their careers to care for children and home. Meanwhile, men are using their wages to support a family unit, not just themselves. If both husbands and wives worked part-time in the market and part-time at home, women and men would have similar social security wage records, and marital status could safely be ignored at both the contribution and the benefit stages.[83] However, such a work pattern is unlikely in the near future, and the years spent at home cannot realistically be credited by assigning that work some market wage. For that reason, social security offers one of those instances when government should take marriage officially into account.

A sensible way to proceed would be to split the earnings of the worker into two accounts, thus allowing the stay-at-home spouse to build up entitlements in his or her own name. Income splitting would occur whenever a couple filed a joint tax return; two-earner couples would add their income and split it.[84] This reform acknowledges that families are partnerships, supported by market and nonmarket labor, and that it is next to impossible to appraise work done in the home at market rates. The system would allow more equitable treatment of divorced spouses as well. Rather than basing a wife's benefit on her former husband's earning record, the reform would grant her credit only for the actual time of the marriage, allowing her to continue to build her account with her own earnings or with another husband. Subsequent to the divorce, the earnings of her ex-spouse would become irrelevant to her; this makes sense, considering that he may have a new wife with whom to split earnings.

Income splitting for social security purposes would not pay wages to the housewife. But as long as the present system is based on wages, looking at the family rather than the individual is one way to avoid penalizing women for choosing to work at home rather than in the marketplace.[85] Unlike alimony, social security is the product of a relationship between government and workers, not between spouses. The present social security law does not allow spouses to bargain over the disposition of future social security benefits: women must accept what they are paid by government.[86] Even if the law were changed to allow spouses to treat future social security payments like pensions, which can be negotiated, that would not address the myriad inequities inherent in the practice of taking marital status into account only at retirement.[87]

Social security was originally conceived as a pension that could be carried from job to job. Extending a form of coverage to homemakers, whether men or women, will acknowledge that work done for the family is a kind of job; it will not perpetuate the assumption that only one spouse will take on the nonmarket role. While individuals may not be much aware of how their work decisions will change their retirement income—and in our politically determined social security system, future payments are uncertain to begin with—income splitting in calculating benefits would expand choice by not penalizing today's husbands and wives for acting contrary to yesterday's assumptions.

V

The family is a resilient human institution, enduring and evolving without much explicit official attention. The family remains a private space, governed by values different from the public world, even as it sustains that world.[88] The point is not, of course, that the family is unaffected by external forces. To the contrary: changes in economic structure, in social norms and values, and in the political understanding of family members have all reconstituted the forms of family life. The argument, rather, is that policy should not outrun personal preference.

For some contemporary feminists, the family resembles a patriarchal prison, limiting and oppressive not just to women, compelled to be homemakers, but to men as well, denied the possibility of fully realizing their own feelings. As historian Carl Degler writes, "The equality of women and the instution of the family have long been at odds with each other. . . . The family's existence assumes that a woman will subordinate her individual interest to those of others—the members of her family."[89] Although men and women have called that assumption into question and they have altered their relationships in myriad ways, tension will still remain between political and economic equality in the public sphere and inherently unequal relations in the private sphere. This tension is endemic to the institution; it cannot be undone by ideologically motivated wish or government dictate.

While the family has evolved, there are apparent limits to its evolution, even when pressed to change by the society. Adult commitments to an extended relationship, entailing central responsibility for raising their children, have withstood the most ambitious dreams of the social engineers— or so one interesting, nearly century-long experiment, the Israeli kibbutz, reveals.[90]

The founders of the kibbutz had in mind a world very different from the Eastern European ghettos they had left behind. Equality between the sexes, not the strict sexual separation ordained by their Orthodox Jewish heritage, was the guiding principle of the kibbutz. Sexual division of labor was banished. Women and men worked in the factories and the fields, the kitchens and the laundries, because it was felt that both sexes could perform almost any job equally well. Families were reshaped. Although the kibbutz encouraged couples to marry and have children, it took steps to separate children from their parents. In most kibbutzim, an infant was removed from its parents' quarters shortly after birth and reared with other children by an adult assigned to run the children's house. Parents saw their children frequently but enjoyed no monopoly on the attention of their offspring, for everyone in the kibbutz became a parent to all the children.

Over time, however, more traditional family norms have reemerged on the kibbutz. Women are routinely assigned to domestic work: 90 percent of housekeeping jobs are now women's jobs. Agricultural labor was too hard for women, the men argued, and the constant threat of terrorist attack demanded that men work in the fields to protect the community. "Whereas other women cook *and* sew *and* launder *and* care for children, kibbutz women cook *or* sew *or* launder *or* care for children. The latter regimen, to be sure, is much easier, but it is also much less stimulating, and for educated women it can be downright boring."[91] The ideology of sexual equality remains, but no longer does it accurately describe life in many kibbutzim.

Family life has also become more conventional as parents have reclaimed responsibility for raising their own offspring. Grandparents who belatedly discovered the pleasures of parenting have formed relationships with their grandchildren closer than those they had with their own sons and daughters. Fully two-thirds of the women and half the men of the kibbutz favor abolishing the practice of children living apart from their parents. "The family is more important than anything," one woman reports. "I wouldn't invest one-fourth the thought to my work that I invest in my family, under no circumstances."[92] Although the kibbutz "family" would be unrecognizable to most American suburbanites, it has grown far more similar to the American norm than the founders thought possible.

To those who would abolish the family, this brief history of family life on the kibbutz tells a dreary tale. But neither the kibbutz story nor, certainly, current American experience suggests a return to the good old days. On the contrary, men and women are increasingly determining for themselves what mix of detachment and freely given affection most closely corresponds to their own sense of who they are.[93] "Changing norms of what a woman is supposed to do as wife and mother and what a man is supposed to do as husband and father are transforming the institutions of the work place and the family," writes Daniel Yankelovich in *New Rules*. "Probably no set of shifting norms carries greater significance for the culture."[94]

The traditional family coexists alongside the many other kinds of relationships that are increasingly preferred. The idea that government might effectively promote one model of the family defies history, for no state—at least no politically tolerable state—has succeeded in that endeavor. It is also a wrongheaded idea, which ignores the breadth of resolutions that individuals create for themselves. Expanding the opportunity for participation in family life, strengthening the capacity of individuals to maintain stable relationships, and nurturing the emergent tolerance of varying forms: those constitute a framework for a humane family policy. A more aggressive course risks contributing to the demise of the very institution that the intervention means to save. Families deserve the respect of policy makers that can best be shown, not through a Family Protection Act, but through a government that intervenes only on a principled and unobtrusive basis.

Conclusion

> . . . The future was
> successive and successful answers to those
> questions it made sense to ask. How far from the
> earth itself could we project? And what was light?
> In the calculus of variations, what was the mean
> process of behavior in a species, in a
> social class? Could we compute a place for
> each of us within the equalizing
> sameness of plan? If we overlooked nothing,
> no single difference of temperament or will,
> if it were all accounted for and stored and if we
> watched it periodically and found it yielded
> more and newer orders, it would teach us how to
> master what was probable and make it pure,
> assign it a completeness like the past's.
>
> James McMichaels, *Four Good Things* (1981)

Our intention in this book has been to propose a way of thinking about law and policy for men and women that is at once fair and within the realm of possibility. We reject a government strategy aimed at producing some fixed set of outcomes, either sex-based indistinguishability or sex-based differentiations. Instead, we have argued that a superior standard would expand the sphere of liberty and equalize the capacity of both sexes to make life choices. In such a world, public processes are opened up to men and women, who are then better able to make determinations about their own lives because less fettered by limitations rooted in sexual stereotypes. This view holds choice paramount and results irrelevant, except when those results suggest that choices are being skewed by what government does.

Our position differs from proposals advanced, on the one side, by leftist feminists and, on the other, by those committed to biological determinism. The leftist feminists view women as an oppressed class, similar in most relevant respects to blacks. But the review of nineteenth century legislation concerning women's roles in chapter 2 shows that most laws setting women apart were rooted in paternalism toward frail womanhood—a misplaced paternalism, to be sure, but wholly different from the animosity that underlay laws aimed at keeping blacks in their place. Blacks were widely held to be inferior; men and women, unlike whites and blacks, lived together in mutually supportive relationships, and that fact too shaped the law. While historically the state placed limits on women and treated them as less competent, it never denied women's basic humanity.

Laws that purport to help women—the regulation of working conditions, for instance, also canvassed in chapter 2—usually end up doing them harm. For that reason among others, a gender-neutral public realm is our goal. To advocate new kinds of sex-specific laws—for instance, offering only women child care or special treatment in jobs or training—risks perpetuating old prejudices about women's incapacities to make it on their own; such rules also limit men's choices, and so violate the norm of equal liberty. Treating women as equal citizens fully able to participate in the public realm means not only extending rights but also imposing duties, since as we point out in chapter 5, laws that exclude women from the responsibilities of civic life embody damagingly stereotypical assumptions about their proper place. All individuals should be free to determine how they will divide their lives between what, in chapter 1, we term the public and private spheres, but some obligations—voting, jury duty, and national service—are the minima necessary to sustain a sex-neutral individualism in a vital state.

Nondiscrimination is an essential element of liberty. Yet as we make plain in chapter 6, nondiscrimination alone does not guarantee gender justice; allowing people to make their own life plans does not mean abandoning them to the vagaries of luck or a ruthless market. Government exists to support as well as to leave alone, to inform individuals of the range of available choices as well as to assure that men and women are treated as individuals. The equal liberty principle offers guidance here as well, because it advances a general rule about the nature of public support: that support should expand rather than contract choice. It is preferable that such help be nonobtrusive, with the hand of government as invisible as possible; that it take the form of direct aid, not grants-in-kind which tend to skew preferences; and that it be offered to those most in need regardless of sex or marital status, especially those supporting dependents, thus enabling the commonwealth to concentrate its scarce resources on helping future citizens reach autonomous adulthood.

Even as we reject the leftist feminist view that women are too oppressed to enter the public arena on equal terms with men, and so need special help, we also eschew the naturalist idea, spelled out in chapter 3, that unalterable genetic differences between the sexes will forever keep women out of the mainstream of public life. We accept the existence of some genetic differences—indeed believe that procreative functions do not exhaust those differences—without concluding that they are sufficient to warrant separate treatment of men and women. The impact of genetic differences on the ultimate life choices of men and women is better determined, not by government, but by individuals voting with their feet. Meanwhile, since research consistently shows that differences within each sex are far greater than between-sex differences for most matters of public significance, there is good reason to call for gender-neutral processes that allow individuals to make what they will of their sex.

Our agnosticism about the implications of biological sex differences mirrors our agnosticism about the "proper" ratio of men and women in various public and private roles. Natural variations or socialization may lead to a world in which men dominate some sectors and women others, but if government has done what it can to open up the processes of decision, there is no reason to sound the alarm. Considerable change will occur—that much is apparent from the transformations of the past fifteen years, detailed in part II—but if women continue to place primary emphasis on family life or tend to remain in traditional female jobs, while men persist in emphasizing careers over family, there is little that government can—or should—do to alter those outcomes.

This is not to say that, in our estimation, all processes of decision have already been opened up and the only remaining problem is the willingness of individuals to take responsibility for the choices available to them; in part II we make it clear that there is some considerable distance to be travelled. Our survey of present law and policy concerning gender points out that traditional assumptions about the proper behavior of men and women remain imbedded in the rules. In subtle and not so subtle ways, they dot the tax code, regulation of sexual conduct, and the social security laws. Equal liberty, if taken seriously, would change much of this society's gender policy.

Substantial progress in the design of domestic policy has not, of course, been characteristic of the 1980s, and it is worth asking whether the equal liberty principle—indeed, any principle more elevated than *triage*—is not merely the expression of some utopian sentiment, of interest only in some far-away future when $200 billion deficits have receded into dim memory. We would argue instead that an emphasis on liberty, elaborated in rules for allocating resources among competing claimants, makes particular sense in a time of scarcity.

When the public pie is expanding rapidly, as occurred during the 1960s and 1970s, the fairness with which slices of that pie are parcelled out is, relatively, of secondary importance: if one class of claimants—the handicapped, say, or senior citizens or women—doesn't get what it wants today, that group can anticipate that tomorrow's budget is likely to reflect its demands. It is only when the size of the pie is constant that allocation becomes all-important, for the policy questions turn into tough tradeoffs; the issue is not "this year or next year?" but "how much positive support—if any?" While coalition politics often demands that public benefits be extended beyond the neediest, the reality of constricted public budgets requires more coherent policies, of the sort proposed in part II, to allow assistance where principle demands without bankrupting the economy.

So too, the principle of nondiscrimination assumes particular significance in a static or slow-growing economy. If, because of new opportunities, many choices are at hand, it does not matter greatly that some potential options are closed because of tradition or prejudice, for there are always other alternatives. But where the sum of the options is itself constricted, where there is not sufficient growth to muffle potential discontent, then fairness in selection—adopting rules that do not honor caste, class or sex lines—becomes of paramount importance. Nor is it irrelevant, when government spending on new domestic initiatives is at a minimum, that policing against discrimination and providing information about available options—key functions in a liberty-enhancing state—are far less costly than a 1980s version of the Great Society, in which government would take on a more directly interventionist role.

Our distrust of intervention is premised on the belief that any preset outcome imposes a notion of the good life on individuals whom we presume are better able to choose for themselves. What we as a society want in the way of gender distribution is not well settled. This is why we have argued for a policy approach that treats men and women as equal citizens with the same rights and responsibilities in the political realm, while enabling them to make choices about the communities they will embrace, the work they will engage in, the families they will raise. Allowing individuals to choose, giving them the unobtrusive support and information they need to make choices, and tolerating the results of those choices are the essential elements of the equal liberty principle—the essential elements of gender justice.

Notes

Introduction

1. See Maren Lockwood Carden, *The New Feminist Movement* (New York: Russell Sage, 1974); Gayle Graham Yates, *What Women Want: The Ideas of the Movement* (Cambridge: Harvard University Press, 1975); Jo Freeman, *The Politics of Women's Liberation* (New York: David McKay, 1975).

2. See Andrea Dworkin, "Safety, Shelter, Rules, Form, Love: The Promise of the Ultra Right," *Ms.* 7 (June 1979): 62; Deirdre English, *"The War Against Choice," Mother Jones* 6 (February/March 1981): 16; Seymour Martin Lipset and Earl Raab, "The Election and the Evangelicals," *Commentary* 71 (March 1981): 25. The monthly *Phyllis Schlafly Report* regularly spells out the New Right's position on these issues.

The link between abortion and gender justice more generally was made clear by the director of the Life Amendment Political Action Committee. "If women have equality, what will happen to the unborn child?" Quoted in Lisa Wohl, "Decoding The Election Game Plan of the New Right," *Ms.* 8 (August 1979): 57.

3. Julia Kristeva, "Women's Time," *Signs* 7 (1981): 13, 26.

4. Jessie Bernard, *Women and the Public Interest* (Chicago: Aldine, 1971), 236.

5. Midge Decter, *The New Chastity and Other Arguments Against Women's Liberation* (New York: Coward, McCann and Geoghegan, 1972), 52.

Compare Betty Friedan's comment that "our daughters take their own personhood and identity for granted." Betty Friedan, "Feminism Takes a New Turn," *New York Times Magazine,* 18 December 1979, 40. See generally Betty Friedan, *The Second Stage* (New York: Summit, 1981).

Chapter 1

1. See Mancur Olson, *The Logic of Collective Action* (Cambridge: Harvard University Press, 1965).

2. Compare Richard Wasserstrom, *Philosophy and Social Issues* (Notre Dame, Indiana: University of Notre Dame Press, 1980) with Steven Goldberg, *The Inevitability of Patriarchy* (New York: William Morrow, 1974).

3. See, e.g., Laurence H. Tribe, "Ways Not to Think About Plastic Trees," *Yale Law Journal* 83 (1974): 1315.

4. Robert Nozick, *Anarchy, State, and Utopia* (New York: Basic Books, 1974), 309.

5. Immanuel Kant, *Foundations of the Metaphysics of Morals* (1785; reprint, Indianapolis: Bobbs-Merrill, 1959).

6. David A. J. Richards, "The Individual, the Family, and the Constitution: A Jurisprudential Perspective," *New York University Law Review* 55 (1980): 1, 9.

7. See, e.g., Nicholas Hobbs, ed., *Issues in the Classification of Exceptional Children* (San Francisco: Jossey Bass, 1975); James S. Coleman, et al., *Youth: Transition to Adulthood* (Chicago: University of Chicago Press, 1974).

8. See, e.g., Jean Jacques Rousseau, *The Social Contract* (1762; reprint, New York: Washington Square Press, 1967); John Rawls, *A Theory of Justice* (Cambridge: Harvard University Press, 1971).

9. John Stuart Mill, *On Liberty* (1859; reprint, Indianapolis: Hackett, 1978), 5.

10. See Kant, *Metaphysics of Morals,* supra note 5; Rawls, *Theory of Justice,* supra note 8.

11. W. J. Bate, ed., *Selected Works of Edmund Burke* (New York: Modern Library, 1960), 346.

12. See, e.g., Bruce Ackerman, *Social Justice in the Liberal State* (New Haven: Yale University Press, 1980).

13. Compare Janet Radcliffe Richards, *The Sceptical Feminist* (London: Routledge & Kegan Paul, 1980), 64–74.

14. Mill, *On Liberty,* supra note 9: 9.

15. See Nozick, *Anarchy,* supra note 4.

16. See, e.g., Charles Schultz, *The Public Use of Private Interest* (Washington, D.C.: Brookings, 1970); Richard Posner, *Economic Analysis of Law* (Boston: Little, Brown, 1972); Ronald Dworkin, "Why Liberals Should Believe in Equality," *New York Review of Books,* 3 February, 1983, 32.

17. See Isaiah Berlin, "Two Concepts of Liberty," in *Four Essays on Liberty* (Oxford: Oxford University Press, 1969).

18. See generally Jean Bethke Elshtain, *Public Man, Private Woman* (Princeton: Princeton University Press, 1981). Compare Michael Walzer, *Spheres of Justice* (New York: Basic Books, 1983).

19. Henry Kariel, "Nietzche's Preface to Constitutionalism," *Journal of Politics* 2 (1963): 211.

20. See Daniel Bell, *The Cultural Contradictions of Capitalism* (New York: Basic Books, 1976).

21. Compare Christopher Lasch, *Haven in a Heartless World* (New York: Basic Books, 1977).

22. See Berlin, "Two Concepts of Liberty," supra note 17.

23. See Betty Friedan, *The Feminine Mystique* (New York: W. W. Norton, 1963); James Levine, *Who Will Raise the Children? New Options for Fathers and Mothers* (Philadelphia: Lippincott, 1976).

24. See Frederick Engels, *The Origin of the Family, Private Property and the State* (1884; reprint, New York: International Publishers, 1972); Eli Zaretsky, *Capitalism, the Family, and Personal Life* (New York: Harper Colophon, 1976).

25. Simone de Beauvoir, "Sex, Society and the Female Dilemma: A Dialogue Between Simone de Beauvoir and Betty Friedan," *Saturday Review,* 14 June 1975, 12, 18.

26. See Benjamin Barber, *Liberating Feminism* (New York: Delta, 1976).

27. See chapter 2.

28. See chapter 6.

29. See Richards, *Sceptical Feminist,* supra note 13: 79–84.

30. See chapters 7 and 8.

31. See, e.g., Walter Nicholson, *Microeconomic Theory* (Hinsdale, Ill.: Dryden, 1978).

32. Mill, *On Liberty,* supra note 9: 74.

33. Fyoder Dostoyevsky, "Notes from the Underground," in *Three Short Novels,* trans. C. Garnett (New York: Dell, 1960), 25, 45–46.

34. John Kenneth Galbraith, *The Affluent Society,* 3rd ed. (New York: Mentor, 1976), 254.

35. See Frank and Fritzie Manuel, *Utopian Thought in the Western World* (Cambridge: Harvard University Press, 1979); Norman Cohn, *Pursuit of the Millennium* (New York: Harper, 1961); John L. Thomas, *Alternative America* (Cambridge: Harvard University Press, 1983); Elisabeth Hansot, *Perfection and Progress: Two Modes of Utopian Thought* (Cambridge: MIT Press, 1974).

36. Wasserstrom, *Philosophy and Social Issues,* supra note 2: 24, 25.

37. Ibid., 29.

38. Elizabeth H. Wolgast, *Equality and the Rights of Women* (Ithaca: Cornell University Press, 1980).

39. Compare Walzer, *Spheres of Justice,* supra note 18.

40. Wolgast, *Equality,* supra note 38: 131.

41. Ibid., 135, 136, 157.

42. Alison Jaggar, "On Sexual Equality," *Ethics* 84 (1974): 275.

43. Cited and discussed in Jaggar, "On Sexual Equality."

44. See Ivan Illich, *Gender* (New York: Pantheon, 1982).

45. Tribe, "Plastic Trees," supra note 3: 1338.

46. David Pole, *Conditions of Rational Inquiry* (London: Athlone Press, 1981), 92.

47. See chapter 4.

48. Lewis Coser, *The Functions of Social Conflict* (Glencoe, Ill.: Free Press, 1956), 154.

49. Elshtain, *Public Man, Private Woman,* supra note 18: 299.

50. George Simmel, *Conflict,* trans. Kurt Wolff (Glencoe, Ill.: Free Press, 1955), 108. See also Coser, *Social Conflict,* supra note 48.

Chapter 2

1. The history of women in America is both a new field—the landmark work, Eleanor Flexner, *Century of Struggle* (Cambridge: Harvard University Press, 1959), was written only a quarter-century ago—and an exciting one. Among the most illuminating studies are Carl N. Degler, *At Odds* (New York: Oxford University Press, 1980); Sheila M. Rothman, *Woman's Proper Place* (New York: Basic Books, 1978); Ann Douglas, *The Feminization of American Culture* (New York: Random House, 1977); William H. Chafe, *The American Woman: Her Changing Social, Economic, and Political Roles, 1920–1970* (New York: Oxford University Press, 1972); Robert W. Smuts, *Women and Work in America* (New York: Columbia University Press, 1959).

2. Richard Morris, *Studies in the History of American Law* (Philadelphia: J. M. Mitchell Company, 1959), 71.

3. Quoted in Aileen Kraditor, ed., *Up from the Pedestal* (New York: Quadrangle, 1970).

4. Sir William Blackstone, *Commentaries on the Laws of England* (1765; reprint, New York: Banks, 1914), 111.

5. John Stuart Mill, *The Subjection of Women* (1869; reprint, Cambridge: MIT Press, 1970), 35.

The leading American critic of the legal condition of women was Tom Paine, who wrote of women as "robbed of freedom and will by the Laws." Quoted in Flexner, *Century of Struggle,* supra note 1: 14–15.

6. Mill, *Subjection of Women,* supra note 5.

7. *Congressional Globe,* 36th Congress, 2nd session, 1866, part 1: 66.

8. John Stuart Mill, *On Liberty* (1859; reprint, Indianapolis: Hackett, 1978), 9, 10.

9. Johann Fichte, *The Science of Rights,* trans. A. E. Kroeger (1796; reprint, London: Trubner and Company, 1889), 440.

10. Gerald Dworkin, "Paternalism," in Richard Wasserstrom, ed., *Morality and the Law* (Belmont, California: Wadsworth, 1971), 118. See also John Hodson, "The Principle of Paternalism," *American Philosophical Quarterly* 14 (1977): 61; Joel Feinberg, "Legal Paternalism," *Canadian Journal of Philosophy* 1 (1971): 195; William C. Powers, "Autonomy and the Legal Control of Self-Regarding Conduct," *Washington Law Review* 51 (1975): 33.

11. See Rothman, *Woman's Proper Place,* supra note 1.

12. *Congressional Globe,* 36th Congress, 2nd session, 1866, part 1: 66.

13. Bradwell v. Illinois, 83 U.S. 130, 141 (1873).

14. Blackstone, *Commentaries,* supra note 4: 33.

15. Mill, *Subjection of Women,* supra note 5: 35.

16. Quoted in Flexner, *Century of Struggle,* supra note 1: 88.

17. Quoted in Elizabeth Cady Stanton, ed., *History of Woman Suffrage,* vol. 1 (1902; reprint, New York: Arno Press, 1969), 61.

18. Quoted in Leo Kanowitz, *Women and the Law* (Albuquerque: University of New Mexico Press, 1969).

19. Quoted in Flexner, *Century of Struggle,* supra note 1: 115–16.

20. Mill, *Subjection of Women,* supra note 5: 76.

21. Ibid.

22. Lucretia Mott, "Discourse on Woman" (1849), excerpted in Wendy Martin, ed., *The American Sisterhood* (New York: Harper & Row, 1972), 55, 56.

23. Sarah Grimke, "Legal Disabilities of Women, Letters on Equality of the Sexes," (1837), reprinted in Martin, *American Sisterhood,* supra note 22: 40.

24. Charlotte Perkins Gilman, *Women and Economics* (1898; reprint, New York: Harper & Row, 1966), 338. Gilman vividly dramatizes this point in her novella, *The Yellow Wallpaper* (1899; reprint, New York: Feminist Press, 1973).

25. Roger Traynor, "Is This Conflict Really Necessary?" *Texas Law Review* 37 (1959): 655, 672.

26. Compare the treatment of this issue in Judith Baer, *The Chains of Protection: The Judicial Response to Women's Labor Legislation* (Westport, Conn.: Greenwood, 1978).

27. Quoted in Flexner, *Century of Struggle,* supra note 1: 208 n. 12.

See generally Edith Abbott, *Women In Industry* (New York: Appleton, 1909); Robert Smuts, *Women and Work in America,* supra note 1.

28. Lochner v. New York, 198 U.S. 45 (1905).

29. People v. Williams, 189 N.Y. 131, 133; 81 N.E. 778, 780 (1907).

30. Quoted in Chafe, *American Woman,* supra note 1: 128.

31. Muller v. Oregon, 208 U.S. 412, 421–22 (1908).

32. Adkins v. Children's Hospital of the District of Columbia, 261 U.S. 525 (1923).

33. Ibid., 553.

34. Comment, "Constitutional Law: Police Power: Minimum Wage for Women," *California Law Review* 11 (1923): 353, 357. See also Thomas Reed Powell, "The Justiciability of Minimum Wage Legislation," *Harvard Law Review* 37 (1924): 545.

35. Quoted in Chafe, *American Woman,* supra note 1: 124.

36. Ibid., 128, 129.

37. Sophonsiba Breckenridge, "Legislative Control of Women's Work," *Journal of Political Economy* 14 (1906): 107, 108.

38. See Chafe, *American Woman,* supra note 1: 125. Compare Elizabeth Baker, *Protective Labor Legislation* (New York: AMS Press, 1969).

39. Baer, *Chains of Protection,* supra note 26: 15.

40. Chafe, *American Woman,* supra note 1: 125.

41. Quoted in Chafe, *American Woman,* supra note 1: 126.

42. See Note, "Rights of Women in the Toxic Workplace," *California Law Review* 65 (1977): 1113.

43. Quoted in Kenneth Davidson, Ruth Bader Ginsberg, and Herma Hill Kay, *Text, Cases and Materials on Sex-Based Discrimination* (St. Paul: West Publishing, 1974), 17.

After the Michigan Supreme Court struck down a law restricting women's work weeks to fifty-four hours, women employed by Hostess Cupcakes, obliged by the company to work as many as sixty-nine hours, sued to restore the maximum hours law. Janet Flammang, *The Political Consciousness of American Women: A Critical Analysis of Liberal Feminism in America* (Ph.D. diss., University of California at Los Angeles, 1980), 445.

44. We discuss this issue at greater length in chapter 7.

45. Isaiah Berlin, *Four Essays on Liberty* (Oxford: Oxford University Press, 1969), 157.

46. See John Coons and Stephen Sugarman, *Education by Choice* (Berkeley: University of California Press, 1978).

47. George Fitzhugh, *Sociology for the South* (Richmond, Va.: A. Morris, 1854), 105.

48. Eugene Genovese, *Roll, Jordan, Roll: The World the Slaves Made* (New York: Vintage Books, 1972), 5.

49. Compare Nathan Glazer, *Affirmative Discrimination* (New York: Basic Books, 1978); see chapter 6.

Chapter 3

1. See Heidi Hartmann, "The Unhappy Marriage of Marxism and Feminism: Towards a More Progressive Union," in Lydia Sargent, ed., *Women and Revolution* (Boston: South End Press, 1980).

2. See, e.g., Alice Rossi, "The Bio-Social Aspects of Parenting," *Daedalus* 106 (Spring 1977): 1; Selma Fraiberg, *Every Child's Birthright* (New York: Basic Books, 1977).

3. Gayle Rubin, "The Traffic in Women: Notes on the 'Political Economy' of Sex," in Rayna Reiter, ed., *Toward an Anthropology of Women* (New York: Monthly Review Press, 1975).

4. Benjamin Barber, *Liberating Feminism* (New York: Delta, 1976) is especially useful in sorting out the puzzles posed by feminism and naturalism.

5. These positions are usefully described in Alison Jaggar and Paula Struhl, eds., *Feminist Frameworks: Alternative Theoretical Accounts of the Relations Between Women and Men* (New York: McGraw-Hill, 1978) and Alison Jaggar, *Feminist Politics and Human Nature* (Totowa, New Jersey: Rowman and Allanheld, 1983).

6. On liberal feminism, see Zillah Eisenstein, *The Radical Future of Liberal Feminism* (New York: Longman, 1981); Gayle Yates, *What Women Want: The Ideas of the Movement* (Cambridge: Harvard University Press, 1975); Jo Freeman, *The Politics of Women's Liberation* (New York: David McKay, 1975); Jessie Bernard, *Women and the Public Interest* (Chicago: Aldine, 1971); Betty Friedan, *The Second Stage* (New York: Summit, 1981).

7. See, e.g., Kate Millett, *Sexual Politics* (New York: Avon, 1970).

8. Mary Daly, *Gyn/Ecology* (Boston: Beacon Press, 1977), 1.

9. See, e.g., Susan Griffin, *Woman and Nature: The Roaring Inside Her* (New York: Harper & Row, 1978).

10. Susan Brownmiller, *Against Our Will: Men, Women and Rape* (New York: Simon & Schuster, 1975), 14–15.

11. Catherine A. MacKinnon, "Feminism, Marxism, Method and the State," *Signs* 7 (1982): 515, 516.

12. Charlotte Bunch, "Lesbians in Revolt," in Nancy Myron and Charlotte Bunch, eds., *Lesbianism and the Woman's Movement* (Baltimore: Diana Press, 1975), 36.

13. Jaggar, *Feminist Politics,* supra note 5: 275–82.

14. See, e.g., Ti-Grace Atkinson, "Radical Feminism," in *Notes from the Second Year: Women's Liberation* (New York: Radical Feminism, 1970), 33; Daly, *Gyn/Ecology,* supra note 8; Jill Johnston, *Lesbian Nation* (New York: Simon & Schuster, 1973); Jean Baker Miller, *Toward a New Psychology of Women* (Boston: Beacon Press, 1976); Susan Griffin, *Woman and Nature,* supra note 9; Hester Eisenstein, *Contemporary Feminist Thought* (London: Unwin, 1984), 105–47. In *The Female World* (New York: Free Press, 1981), Jessie Bernard charts a history, as well as a future, in which men have no apparent place.

15. Shulamith Firestone, *The Dialectic of Sex* (New York: William Morrow, 1970), 1, 226–42, 11.

16. See Jaggar, *Feminist Politics,* supra note 5: 93; Evelyn Fox Keller, "Feminism and Science," *Signs* 7 (1982): 589.

17. See, e.g., Zillah Eisenstein, ed., *Capitalist Patriarchy and the Case for Socialist Feminism* (New York: Monthly Review Press, 1979), and Sargent, *Women and Revolution,* supra note 1, for collections of Marxist feminist writing.

18. See, e.g., Margaret Benston, "The Political Economy of Women's Liberation," *Monthly Review* 21 (September 1969): 13; Peggy Morton, "A Woman's Work Is Never Done, or: The Production, Maintenance and Reproduction of Labor Power," in Edith Altbach, ed., *From Feminism to Liberation* (Cambridge, Mass.: Schenkman, 1971), 211; Helieth Sallisti, *Women in Class Society* (New York: Monthly Review Press, 1975); Eli Zaretsky, *Capitalism, the Family and Personal Life* (New York: Harper Colophon, 1976).

19. Shelia Rowbotham, *Woman's Conscience, Man's World* (Middlesex, England: Penguin, 1973).

20. See, e.g., Giuliana Ponysei, "Wages for Housework," and Carol Lopate, "Women and Pay for Housework," in Jaggar and Stuhl, *Feminist Frameworks,* supra note 5.

21. Lisa Vogel, "Questions on the Women Question," *Monthly Review* 31 (June 1979): 39, 54.

22. Jaggar, *Feminist Politics,* supra note 5: 149.

23. Ibid., 130. See also Juliet Mitchell, *Women's Estate* (New York: Pantheon, 1971); Ann Ferguson and Nancy Folbre, "The Unhappy Marriage of Patriarchy and Capitalism," in Sargent, *Women and Revolution,* supra note 1; Barbara Ehrenreich and Deirdre English, *For Her Own Good* (Garden City, New York: Doubleday-Anchor, 1978).

24. Jaggar, *Feminist Politics,* supra note 5: 147, 132, 336.

25. "The Redstockings Manifesto," in Robin Morgan, ed., *Sisterhood is Powerful* (New York: Vintage, 1970), 533, 534.

26. Eisenstein, *Liberal Feminism,* supra note 6: 14.

27. Rowbotham, *Woman's Conscience,* supra note 19: 34.

28. Simone de Beauvoir, *The Second Sex* (New York: Knopf, 1953), 376.

29. Thomas Kuhn, *The Structure of Scientific Revolutions,* 2d ed. (Chicago: University of Chicago Press, 1970), 109.

30. Ibid., 94.

31. Ann Popkin, "The Personal Is Political: The Women's Liberation Movement," in Dick Cluster, ed., *They Should Have Served That Cup of Coffee* (Boston: South End Press, 1978), 199, 200.

32. Quoted in Irving Howe, "The Middle-Class Mind of Kate Millett," in Judith Bardwick, ed., *Readings on the Psychology of Women* (New York: Harper & Row, 1972), 181, 184.

33. Simone de Beauvoir, *Second Sex,* supra note 28: 674. See also Jane Larkin Crain's criticism of this determinist approach as reflected in feminist fiction, "Feminist Fiction," *Commentary* (December 1974), 58, and the discussion of "false consciousness" in chapter 4.

34. Mary Midgeley, *Beast and Man: The Roots of Human Nature* (Ithaca: Cornell University Press, 1978), draws on similar materials but reaches a quite different conclusion concerning human capacity to evolve.

35. For summaries of biological and psychological differences between men and women, see, e.g., Alice S. Rossi, "Gender and Parenthood," *American Sociological Review* 49 (1984): 1; Jo Durden-Smith and Diane deSimone, *Sex and the Brain* (New York: Warner, 1983); Jacquelynne E. Parsons, *The Psychobiology of Sex Differences and Sex Roles* (New York: McGraw-Hill, 1980); Walter R. Gove and G. Russell Carpenter, eds., *The Fundamental Connection between Nature and Nurture* (Lexington, Mass: Lexington, 1982); Carol Gilligan, *In a Different Voice* (Cambridge: Harvard University Press, 1982); E. O. Wilson, *On Human Nature* (New York: Bantam, 1978).

36. Quoted in Durden-Smith and DeSimone, *Sex and the Brain,* supra note 35: 48.

37. Steven Goldberg, *The Inevitability of Patriarchy* (New York: William Morrow, 1974), 75.

38. Lionel Tiger and Robin Fox, *The Imperial Animal* (New York: Holt, Rinehart, and Winston, 1971). See also Lionel Tiger, *Men in Groups* (New York: Random House, 1969); George Gilder, *Sexual Suicide* (New York: Quadrangle, 1973).

39. See Konrad Lorenz, *On Aggression* (New York: Harcourt, Brace and World, 1966); Lionel Tiger, *Men in Groups,* supra note 38; Robert Audrey, *The Territorial Imperative* (New York: Atheneum, 1966); Goldberg, *Patriarchy,* supra note 37; Gilder, *Sexual Suicide,* supra note 38.

40. Goldberg, *Patriarchy,* supra note 37: 106–107.

41. Ibid.

42. Tiger and Fox, *Imperial Animal,* supra note 38: 146.

43. Barber, *Liberating Feminism,* supra note 4: 85.

44. Lionel Tiger and Joseph Shepher, *Women in the Kibbutz* (New York: Harcourt Brace Jovanovich, 1975).

45. Wilson, *On Human Nature,* supra note 35: 154–55.

46. Ibid., 7.

47. Charles Lindblom and David Cohen, *Usable Knowledge* (New Haven: Yale University Press, 1979).

48. Jean Bethke Elshtain, *Public Man, Private Woman* (Princeton: Princeton University Press, 1981).

49. Rubin, "Traffic in Women," supra note 3: 157.

50. Edmund Burke, "Reflections on the Revolution in France," in W. J. Bate, ed., *Selected Works of Edmund Burke* (New York: Modern Library, 1960).

51. Mitchell, *Women's Estate,* supra note 23: 63.

52. Charlotte Bunch, *Personal Politics* (New York: Vintage, 1979), 178.

53. Elshtain, *Public Man, Private Woman,* supra note 48: 256.

54. Firestone, *Dialectic of Sex,* supra note 15.

Compare Kate Millett's unqualified support for "the end of the present chattel status and denial of right to minors." *Sexual Politics,* supra note 7: 92.

55. See John Rothschild and Susan Berns Wolf, *The Children of the Counterculture* (Garden City, New York: Doubleday, 1976).

56. See de Beauvoir, *Second Sex,* supra note 28: 65.

57. Elshtain, *Public Man, Private Woman,* supra note 48, offers useful insights on these issues from a different perspective. See also chapter 6.

58. Dorothy Dinnerstein, *The Mermaid and the Minotaur: Sexual Arrangements and Human Malaise* (New York: Harper & Row, 1977); Nancy Chodorow, *The Reproduction of Mothering: Psychoanalysis and the Sociology of Gender* (Berkeley: University of California Press, 1978).

59. Dinnerstein, *Mermaid,* supra note 58: 5.

60. Chodorow, *Mothering,* supra note 58: 33.

61. Dinnerstein, *Mermaid,* supra note 58: 256.

62. Chodorow, *Mothering,* supra note 58: 219.

63. Germaine Greer, *The Female Eunuch* (New York: McGraw-Hill, 1971), 326, 328.

64. Mitchell, *Women's Estate,* supra note 23: 174.

65. See, e.g., Jaggar, *Feminist Politics,* supra note 5: 303–50.

66. Elizabeth Cady Stanton, ed., *History of Woman Suffrage,* vol. 1 (1902; reprint, New York: Arno Press, 1969), 73.

67. William O'Neill, *Everyone Was Brave* (Chicago: Quadrangle, 1969), 69.

68. See Kirsten Amundsen, *A New Look at the Silenced Majority* (Englewood Cliffs, New Jersey: Prentice-Hall, 1977).

During the Reagan administration, surveys of the president's popularity found a 10 percent difference between the level of support he enjoyed from men and women. Such a gap is unprecedented. If sustained, it would argue for greater gender-specific politics than has thus far been the case.

69. Elizabeth Janeway, *Man's World, Woman's Place* (New York: Delta, 1971), 232.

70. Betty Friedan, *The Feminine Mystique* (New York: W. W. Norton, 1963).

71. Rubin, "Traffic in Women," supra note 3: 198.

72. Peter Clecak, *Radical Paradoxes; Dilemmas of the American Left: 1945–1970* (New York: Harper & Row, 1974), 9, 30.

As Michael Oakeshott writes in a related context, the radical sees infinite possibilities but ultimately presses for the "imposition of a uniform condition of perfection upon human conduct." *Rationalism in Politics* (New York: Basic Books, 1962), 5–6.

British feminists have tried to relate gender issues to the political agenda of the Labor Left. See Shelia Rowbotham, Lynne Segal and Hilary Wainwright, *Beyond the Fragments: Feminism and the Making of Socialism* (Boston: Alyson, 1981).

73. Julia Kristeva, "Woman's Time," *Signs* 7 (1981): 13, 27.

74. Barber, *Liberating Feminism,* supra note 4: 19.

75. Janet Flammang, "Feminist Theory: The Question of Power," *Current Perspectives in Social Theory* 4 (1983): 37, 73.

76. Wilson, *On Human Nature,* supra note 35: 7.

77. J. J. C. Smart and Bernard Williams, *Utilitarianism For and Against* (Cambridge: Cambridge University Press, 1973), 80.

78. G. Russell Carpenter, "The Social Control of Biology," in Gove & Carpenter, *Nature and Nurture,* supra note 35: 283.

79. See generally C. A. Campbell, *In Defense of Free Will* (London: Allen and Unwin, 1967); John Lucas, *The Freedom of the Will* (Oxford: Oxford University Press, 1970); Robert Nozick, *Philosophical Explanations* (Cambridge: Harvard University Press, 1981), 291–398.

80. Michael Polanyi, *Personal Knowledge* (Chicago: University of Chicago Press, 1958), 312, 309.

81. Isaiah Berlin, *Four Essays on Liberty* (Oxford: Oxford University Press, 1969), 55–56.

82. Ibid., 63.

83. Nozick, *Philosophical Explanations,* supra note 79: 2.

84. Ibid., 312.

85. This point is examined in depth in chapter 4.

86. See Midge Decter, *The New Chastity and Other Arguments Against Women's Liberation* (New York: Coward, McCann and Geoghogan, 1972), 51, 52 (emphasis added).

87. Susanne Langer, *Philosophical Sketches* (Baltimore: Johns Hopkins University Press, 1962), 178.

88. Ibid.

89. Clifford Geertz, *The Interpretation of Cultures* (New York: Basic Books, 1973), 52.

Chapter 4

1. Compare Robert A. Nisbet, *The Quest for Community,* revised ed. (Oxford: Oxford University Press, 1969) with Grant McConnell, *Private Power and American Democracy* (New York: Random House, 1970).

2. Michael Walzer, *Radical Principles* (New York: Basic Books, 1980), 6.

3. Compare William M. Sullivan, *Reconstructing Public Philosophy* (Berkeley: University of California Press, 1981), which faults the liberal tradition on these grounds.

4. "What made liberalism endurable for all these years was the fact that the individualism it generated was imperfect, tempered by older constraints and loyalties, by stable patterns of local, ethnic, religious, and class relationships." Jean Bethke Elshtain, "Feminism, Family, and Community," *Dissent* (Fall 1982): 422, 446.

5. Claude S. Fischer, et al., *Networks and Places* (New York: Free Press, 1978), 202.

6. Quoted in Fischer, *Networks and Places,* supra note 5: 196.

7. This is the view of many of the radical feminists discussed in chapter 3. In the social sciences, it is implicit in the treatment of marriage and family in Judith Blake Davis, "The Changing Status of Women in Developed Countries" *Scientific American* 231 (September 1974): 144; Jessie Bernard, *Women and the Public Interest* (Chicago: Aldine-Atherton, 1971), 63–103; and Eli Zaretsky, *Capitalism, the Family, and Personal Life* (New York: Harper Colophon, 1976).

8. We do not deny that resource constraints may be powerful constraints on choice—in fact, they are likely to be more constraining than the socialization discussed in this chapter. Resource constraints may also affect women more strongly, for two reasons: (1) women generally earn less than men; (2) women generally have more child care responsibilities, both in and out of marriage. How choice-enhancing policies with respect to such resource constraints might look are discussed in chapters 6–8.

9. The concept is developed in the writings of Jürgen Habermas. See, e.g., Thomas McCarthy, *The Critical Theory of Jürgen Habermas* (Cambridge: MIT Press, 1979); Raymond Geuss, *The Idea of a Critical Theory* (Cambridge: Cambridge University Press, 1981). See also Herbert Marcuse, *One-Dimensional Man* (Boston: Beacon Press, 1966).

10. See Janet Radcliffe Richards, *The Sceptical Feminist* (London: Routledge and Kegan Paul, 1980).

11. John E. Coons and Stephen D. Sugarman, "A Case for Choice," in *Parents, Teachers, and Children: Prospects for Choice in American Education* (San Francisco: Institute for Contemporary Studies, 1977), 129, 148.

12. Carol Gilligan, *In a Different Voice* (Cambridge: Harvard University Press, 1982).

13. Jill Johnston, *Lesbian Nation* (New York: Simon & Schuster, 1973), 174. See also Mary Daly, *Gyn/Ecology* (Boston: Beacon Press, 1977); Susan Griffin, *Woman and Nature: The Roaring Inside Her* (New York: Harper & Row, 1978).

14. See chapter 3.

15. See, e.g., Lionel Tiger and Robin Fox, *The Imperial Animal* (New York: Holt, Rinehart, and Winston, 1971), 146.

16. See generally Alan Crawford, *Thunder on the Right* (New York: Pantheon, 1980).

17. Marabel Morgan, *The Total Woman* (Old Tappan, New Jersey: F. H. Revell, 1973).

18. Nisbet, *Quest for Community,* supra note 1:81. Compare Alasdair MacIntyre, *After Virtue* (Notre Dame, Indiana: University of Notre Dame Press, 1981). The longing for traditional forms of community is shared by a group of social scientists who have been labelled neoconservatives. See generally Peter Steinfels, *The Neoconservatives* (New York: Simon & Schuster, 1979).

19. See generally Sheldon S. Wolin, *Politics and Vision* (Boston: Little, Brown, 1960); Lewis Coser, *Greedy Institutions* (New York: Free Press, 1974).

20. J. L. Talmon, *Political Messianism* (London: Martin Secker and Warburg, 1960), 20.

21. Ivan Illich, *Gender* (New York: Pantheon, 1982). See also his *Tools for Conviviality* (New York: Harper & Row, 1973) and *Shadow Work* (Salem, New Hampshire: Marion Boyars, 1981).

22. Christopher Lasch says much the same thing, in criticizing the new elite that "has torn away the veil of chivalry that once tempered the exploitation of women . . . (and) has expropriated the worker's knowledge and the mother's 'instinct'. . . ." *The Culture of Narcissism* (New York: Warner, 1979), 375.

23. Germaine Greer, *Sex and Destiny* (New York: Harper & Row, 1984). Compare her *The Female Eunuch* (New York: McGraw-Hill, 1971).

24. Roberto Mangabeira Unger, *Knowledge and Politics* (New York: Free Press, 1975); Michael Walzer, *Radical Principles,* supra note 2; Raymond Williams, *Culture and Society* (New York: Columbia University Press, 1960); Daniel Bell, *The Cultural Contradictions of Capitalism* (New York: Basic Books, 1976); Benjamin R. Barber, *Liberating Feminism* (New York: Delta, 1976); and *Strong Democracy* (Berkeley: University of California Press, 1984); Philip Selznick, *Law, Society, and Industrial Justice* (New York: Russell Sage, 1964); Christopher Jencks, "The Social Basis of Unselfishness," in Herbert J. Gans, et al., eds., *On the Making of Americans: Essays in Honor of David Riesman* (Philadelphia: University of Pennsylvania Press, 1979), 63.

25. Quoted in Wolin, *Politics and Vision,* supra note 19: 424.

26. Ibid., 281.

27. Talmon, *Political Messianism,* supra note 20: 20.

28. Barber, *Liberating Feminism,* supra note 24: 138–39. In his later work, Barber has proposed a program to rejuvenate politics, but it is so broad as to appear utopian. See his *Strong Democracy,* supra note 24: 261–311.

29. Walzer, Radical Principles, supra note 2: 35.

30. Barber, *Strong Democracy,* supra note 24.

31. Williams, *Culture and Society,* supra note 24.

32. Unger, *Knowledge and Politics,* supra note 24: 217.

33. See, e.g., Jencks, "Unselfishness," supra note 24: 69. See also Richard Titmuss, *The Gift Relationship* (New York: Pantheon, 1971). Titmuss argues that it is the capacity to nurture empathy that enabled Britain to secure blood from its citizens without promising money or blood in exchange.

34. See Barber, *Strong Democracy,* supra note 24.

35. Williams, *Culture and Society,* supra note 24: 334–35.

36. Ibid., 335.

37. John Rawls, "Fairness to Goodness," *Philosophical Review* 84 (1975): 536, 550.

38. Unger, *Knowledge and Politics,* supra note 24: 280.

39. Michael J. Sandel, *Liberalism and the Limits of Justice* (Cambridge: Cambridge University Press, 1982), 183.

40. Jean Bethke Elshtain, "Antigone's Daughters: Reflections on Female Identity and the State," in Irene Diamond, ed., *Families, Politics, and Public Policy* (New York: Longman, 1983), 300.

Chapter 5

1. See, generally Raoul Berger, *Government by Judiciary* (Cambridge: Harvard University Press, 1977); Jesse Choper, *Judicial Review and the National Political Process* (Chicago: University of Chicago Press, 1980); John Hart Ely, *Democracy and Distrust* (Cambridge: Harvard University Press, 1980); Michael J. Perry, *The Constitution, the Courts, and Human Rights* (New Haven: Yale University Press, 1982).

2. Paul Brest, "The Conscientious Legislator's Guide to Constitutional Interpretation," *Stanford Law Review* 27 (1975): 585. See generally, Donald G. Morgan, *Congress and the Constitution* (Cambridge: Harvard University Press, Belknap Press, 1966).

3. See, e.g., William K. Muir, Jr., *Prayer in the Public Schools: Law and Attitude Change* (Chicago: University of Chicago Press, 1967).

4. See Alexander Bickel, *The Least Dangerous Branch* (Indianapolis: Bobbs-Merrill, 1962), 64; Eugene V. Rostow, "The Democratic Character of Judicial Review," *Harvard Law Review* 66 (1952): 193.

5. Michael M. v. Superior Court of Sonoma County, 450 U.S. 464, 478 (1981) (concurring opinion). Even race-conscious preferential programs are said to promote the irrelevance of race in the long run. See University of California Regents v. Bakke, 438 U.S. 265, 325 (1978) (Opinion of Justices Brennan, White, Marshall, and Blackmun, concurring in the judgment in part and dissenting).

6. See U.S. v. Carolene Products Co., 304 U.S. 144, 152–53, n. 4 (1938). See generally Ely, *Democracy and Distrust,* supra note 1; Louis Lusky, *By What Right?* (Charlottesville, Va.: The Michie Company, 1975).

7. See generally Charles L. Black, "The Lawfulness of the Segregation Decisions," *Yale Law Journal* 69 (1960): 421.

8. Frontiero v. Richardson, 411 U.S. 677, 685 (1973). Compare Ely, *Democracy and Distrust,* supra note 1: 166–69.

9. Compare John H. Garvey, "Freedom and Choice in Constitutional Law," *Harvard Law Review* 94 (1981): 1756. The question of whether the word *equal* adds anything to arguments for respect or autonomy is hotly debated by philosophers. Compare J. R. Lucas, "Against Equality," *Philosophy* 40 (1965): 296, with Stanley I. Benn, "Egalitarianism and the Equal Consideration of Interests," in J. Roland Pennock and John W. Chapman, eds., *Equality: Nomos IX* (New York: Atherton Press, 1967), 61.

10. See generally Kenneth L. Karst, " 'A Discrimination So Trivial': A Note on Law and the Symbolism of Women's Dependency," *Ohio State Law Journal* 35 (1974): 546.

11. See John Plamenatz, "Diversity of Rights and Kinds of Equality," in Pennock and Chapman, *Equality,* supra note 9: 79; Richard A. Wasserstrom, *Philosophy and Social Issues: Five Studies* (Notre Dame, Indiana: University of Notre Dame Press, 1980).

12. David A. J. Richards, "The Individual, the Family, and the Constitution: A Jurisprudential Perspective," *New York University Law Review* 55 (1980): 1.

13. Sidney Hook, *Philosophy and Public Policy* (Carbondale: Southern Illinois University Press, 1980), 81. ("The proposal to treat human beings equally in certain respects does not rest upon any assertion of biological equality, but advances a moral justified by its consequences.")

14. John Stuart Mill, *The Subjection of Women* (1869) in *Essays on Sex Equality* by John Stuart Mill and Harriet Taylor Mill (Chicago: University of Chicago Press, 1970).

15. Kenneth L. Karst, "The Supreme Court, 1976 Term—Foreword: Equal Citizenship Under the Fourteenth Amendment," *Harvard Law Review* 91 (1977): 1, 55; see also Paul Brest, "The Substance of Process," *Ohio State Law Journal* 42 (1981): 131.

16. Leo Kanowitz, *Equal Rights, The Male Stake* (Albuquerque: University of New Mexico Press, 1981).

17. John D. Johnston, Jr., "Sex Discrimination and the Supreme Court—1971–1974," *New York University Law Review* 49 (1974): 617, 624.

18. Karst, "Supreme Court, 1976," supra note 15: 4.

19. See generally Benjamin Barber, *Strong Democracy* (Berkeley: University of California Press, 1984).

20. Henry Sumner Maine, *Ancient Law* (New York: C. Scribner, 1864), 149–51.

21. See Paul Brest, "The Supreme Court, 1975 Term—Foreword: In Defense of the Antidiscrimination Principle," *Harvard Law Review* 90 (1976): 1.

22. Barbara A. Brown, Thomas Emerson, Gail Falk, and Ann E. Freedman, "The Equal Rights Amendment: A Constitutional Basis for Equal Rights for Women," *Yale Law Journal* 80 (1971): 871, 891–92 (emphasis added); see also Richard Wasserstrom, "Racism, Sexism, and Preferential Treatment: An Approach to the Topics," *University of California-Los Angeles Law Review* 24 (1977): 581.

23. 404 U.S. 71 (1971).

24. 411 U.S. 677 (1973).

25. Its failure to do so was strongly criticized. See, e.g., Ruth Bader Ginsburg, "Gender in the Supreme Court: The 1973 and 1974 Terms," *Supreme Court Review* 1975: 1; Johnston "Sex Discrimination," supra note 17.

26. 411 U.S. 677, 682 (1973). Compare Mississippi University for Women v. Hogan, 458 U.S. 718 (1982).

27. 411 U.S. 677, 684 (1973).

28. Compare Ely, *Democracy and Distrust,* supra note 1: 166–69.

29. 429 U.S. 190 (1976).

30. Kahn v. Shevin, 416 U.S. 351 (1974). See generally Leo Kanowitz, " 'Benign' Sex Discrimination: Its Troubles and Their Cure," *Hastings Law Journal* 31 (1980): 1379.

31. Geduldig v. Aiello, 417 U.S. 484 (1974). See also General Electric Co. v. Gilbert, 429 U.S. 125 (1976). Compare Nashville Gas Co. v. Satty, 434 U.S. 136 (1977). See generally David L. Kirp and Dorothy Robyn, "Pregnancy, Justice, and the Justices," *Texas Law Review* 57 (1979): 947.

32. 429 U.S. 190, 197 (1976) (emphasis added).

33. Ibid., 224 (Rehnquist, J., dissenting).

34. Ibid., 221 (Rehnquist, J., dissenting).

35. Compare Parham v. Hughes, 441 U.S. 347 (1979) with Caban v. Mohammed, 441 U.S. 380 (1979).

36. Compare Kahn v. Shevin, 416 U.S. 351 (1974) with Orr v. Orr, 440 U.S. 268, 283 (1979).

37. Personnel Administrator of Massachusetts v. Feeney, 442 U.S. 256, 273 (1979).

38. Rostker v. Goldberg, 453 U.S. 57 (1981): Michael M. v. Superior Court of Sonoma County, 450 U.S. 464 (1981).

39. Rostker v. Goldberg, 453 U.S. 57, 78 (1981).

40. Michael M. v. Superior Court of Sonoma County, 450 U.S. 464, 479 (1981).

41. People v. Hernandez, 61 Cal.2d 529, 531, 393 P.2d 673, 674, 39 Cal. Rptr. 361, 362 (1964).

42. 450 U.S. 464, 473–74 (1981).

43. Cass R. Sunstein, "Public Values, Private Interests, and the Equal Protection Clause," *Supreme Court Review* 1982: 127; Peter Westen, "The Empty Idea of Equality," *Harvard Law Review* 95 (1982): 537.

44. 404 U.S. 71 (1971).

45. 421 U.S. 7 (1975).

46. Kirchberg v. Feenstra, 450 U.S. 455 (1981).

47. Mississippi University for Women v. Hogan, 458 U.S. 718 (1982).

48. Craig v. Boren, 429 U.S. 190, 211 (1976). Chief Justice Roger Taney once voiced a similar sentiment: "[The Constitution] speaks not only in the same words, but with the same meaning and intent with which it spoke when it came from the hands of its framers, and was voted on and adopted by the people of the United States." Dred Scott v. Sanford, 60 U.S. (19 How.) 393, 426 (1857). See generally Walter Benn Michaels, "Book Review," *Texas Law Review* 61 (1982): 765.

49. Vorchheimer v. School District, 400 F. Supp. 326, 340–41 (E. D. Pa. 1975), *rev'd* 532 F.2d 880 (3rd Cir. 1976), *aff'd by an equally divided court*, 430 U.S. 703 (1972).

50. See generally John D. Johnston, Jr., and Charles L. Knapp, "Sex Discrimination by Law: A Study in Judicial Perspective" *New York University Law Review* 46 (1971): 675, and Blanche Crozier, "Constitutionality of Discrimination Based on Sex," *Boston University Law Review* 15 (1935): 723, for insightful discussions of the early case law, and the perspective that it reflects.

51. Among the most thoughtful of the recent appraisals is Wendy Williams, "The Equality Crisis: Some Reflections on Culture, Courts, and Feminism," *Women's Rights Law Reporter* 7 (1982): 175. See also Ann Freedman, "Sex Equality, Sex Differences, and the Supreme Court," *Yale Law Journal* 92 (1983): 913; Catherine MacKinnon, "Feminism, Marxism, Method, and the State: Toward Feminist Jurisprudence," *Signs* 8 (1983): 635; Note, "Toward a Redefinition of Sexual Equality," *Harvard Law Review* 95 (1981): 487.

52. Elizabeth H. Wolgast, *Equality and the Rights of Women* (Ithaca: Cornell University Press, 1980).

53. Freedman, "Sex Equality," supra note 51: 965.

54. MacKinnon, "Feminism," supra note 51: 645.

55. 429 U.S. 190, 212 (1976) (Stevens, J., concurring).

56. Michael M. v. Superior Court of Sonoma County, 450 U.S. 464, 476 (1981).

57. Frontiero v. Richardson, 411 U.S. 677, 687 (1973).

58. Kahn v. Shevin, 416 U.S. 351 (1974).

59. In *Frontiero*, for instance, as the Court observes, servicewomen are disadvantaged vis-à-vis servicemen. The spouses of servicemen who enjoy automatic access to benefits are

better off than the spouses of servicewomen. Compare Schlesinger v. Ballard, 419 U.S. 498 (1975) and Two v. United States, 471 F.2d 287 (9th Cir. 1972) *cert denied*, 412 U.S. 931 (1973) (different criteria for promotion of male and female Navy officers asserted, in *Ballard*, to benefit women, and in *Two* to discriminate against women).

60. See Muller v. Oregon, 208 U.S. 412 (1908).

61. Weinberger v. Wiesenfeld, 420 U.S. 636 (1975).

62. Wengler v. Druggist Mutual Insurance Co., 446 U.S. 142 (1980).

63. Kahn v. Shevin, 416 U.S. 351 (1974).

64. Califano v. Webster, 430 U.S. 313 (1977).

65. Schlesinger v. Ballard, 419 U.S. 498 (1975).

66. Nancy S. Erickson, "*Kahn, Ballard,* and *Wiesenfeld:* A New Equal Protection Test in 'Reverse' Sex Discrimination Cases?" *Brooklyn Law Review* 42 (1975): 1, 53 (emphasis in original).

67. See Ruth Bader Ginsburg, "Women, Equality, and the *Bakke* Case," *Civil Liberties Review* 4 (November/December 1977): 8. But see Kanowitz, " 'Benign' Sex Discrimination," supra note 30.

68. 420 U.S. 636 (1975).

69. Ibid., 643, 648.

70. Ibid., 652, quoting Stanley v. Illinois, 405 U.S. 645, 651 (1972). But see Quilloin v. Walcott, 434 U.S. 246 (1978).

71. See James A. Levine, *Who Will Raise the Children? New Options for Fathers (and Mothers)* (Philadelphia: Lippincott, 1976).

72. Orr v. Orr, 440 U.S. 268, 282, 279, n. 9 (1979).

73. Ibid., 283.

74. 430 U.S. 313 (1977) (per curiam).

75. See Ginsburg, "Women, Equality," supra note 67: 13–14.

76. See generally Frank I. Michelman, "Welfare Rights in a Constitutional Democracy," *Washington Law Quarterly* 1979: 659; John Hart Ely, "Toward a Representation-Reinforcing Mode of Judicial Review," *Maryland Law Review* 37 (1978): 451.

77. 419 U.S. 522 (1975). Compare Strauder v. West Virginia, 100 U.S. 303 (1880).

78. 419 U.S. 522, 531–32 (1975) (quoting from Ballard v. United States, 329 U.S. 187, 193–94 (1946)).

79. Rostker v. Goldberg, 453 U.S. 57 (1981).

80. Ibid., 77, quoting Senate Report 96–826.

81. The percentage of women in the military has risen from 0.78 percent in 1966 to nearly 10 percent in 1984. See Michael Levin, "Women as Soldiers—The Record So Far," *The Public Interest* 76 (Summer 1984): 31.

82. See Williams, "Equality Crisis," supra note 51: 189–90.

83. *Harvard Law School Record* (March 23, 1973): 15.

84. 453 U.S. 57, 86 (Marshall, J., dissenting).

85. See Brown, et al., "Equal Rights Amendment," supra note 22: 900–902; Kathryn L. Powers, "Sex Segregation and the Ambivalent Directions of Sex Discrimination Law," *Wisconsin Law Review* 1979: 55. Senator Cook derided a proposed privacy amendment to the ERA as the "potty amendment." *Congressional Record* 118 (1979): 9531.

86. Vorchheimer v. School District, 430 U.S. 703 (1979).

87. See Mark G. Yudof, David L. Kirp, Tyll van Geel, and Betsy Levin, *Educational Policy and the Law* (Berkeley: McCutchan Publishing Corp., 1982), Chapter 5.

88. 458 U.S. 718 (1982).

89. Ibid., 724, 729.

90. Ibid, 730 n. 16.

91. Ibid., 745 (Powell, J., dissenting).

92. This categorization is borrowed from Williams, "Equality Crisis," supra note 51.

93. Roe v. Wade, 410 U.S. 113, 169 (1973) (Stewart, J., concurring). See generally John A. Robertson, "Procreative Liberty and the Control of Conception, Pregnancy, and Childbirth," *Virginia Law Review* 69 (1983): 405.

94. Cleveland Board of Education v. LaFleur, 414 U.S. 632, 647 (1974).

95. Geduldig v. Aiello, 417 U.S. 484, 496–97, n. 20 (1974). See also General Electric Company v. Gilbert, 429 U.S. 125 (1976). Compare Nashville Gas Co. v. Satty, 434 U.S. 136 (1977). We include suits concerning claims of nondiscrimination on the basis of sex based on Title VII of the 1964 Civil Rights Act, 42 U.S.C.A. §2000e et seq., in the category of constitutional jurisprudence for these purposes, because of the important parallelism in the treatment of the wrong.

96. 429 U.S. 125, 161–62, n.5 (1976) (Stevens, J., dissenting).

97. See Kirp and Robyn, "Pregnancy, Justice," supra note 31.

98. Maher v. Roe, 432 U.S. 464, 474 (1977).

99. Harris v. McRae, 448 U.S. 297 (1980).

100. "Although Congress has opted to subsidize medically necessary services generally, but not certain medically necessary abortions, the fact remains that the Hyde Amendment leaves an indigent woman with at least the same range of choice in deciding whether to obtain a medically necessary abortion as she would have if Congress had chosen to subsidize no health care costs at all." 448 U.S. 297, 316–17.

101. Ibid., 333–34 (Brennan, J., dissenting).

102. See Planned Parenthood of Central Missouri v. Danforth, 428 U.S. 52, 67–71 (1976), which denied that fathers had the right to veto abortions. Compare Orr v. Orr, 440 U.S. 268 (1979); Stanley v. Illinois, 405 U.S. 645 (1972).

103. Compare Griswold v. Connecticut, 381 U.S. 479 (1965), where the right to use contraceptives appears to reside in the couple, not the individual.

104. In a world where interuterine transplants are fast becoming a reality, the burden on the woman could be lessened as well.

105. Rostker v. Goldberg, 453 U.S. 57 (1981). See Seth Cropsey, "Women in Combat?" *Public Interest* 61 (1980): 58; Martin Binkin and Shirley J. Bach, *Women in the Military* (Washington, D.C.: Brookings, 1977).

106. Dothard v. Rawlinson, 433 U.S. 321, 335–36 (1977). Although the Rawlinson case was brought under Title VII of the Civil Rights Act of 1964, prohibiting discrimination on the basis of sex, "the parties do not suggest . . . that the Equal Protection Clause requires more rigorous scrutiny of a State's sexually discriminatory employment policy than does Title VII." Ibid., 334, n. 20.

107. See, e.g., Susan Brownmiller, *Against Our Will* (New York: Simon & Schuster, 1975).

108. 433 U.S. 321, 336 (1977). See generally Note, "The Equal Rights Amendment and the Military," *Yale Law Journal* 82 (1973): 1533.

109. Goesaert v. Cleary, 335 U.S. 464 (1948).

110. Kenneth L. Karst, "The Freedom of Intimate Association," *Yale Law Journal* 89 (1980): 624, 692.

111. Joel Feinberg, *Social Philosophy* (Englewood Cliffs, New Jersey: Prentice-Hall, 1973), 7. See also Gerald C. MacCallum, Jr., "Negative and Positive Freedom," *The Philosophy Review* 76 (1967): 312, 313.

112. Feinberg, *Social Philosophy,* supra note 111: chapter 2, discussing John Stuart Mill, *On Liberty* (1859).

113. See Isaiah Berlin, *Four Essays on Liberty* (Oxford: Oxford University Press, 1969).

114. See MacCallum, "Freedom," supra note 111: 319–27. Professor MacCallum argues that "disputes about the nature of freedom are certainly historically best understood as a series of attempts by parties opposing each other on very many issues to capture for their own side the favorable attitudes attaching to the notion of freedom." Id., 313.

115. See, e.g., Youngberg v. Romeo, 457 U.S. 307 (1982); Harris v. McRae, 448 U.S. 297, 316 (1980); Maher v. Roe, 432 U.S. 464, 473–74 (1977); Norwood v. Harrison, 413 U.S. 455, 462 (1973); Dandridge v. Williams, 397 U.S. 471 (1970). See John H. Garvey, "Freedom and Equality in the Religion Clauses," *Supreme Court Review* 1981: 193; Albert M. Bendich, "Privacy, Poverty, and the Constitution," *California Law Review* 54 (1966): 407. But see Frank Michelman, "The Supreme Court 1968 Term—Foreword: On Protecting the Poor Through the Fourteenth Amendment," *Harvard Law Review* 83 (1969): 7.

116. See Ingram v. O'Bannon, 534 F. Supp. 385 (E.D. Pa. 1982); Black v. Beame, 419 F. Supp. 599 (S.D.N.Y. 1976). But see De La Cruz v. Tormey, 582 F.2d 45 (9th Cir. 1978).

117. See Feinberg, *Social Philosophy,* supra note 111.

118. As Professor MacCallum said, "Whenever the freedom of some agent . . . is in question, it is always freedom from some constraint or restriction on, interference with, or barrier to doing, not doing, becoming, or not becoming something." "Freedom," supra note 111: 314.

119. J. R. Lucas, "Because You Are a Woman," *Philosophy* 48 (1973): 161, 166.

120. See, e.g., John Stuart Mill, *On Liberty* (1859; reprint, Indianapolis: Hackett, 1978).

121. See generally, Richard Posner, *Economic Analysis of Law,* 2d ed. (Boston: Little, Brown, 1977). Compare Thomas Schelling, *Micromotives and Macrobehavior* (New York: W. W. Norton, 1978).

122. See, e.g., David Truman, *The Governmental Process: Political Interests and Public Opinion* (New York: Knopf, 1951); Robert Dahl, *Democracy in the United States: Promise and Performance* (Chicago: Rand McNally, 1976). Compare Albert Hirschman, *Exit, Voice, and Loyalty* (Cambridge: Harvard University Press, 1970).

123. See City of Los Angeles Department of Water and Power v. Manhart, 435 U.S. 702 (1978). For discussion of these issues, see Sydney J. Key, "Sex-Based Pension Plans in Perspective: *City of Los Angeles Department of Water and Power v. Manhart,*" *Harvard Women's Civil Rights Law Review* 2 (1979): 1; William Van Alstyne, "Equality for Individuals or Equality for Groups: Implications of the Supreme Court Decision in the *Manhart* Case," *AAUP Bulletin* 62 (1978): 150; George Rutherglen, "Sexual Equality in Fringe-Benefit Plans," *Virginia Law Review* 65 (1979): 199; Bernard D. Meltzer, "The *Weber* Case: The Judicial Abrogation of the Antidiscrimination Standard in Employment," *University of Chicago Law Review* 47 (1980): 423; Michael Evan Gold, "Of Giving and Taking: Applications and Implications of *City of Los Angeles Department of Water and Power v. Manhart,*" *Virginia Law Review* 65 (1979): 663; Lea Brilmayer, Richard W. Hekeler, Douglas Laycock, and Teresa A. Sullivan, "Sex Discrimination in Employer Sponsored Insurance Plans: A Legal and Demographic Analysis," *University of Chicago Law Review* 47 (1980): 505.

124. 435 U.S. 702, 727–28 (Burger, C. J., dissenting). See also Spencer Kimball, "Reverse Sex Discrimination: *Manhart,*" *American Bar Foundation Research Journal* 1979: 83, 119.

125. Frontiero v. Richardson, 411 U.S. 677 (1973).

126. Weinberger v. Wiesenfeld, 420 U.S. 636 (1975).

127. U.S. Department of Labor, Bureau of Labor Statistics, *Special Labor Force Report,* "Marital and Family Characteristics of Workers," (Washington, D.C.: Government Printing Office, 1970), 130. The earnings for working wives amount to one-quarter of average family income. See Carolyn Shaw Bell, "Working Wives and Family Income," in Jane Roberts Chapman, ed., *Economic Independence for Women* (Beverly Hills, Cal.: Sage Publications, 1976), 239, 240.

128. Compare Mathews v. Lucas, 427 U.S. 495 (1976) (upholding denial of social security benefits to illegitimate children on similar grounds).

129. See Califano v. Goldfarb, 430 U.S. 199 (1977); Wengler v. Druggists Mutual Insurance Co., 446 U.S. 142 (1980).

130. See generally Hermine Herta Meyer, *The History and Meaning of the Fourteenth Amendment* (New York: Vantage Press, 1977), Friedrich August von Hayek, *The Constitution of Liberty* (Chicago: University of Chicago Press, 1960).

131. See generally Herman Belz, *A New Birth of Freedom* (Westport, Conn.: Greenwood Press, 1976); Jacobus tenBroek, *Equal Under Law* (New York: Collier Books, 1965); John P. Frank and Robert F. Munro, "The Original Understanding of 'Equal Protection of the Laws,' " *Washington University Law Quarterly* (1972): 421.

132. Thomas M. Cooley, *A Treatise on the Constitutional Limitations Which Rest Upon the Legislative Power of the States of the American Union,* 3rd ed. (Boston: Little, Brown, 1874). See generally Phillip S. Paludan, *A Covenant With Death: The Constitution, Law, and Equality in the Civil War Era* (Urbana: University of Illinois Press, 1975).

133. Cooley, Constitutional Limitations, supra note 132: 459. When Cooley argued that the states were not free to deny the equal protection of the laws even before the adoption of the Civil War Amendments, he presumably meant that state constitutions implicitly or explicitly forbade such legislation. He devoted a whole section of his treatise on *Constitutional Limitations* to impartial legislation, mostly emphasizing state and federal due process provisions. Id., 456–66. He made only minimal references to the newly enacted Equal Protection Clause.

At a minimum the Fourteenth Amendment was designed to undo the Black Codes enacted in the winter of 1856–66 by all the rebel states except Texas. Paul Dimond, "Strict Construction and Judicial Review of Racial Discrimination Under the Equal Protection Clause: Meeting Raoul Berger on Interpretivist Grounds," *Michigan Law Review* 80 (1982): 462, 474–75. The Civil Rights Act of 1866, which the Fourteenth Amendment was designed to sanction (see Berger, *Government by Judiciary,* supra note 1: 18–36; Frank and Munro, " 'Equal Protection," supra note 131: 440–41), sheds some light on the meaning of equal protection, though most scholars believe that the amendment encompasses more than the Act. See Alexander Bickel, "The Original Understanding and the Segregation Decision," *Harvard Law Review* 69 (1955): 1; but see Berger, *Government by Judiciary,* supra note 1. The Act gave citizens of every race, irrespective of previous condition of servitude, the same rights to make and enforce contracts, to be a party to litigation, to give evidence, to inherit, and to hold and convey property, notwithstanding any state law or custom to the contrary. After the laundry list of specific concerns, the Act broadly stated that all citizens were entitled "to the full and equal benefit of all laws and proceedings for the security of person and property, as is enjoyed by white citizens, and shall be subject to like punishment, pains, and penalties, and to none other. . . ." 42 U.S.C. § 1983.

In large measure the Civil Rights Act of 1866 appears designed to give citizens equal access to the machinery of government in the ordering of their private affairs. There is not to be one law of trespass or contract remedies or theft for blacks and another for whites; they are to have equal ability to protect the "security of person and property" through the legal process. In this sense, it is easy to discern why Cooley and others at the time saw equal protection and due process as vitally linked to each other. The notion of fair procedures included the requirement that the law be the same for all, that it subject different persons to the same rules for vindicating entitlements and resolving disputes. See Durkee v. Janseville, 28 Wisc. 464 (1871). As Cooley quotes an 1825 Maine Supreme Court decision,

> On principle it can never be within the bounds of legitimate legislation to enact a special law, or pass a resolve dispensing with the general law in a particular case, and granting a privilege and indulgence to one man, by way of exemption from the operation and effect of such general law, leaving all other persons under its operation. Such a law is neither just nor reasonable in its consequences. It is our boast that we live under a government of laws, and not of men; but this can hardly be deemed a blessing, unless those laws have for their immovable basis the great principles of constitutional equality.

Cooley, *Constitutional Limitations,* supra note 132: 459. Or, Daniel Webster urged in his famous argument in the *Dartmouth College Case,* 17 U.S. (4 Wheat.) 518 (1819), a legislative enactment must be a general law if it is "to be considered the law of the land." Christopher G. Tiedeman, *A Treatise on the Limitations of Police Power in the United States* (St. Louis: The F. H. Thomas Law Book Co., 1886), 71.

134. See Ely, *Democracy and Distrust,* supra note 1: 90–91; Hayek, *Constitution of Liberty,* 130: 188.

135. See Cooley, *Constitutional Limitations,* supra note 136: 456–66.

136. Ibid., 459. See, e.g., State v. Duffy, 7 Nev. 342, 349 (1872). See Frank and Munro, *Equal Protection,* supra note 131: 436.

137. Hayek, *Constitution of Liberty,* supra note 130: 188. State supreme courts were generally not reluctant, except in volatile cases involving the treatment of blacks or other racial minorities, to overturn special legislation as in violation of state constitutions. For example, as early as 1814, the Supreme Judicial Court of Massachusetts, in refusing to uphold the suspension of a general law in favor of an individual, stated that

> it is manifestly contrary to the first principles of civil liberty and natural justice, and to the spirit of our constitution and laws, that any one citizen should enjoy privileges and advantages which are denied to all others under like circumstances; or that any one should be subjected to losses, damages, suits, or actions, from which all others, under like circumstances, are exempted.

Holden v. James, 11 Mass. 396, 403–404 (1814). Similarly, Chancellor Kent, writing in 1816, opined that a law limited to public officials was unconstitutional since it was "not impartial in the imposition which it creates. If the principle be just, it ought to have a general and equal application." William Kent, *Memoirs and Letters of James Kent, L.L.D.* (Boston: Little, Brown, 1898), 163. The Supreme Court of Wisconsin in 1860 stated that the legislature "cannot, under color of making laws to regulate and extend the boundaries of cities or villages, enact for the mere purpose of cutting off or reducing the exemptions of particular individuals, and thus legislate specially for or against certain persons, contrary to the spirit and intent of the constitution." Bull v. Conroe, 13 Wis. 260, 272–73 (1860). Judge Cooley cites numerous state court decisions to the same effect (Cooley, *Constitutional Limitations,* supra note 132: 457–58), and synthesizes them into the following general rule: "[A] statute would not be constitutional which should proscribe a class or a party for opinion's sake, or which should select particular individuals from a class or locality, and subject them to peculiar rules, or impose upon them special obligations or burdens from which others in the same locality or class are exempt."

138. TenBroek, *Equal Under Law*, supra note 131: 237.

139. Compare Sunstein, "Public Values," supra note 43: 131: "In brief, the Court requires differential treatment to be justified by reference to some public value. A justification that rests on the intrinsic value of treating one person differently from another is prohibited." See also Robert Bennett, " 'Mere' Rationality in Constitutional Law: Judicial Review and Democratic Theory," *California Law Review* 67 (1979): 1049; Bruce A. Ackerman, *Social Justice in the Liberal State* (New Haven: Yale University Press, 1980).

140. See Maine, *Ancient Law*, supra note 20. Compare Frank I. Michelman, "Politics and Values or What's Really Wrong with Rationality Review?" *Creighton Law Review* 13 (1979): 487, 496–98.

141. See, e.g., Sunstein, "Public Values," supra note 43: 129–30; Westen, "Equality", supra note 43; Terrance Sandalow, "Racial Preferences in Higher Education: Political Responsibility, Judicial Role," *University of Chicago Law Review* 42 (1975): 653, 654–63.

142. Westen, "Equality," supra note 43: 560, 549. See generally Ronald M. Dworkin, *Taking Rights Seriously* (Cambridge: Harvard University Press, 1977), 273.

143. See generally J. R. Pole, *The Pursuit of Equality in American History* (Berkeley: University of California Press, 1978, 174–76.

In the first half of the nineteenth century, women benefited enormously from the movement away from status and toward individual liberty, even if that movement was more a reflection of economic changes than of changing perceptions of the place of women. Lawrence M. Friedman, *A History of American Law* (New York: Simon & Schuster, 1973), 186. In 1839, Mississippi recognized the legal capacity of women, and by 1850 half of the states had enacted laws recognizing the property rights of married women. Harold M. Hyman and William M. Wieck, *Equal Justice Under Law* (New York: Harper & Row, 1982), 51. These new laws were not extensively debated in legislative bodies, and they did not receive significant attention in the press. Friedman, *American Law*, 186. Litigation arising out of the Married Women's Property Acts was largely initiated by creditors, with very few cases litigated between husbands and wives. Lawrence Friedman describes these laws as the ratification of a "silent revolution." Id.

Friedman's description gives us a clue to the profound difficulties of fitting gender classifications into the scheme of the Fourteenth Amendment. Gender classifications disadvantaging women were largely viewed as paternalistic and benign. Where such paternalism appeared ill-suited and inconsistent with the ethos of liberty and contract, significant changes were made in state laws. Thus sex discrimination simply was not viewed as a problem, and state bans on special legislation and concepts of equality under law were generally not invoked to strike down such discrimination. This inability to recognize sex classifications as inconsistent with the movement away from status and toward liberty and equality under law carried over into the Fourteenth Amendment. It is not so much that those who drafted and approved the amendment rejected its application to gender classifications; rather they focused on the real and pressing problem of racial discrimination.

But status came to take on a larger meaning, referring to the assignment of legal rights and obligations on the basis of ascribed and not achieved characteristics. Hayek, *Constitution of Liberty*, supra note 130: 154; see generally Patrick S. Atiyah, *The Rise and Fall of Freedom of Contract* (London: Oxford University Press, 1979). It is interesting to note in this regard that the Civil War amendments to the Constitution make reference to both types of status distinctions. The Thirteenth Amendment, abolishing slavery, naturally refers to slavery and involuntary servitude. The Fourteenth Amendment makes no reference to slavery at all. But the Fifteenth Amendment states that the rights of citizens of the United States to vote shall not be abridged "on account of race, color, or previous condition of servitude." Arbitrariness lies in classifying persons in accordance with their birthrights (slave status) or other characteristics (race) over which they have little or no control; a reasonable classification takes into account their wills, the things they are able to choose to do or not do within the limits of their capacities and the social order. Hayek, *Constitution of Liberty*, supra note 130: 170. As Senator Howard, a floor leader for the Fourteenth Amendment, said about the Equal Protection Clause, "It abolishes all class legislation in the States and does away with the injustice of subjecting one caste of persons to a code not applicable to another." Frank and Munro, " 'Equal Protection'," supra note 131: 441. Justice Bradley, writing for a majority of the Supreme Court in the Civil Rights Cases in 1883, reaffirmed these essential fourteenth amendment principles, opining that the amendment forbade "class legislation." 109 U.S. 3, 24 (1883).

144. Bradwell v. Illinois, 83 U.S. (16 Wall.) 130 (1873).

145. Minor v. Happersatt, 88 U.S. (21 Wall.) 162 (1874).

The *Minor* decision casts some light on the discomfiture of the nation's highest court with state-sanctioned sex discrimination, despite its tolerance of such inequalities under the law. The Court went to considerable lengths to confirm the fact that women were citizens of the United States and persons under the Constitution. It noted that women were members of the polity, that the Constitution was established by "the people," including women, and that (in contrast to its discredited decision in the *Dred Scott* case on blacks), women had long been treated as citizens for purposes of federal court jurisdiction of controversies between citizens of different states (diversity jurisdiction). The Chief Justice even opined that "there cannot be a nation without a people," and that women had always been citizens, the Fourteenth Amendment not having affected "the citizenship of women any more than it did of men." (88 U.S. 162, 170.)

How then did Mrs. Minor lose her law suit? The Court extensively reviewed the franchise under state constitutions at the time of the adoption of the federal constitution, and found that the states disenfranchised many citizens, including women. Further, the privileges and immunities clause of Article IV of the Constitution, giving the citizens of each state rights in the several states, had never been construed (nor could it be) so as to give a citizen a right to vote in more than one state. In short, in the absence of express language to the contrary, the Court concluded that the right to vote was not among the privileges and immunities protected by the Fourteenth Amendment. (88 U.S. 162, 171.) This conclusion was bolstered by a well-taken point: " If suffrage was one of these privileges or immunities, why amend the Constitution to prevent its being denied on account of race, etc?" (88 U.S. 162, 175.) This reference to the Fifteenth Amendment probably confirmed the worst fears of those feminists who had opposed the Fourteenth Amendment and attempted to revise the Fifteenth Amendment. Women were only vaguely protected by the Constitution, and that protection could easily be negated. See Crozier, "Discrimination," supra note 50.

Neither counsel nor the Court in *Minor* raised the question as to whether a classification by sex, of individuals acknowledged to be citizens and persons under the Constitution, violated the equal protection of the laws. The Court was more interested in the nature of the interest that had been affected than in the nature of the classification creating the inequality under the law.

146. A similar analysis of the race cases in the progressive era has been undertaken by Professor Schmidt. See Benno C. Schmidt, Jr., "Principle and Prejudice: The Supreme Court and Race in the Progressive Era. Part I: The Heyday of Jim Crow," *Columbia Law Review* 82 (1982): 444.

147. 208 U.S. 412 (1908).

148. Lochner v. New York, 198 U.S. 45, 57 (1905).

149. 261 U.S. 525 (1923).

150. Ibid., 553.

151. Crozier, "Discrimination," supra note 50: 745.

152. West Coast Hotel v. Parrish, 300 U.S. 379, 398 (1937).

153. Goesaert v. Cleary, 335 U.S. 464, 465 (1948).

154. In fairness to the majority, it is not entirely clear whether the Court was lightly dismissing any claim of sex discrimination under the Equal Protection Clause, or whether it was simply affirming the traditional authority of the states, embodied in the Twenty-first Amendment, to regulate the liquor trade. See, e.g., California v. LaRue, 409 U.S. 109 (1972). Indeed, the state's brief in *Goesaert* argued that "while discriminations against women as such are invalid, discriminations against them in matters relating to intoxicating liquors have consistently been upheld." See Brief for Appellees at 23, Goesaert v. Cleary, 335 U.S. 464 (1948). The opinion appears more concerned with classifications among women than with gender discrimination itself. Id., 467. The Court also opines that the equal protection claim of women is entirely novel, reflecting new "sociological insight[s]" and "shifting social standards." Id., 466.

155. Zorach v. Clauson, 343 U.S. 306, 313 (1952).

156. Marc Galanter, "Religious Freedoms in the United States: A Turning Point?," *Wisconsin Law Review* 1966: 217, 293.

157. Paul G. Kauper, *Religion and the Constitution* (Baton Rouge: Louisiana State University Press, 1964), 21.

158. See, e.g., Abington School District v. Schempp, 374 U.S. 203 (1963).

159. See West Virginia Board of Education v. Barnette, 319 U.S. 624 (1943).

160. See Mark de Wolfe Howe, *The Garden and the Wilderness* (Chicago: University of Chicago Press, 1965) for a discussion of the historical understanding.

161. See, e.g., Paul G. Kauper, "*Schempp* and *Sherbert:* Studies in Neutrality and Accommodation," *Religion and the Public Order* 1963: 3; Donald A. Giannella, "Religious Liberty, Nonestablishment, and Doctrinal Development, Part I: The Religious Liberty Guarantee," *Harvard Law Review* 80 (1967): 1381; Alan Schwartz, "No Imposition of Religion: The Establishment Clause Value," *Yale Law Journal* 77 (1968): 692.

162. See Philip B. Kurland, *Religion and the Law of Church and State and the Supreme Court* (Chicago: Aldine, 1962).

163. Arlan's Department Store v. Kentucky, 371 U.S. 218 (1962) (case dismissed for want of a substantial federal question).

164. Sherbert v. Verner, 374 U.S. 398 (1963).

165. Schwartz, "No Imposition of Religion," supra note 161: 727. See also Wasserstrom, *Philosophy and Social Issues,* supra note 11: 26–27.

166. See, e.g., Braunfeld v. Brown, 366 U.S. 599 (1961).

167. Compare Cleveland v. United States, 329 U.S. 14 (1946) with People v. Woody, 61 Cal. 2d 716, 394 P.2d 813, 40 Cal. Rptr. 69 (1964).

168. See, e.g., United States v. Seeger, 380 U.S. 163 (1965); In re Jenison, 267 Minn. 136, 125 N.W.2d 588 (1963).

169. See Giannella, "Religious Liberty," supra note 161: 1390.

170. See Galanter, "Religious Freedoms," supra note 156: 289–90.

171. Sherbert v. Verner, 374 U.S. 398 (1963). Compare Harris v. McRae, 448 U.S. 297 (1980) (abortion funds).

172. Wisconsin v. Yoder, 406 U.S. 205 (1972).

173. Donald A. Giannella, "Religious Liberty, Nonestablishment, and Doctrinal Development, Part II: The Nonestablishment Principle," *Harvard Law Review* 81 (1968): 513.

174. See generally E. G. West, ed., *Nonpublic School Aid* (Lexington, Mass.: Lexington Books, 1975).

175. Compare Board of Education v. Allen, 392 U.S. 236 (1968); Committee for Public Education v. Regan, 444 U.S. 646 (1980); Wolman v. Walter, 433 U.S. 229 (1977) with Lemon v. Kurtzman, 403 U.S. 602 (1971) and Committee for Public Education v. Nyquist, 413 U.S. 756 (1973).

176. See generally Herma Hill Kay, *Sex-Based Discrimination* (St. Paul: West Publishing, 1981).

177. Schwartz, "No Imposition of Religion," supra note 161: 727.

Chapter 6

1. See, e.g., Ann Corinne Hill, "Protection of Woman Workers and the Courts: A Legal Case History," *Feminist Studies* 5 (1979): 249; Joan Samuelson, "Employment Rights of Women in the Toxic Workplace," *California Law Review* 65 (1977): 1113.

2. See, e.g., Benna F. Armanno, "The Lesbian Mother: Her Right to Child Custody," *Golden Gate Law Review* 4 (1973): 1; Nan Hunter and Nancy Polikoff, "Custody Rights of Lesbian Mothers: Legal Theory and Litigation Strategy," *Buffalo Law Review* 25 (1976): 691.

3. "The choice is not always between some selfish temptation and some obvious responsible course [but] among values that one can be responsible to." Thomas Schelling, "Command and Control," in James McKie, ed., *Social Responsibility and the Business Predicament* (Washington, D.C.: Brookings, 1974), 79.

4. See, e.g., Daniel Yankelovich and Larry Kaagan, "Proposition 13 One Year Later: What It Is and What It Isn't," *Social Policy* 10 (May/June 1979): 19; Robert Kuttner, *Revolt of the Haves: Tax Rebellions and Hard Times* (New York: Simon & Schuster, 1980); Thomas Schelling, "Economic Reasoning and the Ethics of Policy," *Public Interest* 63 (Spring 1981): 37.

5. See generally Zillah Eisenstein, *The Radical Future of Liberal Feminism* (New York: Longman, 1981).

6. Maggie Tripp, ed., *Woman In The Year 2000* (New York: Arbor House, 1974).

7. See Joyce Gelb and Marian Lief Palley, *Women and Public Policies* (Princeton: Princeton University Press, 1982); Anne Costain, "Representing Women: The Transition from Social Movement to Interest Group," in Ellen Boneparth, ed., *Women, Power and Policy* (New York: Pergamon, 1982), 19.

8. See Carol Jaffe, "Why the United States Has No Child-Care Policy," in Irene Diamond, ed., *Families, Politics and Public Policy* (New York: Longman, 1983), 168; Gilbert Steiner, *The Futility of Family Policy* (Washington, D.C.: Brookings, 1981).

9. See Margaret C. Simms, "Women and Housing: The Impact of Government Housing Policy," in Diamond, *Families,* supra note 8: 123; Irene Diamond, "Women and Housing: The Limitations of Liberal Reform," in Boneparth, *Women, Power and Policy,* supra note 7: 109.

10. See chapter 3 for a fuller discussion of this issue.

11. See Sara Evans, *Personal Politics* (New York: Viking, 1980), 203.

12. *Eagle Forum* (December 1980), quoted in Betty Friedan, *The Second Stage* (New York: Summit, 1981), 232–33.

13. Various versions of the Family Protection Act exist. These provisions are taken from Senator Roger Jepsen's version, S. 1378. *Congressional Record,* 17 July 1981, S-6327–44.

14. Richard Nixon, "The President's Message to the Senate Returning S. 2007 Without His Approval," 9 December 1971, *Weekly Compilation of Presidential Documents VII,* 1971: 1634.

15. "Public Opinion Is Catching Up With the Women's Movement," *Washington Post National Weekly Edition,* 25 June 1984, 37.

16. See, e.g., Brigette Berger, "The Helping Hand Strikes Again," *Public Interest* 65 (Fall 1981): 3; Michael Uink, "Abortion and Birth Control in Canton, China," *Wall Street Journal,* 30 November 1981, 14.

17. Compare Friedrich August von Hayek, *The Road to Serfdom* (Chicago: University of Chicago Press, 1944); Robert Nozick, *Anarchy, State, and Utopia* (New York: Basic Books, 1974).

18. See Mark G. Yudof, "Plato's Ideal and the Perversity of Politics," *Michigan Law Review* 81 (1983): 730.

19. Alexander Hamilton, *Federalist Papers,* No. 78.

20. See, e.g., Herbert Wechsler, *Principles, Politics, and Fundamental Law* (Cambridge: Harvard University Press, 1961). Compare Alexander Bickel, *The Supreme Court and the Idea of Progress* (New York: Harper & Row, 1970); Archibald Cox, *The Role of the Supreme Court in American Government* (London: Oxford University Press, 1976); John Hart Ely, *Democracy and Distrust: A Theory of Judicial Review* (Cambridge: Harvard University Press, 1980).

21. See, e.g., Philip C. Bobbitt, *Constitutional Fate* (New York: Oxford University Press, 1982); Lief H. Carter, *Reason in Law* (Boston: Little, Brown, 1979); Edward Levi, *An Introduction to Legal Reasoning* (Chicago: University of Chicago Press, 1949). But see Roberto Unger, "The Critical Legal Studies Movement," *Harvard Law Review* 96 (1983): 561.

22. See generally Herbert A. Simon, *Models of Man: Social and Rational* (New York: Wiley, 1957).

23. See generally H. L. A. Hart, "American Jurisprudence Through English Eyes: The Nightmare and the Noble Dream," *Georgia Law Review* 11 (1977): 969; Kent Greenawalt, "Discretion and Judicial Decision: The Elusive Quest for Fetters that Bind Judges," *Columbia Law Review* 75 (1979): 359. But see Ronald Dworkin, *Taking Rights Seriously* (Cambridge: Harvard University Press, 1977).

24. David Kirp, "Professionalization as a Policy Choice: British Special Education in Comparative Perspective," *World Politics* 34 (1982): 137.

25. See, e.g., Thomas Szasz, *Sex by Prescription* (Garden City, New York: Doubleday, 1981); Barbara Ehrenreich and Deirdre English, *For Her Own Good* (Garden City, New York: Doubleday-Anchor, 1978).

26. Karl Popper, *The Poverty of Historicism* (Boston: Beacon Press, 1957), 67.

27. See Michael Oakeshott, *Rationalism in Politics* (New York: Basic Books, 1962).

28. Popper, *Poverty of Historicism,* supra note 26: 74.

29. David Braybrooke and Charles E. Lindblom, *A Strategy of Decision* (New York: Free Press, 1963); Aaron Wildavsky, *Speaking Truth to Power* (Boston: Little, Brown, 1979).

30. Charles E. Lindblom, *The Policy-Making Process* (Englewood Cliffs, New Jersey: Prentice-Hall, 1980), 36. See also Charles E. Lindblom, "The Politics of 'Muddling Through,'" *Public Administration Review* 19 (1959): 79.

31. Paul Brest, "The Conscientious Legislator's Guide to Constitutional Interpretation," *Stanford Law Review* 27 (1975): 585.

32. See, e.g., George Akerlof, "The Market for 'Lemons': Quality, Uncertainty, and the Market Mechanism," *Quarterly Journal of Economics* 84 (1970): 488. Compare Gary Becker, *The Economics of Discrimination* (Chicago: University of Chicago Press, 1957).

33. Amy Gutmann, *Liberal Equality* (Cambridge: Cambridge University Press, 1980), 11.

34. See, e.g., Charles Lindblom, *Politics and Markets* (New York: Basic Books, 1977).

35. John Stuart Mill, *On Liberty* (1859; reprint, Indianapolis: Hackett, 1978).

36. See generally Gutmann, *Liberal Equality,* supra note 33. Compare Lawrence M. Mead, "Social Programs and Social Obligations," *Public Interest* 69 (Fall 1982): 17.

37. Compare Frank Michelman, "Foreword: On Protecting the Poor Through the Fourteenth Amendment," *Harvard Law Review* 83 (1969): 7; Michael Walzer, *Spheres of Justice* (New York: Basic Books, 1983).

38. Isaiah Berlin, *Four Essays On Liberty* (Oxford: Oxford University Press, 1969), 125.

39. See Mark S. Granovetter, *Getting A Job: A Study of Contacts and Careers* (Cambridge: Harvard University Press, 1974).

40. Research may also lead to greater disagreement by heightening uncertainty. See Charles Lindblom and David Cohen, *Usable Knowledge* (New Haven: Yale University Press, 1979).

41. Jean Bethke Elshtain, *Public Man, Private Woman* (Princeton: Princeton University Press, 1981), 311.

42. R. M. Hare, *Freedom and Reason* (New York: Oxford University Press, 1965), 177. The coercive tenor of the abortion debate is instructively examined in this light.

43. Ronald Dworkin, "Liberalism," in Stuart Hampshire, ed., *Public and Private Morality* (Cambridge: Cambridge University Press, 1978), 113, 117. See also Philip Selznick, *Law, Society, and Industrial Justice* (New York: Russell Sage, 1964).

44. See chapter 7, where the relevance of outcome measures as suggestive of possible denials of opportunity is addressed.

45. Elshtain, *Public Man, Private Woman,* supra note 41: 353.

46. See Owen Fiss, "Groups and the Equal Protection Clause," *Philosophy and Public Affairs* 2 (1976): 107.

47. See, e.g., Robert Fullinwider, *The Reverse Discrimination Controversy* (Totowa, New Jersey: Roman and Littlefield, 1980). Compare Nathan Glazer, *Affirmative Discrimination* (New York: Basic Books, 1975), who would treat evidence that preferential treatment actually reduced the black-white gap as reason to abandon principled opposition to such a policy. See also the discussion of racial discrimination in chapter 2.

48. U.S. Bureau of the Census, *Statistical Abstract of the United States: 1982-83* (Washington, D.C.: Government Printing Office, 1982), table 73.

49. Quoted in Ruth Bader Ginsburg, "Sexual Equality Under the Fourteenth and Equal Rights Amendments," *Washington University Law Quarterly* 1979: 161, 168.

50. Peter Feline, *Him/Her/Self: Sex Roles in Modern America* (New York: Harcourt Brace Jovanovich, 1975).

51. Robert Fullinwider, "The AT&T Case and Affirmative Action," (College Park, Maryland: Center for Philosophy and Public Policy, University of Maryland, 1981), 6.

52. Andrea Altschuler, "Women and the Formulation of Gender Policy in Five Organizations" (unpublished manuscript, 1981).

53. Daniel Yankelovich, *New Rules* (New York: Random House, 1981), 58, 93, 94.

54. Carl Degler, *At Odds* (New York: Oxford University Press, 1980), 418–35.

55. On the changes in men's lives, see Friedan, *The Second Stage,* supra note 12: 125–62.

56. Nora Ephron, *Crazy Salad* (New York: Knopf, 1975), 55.

57. Maren Carden, *The New Feminist Movement* (New York: Russell Sage, 1974).

58. See Frances Ford FitzGerald, "The Triumphs of the New Right," *New York Review of Books* 28 (19 November, 1981), 19.

59. Friedan, *The Second Stage,* supra note 12: 315.

Chapter 7

1. Karl Marx and Friedrich Engels, *Collected Works* (New York: International Publishers, 1975), 3. Adam Smith, *Wealth of Nations* (New York: Modern Library, 1937), 21–22.

2. Carl Degler, *At Odds: Women and the Family in America from the Revolution to the Present* (New York: Oxford University Press, 1980), 422–23.

3. Morris Zelditch, Jr., "Role Differentiation in the Nuclear Family: A Comparative Study," in Talcott Parsons and Robert F. Bales, eds., *Family, Socialization and Interaction Process* (Glencoe, Ill.: Free Press, 1955), 307, 339.

4. Ralph Smith, ed., *The Subtle Revolution: Women At Work* (Washington, D.C.: Urban Institute, 1979). See also Juanita Kreps, *Sex in the Marketplace* (Baltimore: Johns Hopkins University Press, 1971).

For a historical treatment, see Robert Smuts, *Women and Work In America* (New York: Columbia University Press, 1959); William Chafe, *The American Woman* (London: Oxford University Press, 1972).

5. Degler, *At Odds,* supra note 2: 433.

6. Linda Waite, "U.S. Women at Work," *Population Bulletin* 36, (May 1981): 2, 7. This decline is only partially explicable by growing unemployment.

7. The statistics are drawn from Waite, "Women at Work," supra note 6; Smith, *Subtle Revolution,* supra note 4; Degler, *At Odds,* supra note 2.

8. Waite, "Women at Work," supra note 6: 4.

9. Smith, *Subtle Revolution,* supra note 4: 1.

10. Mary Joe Bane, *Here to Stay* (New York: Basic Books, 1976).

11. Waite, "Women at Work," supra note 6: 4.

12. Stanley Lebergott, *Manpower in Economic Growth* (New York: McGraw-Hill, 1964).

13. T. Aldrich Finegan, "Participation of Married Women in the Labor Force," in Cynthia B. Lloyd, ed. *Sex, Discrimination, and the Division of Labor* (New York: Columbia University Press, 1975), 36.

14. See Gary Becker, *A Treatise on the Family* (Cambridge: Harvard University Press, 1981).

15. See Valerie Oppenheimer, *The Female Labor Force in the United States* (Berkeley: Institute of Population Studies, 1970), 157.

16. See Chafe, *American Woman,* supra note 4; Smith, *Subtle Revolution,* supra note 4.

Worker protection remains an issue, particularly as attention is drawn to the dangers to pregnant women of toxic substances. See Note, "Employment Rights of Women in the Toxic Workplace," *California Law Review* 65 (1977): 1113; Vilma Hunt, "A Brief History of Women Workers and Hazards in the Workplace," *Feminist Studies* 5 (1979): 274.

17. See Edith Abbott, *Women in Industry* (New York: Arno, 1969); Ruth Blumrosen, "Wage Discrimination, Job Segregation, and Title VII of the Civil Rights Act of 1964," *Michigan Journal of Law Reform* 12 (1979): 397, 421–28.

18. Paul Burstein, "Equal Employment Opportunity Legislation and the Income of Women and Nonwhites," *American Sociological Review* 44 (1979): 367, 380.

19. Lester Thurow, "Why Women Are Paid Less Than Men," *New York Times,* 8 March, 1981.

20. Zelditch, "Role Differentiation," supra note 3.

21. See chapter 6.

22. See George Gilder, *Wealth and Poverty* (New York: Basic Books, 1981).

23. Heidi Hartmann, "Capitalism, Patriarchy and Job Segregation By Sex," in Martha Blaxall and Barbara Reagan, eds., *Women and the Workplace* (Chicago: University of Chicago Press, 1976), 137.

24. This research is summarized in Cynthia Lloyd and Beth Niemi, *The Economics of Sex Differentials* (New York: Columbia University Press, 1979), 232–39.

25. See Joan Talbert and Christine Bose, "Wage Attainment Processes: The Retail Clerk Case," *American Journal of Sociology* 33 (1977): 403.

26. In 1968, for instance, the income of two-earner black families was 73 percent as large as similar white families; by 1981, that figure had risen to 84 percent. Factors such as the increase of female-headed black households and the increasing unemployment rates for black males have depressed overall black incomes, however. *New York Times,* 18 July 1983.

Between 1980 and 1984, however, the male-female earnings gap narrowed: the average working woman, who in 1980 earned 60 percent of what a man did, earned 64 percent in 1984. James Smith and Michael Ward, *Women's Wages and Work in the Twentieth Century* (Santa Monica: Rand Corp., 1984).

27. Barbara Bergmann, "The Effect on White Incomes of Discrimination in Employment," *Journal of Political Economy* 79 (1971): 294.

28. Thurow, "Why Women are Paid Less," supra note 19.

29. See generally Greg Duncan, et al., *Years of Poverty, Years of Plenty: The Changing Economic Factors of American Workers and Families* (Ann Arbor: University of Michigan Survey Research Center, 1984), 153–72.

30. See, e.g., B. G. Malkiel and J. A. Malkiel, "Male-Female Pay Differentials In Professional Employment," *American Economic Review* 63 (1973): 693.

31. See, e.g., Gary Becker, *Human Capital: A Theoretical and Empirical Analysis, With Specific Reference to Education* (New York: National Bureau of Economic Research, 1975).

32. See, e.g., Mary Corcoran and Gregory Duncan, "Work History, Labor Force Attachment, and Earnings Differences Between the Races and Sexes," *Journal of Human Resources* 14 (1979): 3; Jacob Mincer and Solomon Polachek, "Family Investments in Human Capital: Earnings of Women," *Journal of Political Economics* 82 (Part 2, March/April 1974): 76.

33. See, e.g., Gary Brown, "How Type of Employment Affects Earnings Difference by Sex," *Monthly Labor Review* 99 (July 1976): 25.

34. Nancy S. Barrett, "Women in the Job Market: Occupations, Earnings, and Career Opportunities," in Smith, *Subtle Revolution,* supra note 4: 41–42.

35. Mincer and Polachek, "Family Investments," supra note 32. This pattern appears to be changing. See Isabel Sawhill, "The Economics of Segregation Against Women: Some New Findings," *Journal of Human Resources* 8 (1973): 383.

36. Dixie Sommers, "Occupational Rankings for Men and Women by Earnings," *Monthly Labor Review* 97 (August 1974): 34.

37. Edward Lazear, "Male-Female Wage Differentials: Has the Government Had Any Effect?" in Cynthia Lloyd, Emily Andrews, and Curtis Gilroy, eds., *Women in the Labor Market* (New York: Columbia University Press, 1979).

38. Waite, "Women at Work," supra note 6: 26.

39. U.S. Department of Labor, Bureau of Labor Statistics, *Perspectives on Working Women* (October 1980), 10.

40. Degler, *At Odds*, supra note 2: 423.

41. Donald Treiman and Kermit Terrell, "Women, Work, and Wages—Trends in the Female Occupational Structure since 1940," in Kenneth Land and Seymour Spilerman, eds., *Social Indicator Models* (New York: Russell Sage, 1975), 157.
See also, U.S. Commission on Civil Rights, *Social Indicators of Equality for Minorities and Women* (Washington, D.C.: U.S. Commission on Civil Rights, 1978).

42. U.S. Department of Labor, Bureau of Labor Statistics, *Employment and Earnings* 25 (1978): 153.

43. Gary Becker, *Economics of Discrimination* (Chicago: University of Chicago Press, 1957).

44. See Janice Madden, *The Economics of Sex Discrimination*, (Lexington: D. C. Heath, 1973); Barbara Bergmann, "Occupational Segregation, Wages and Profits When Employers Discriminate by Race or Sex," *Eastern Economic Journal* (1974): 103; Barbara Bergmann, "Reducing the Pervasiveness of Discrimination," in Eli Ginzberg, ed., *Jobs for Americans* (Englewood Cliffs, New Jersey: Prentice-Hall, 1976).

45. Jean Blumen, "Toward a Homosocial Theory of Sex Roles: An Explanation of the Sex Segregation of Social Institution," in Blaxall and Reagan, *Women and the Workplace*, supra note 23.

46. See, e.g., Lillian Breslow Rubin, *Worlds of Pain* (New York: Basic Books, 1976).

47. See, e.g., Peter Doeringer and Michael Piore, *Internal Labor Markets and Manpower Analysis* (Lexington: D. C. Heath, 1971); Francine Blau and Carol Jusenius, "Economists' Approaches to Sex Segregation in the Labor Market: An Appraisal," Blaxall and Reagan *Women and the Workplace*, supra note 23; 181.

48. See, e.g., Richard Edwards, *Contested Terrain: The Transformation of the Marketplace in America* (New York: Basic Books, 1979).

49. Donald Treiman and Heidi Hartmann, eds., *Women, Work, and Wages* (Washington, D.C.: National Academy Press, 1981), 52.

50. Rosabeth Moss Kanter, *Men and Women of the Corporation* (New York: Basic Books, 1977).

51. See Edmund Phelps, "The Statistical Theory of Racism and Sexism," *American Economic Review* 62 (1972): 659; Henry Aaron, *Politics and the Professors* (Washington, D.C.: Brookings, 1978), 46–48.

52. This discussion borrows generally from Degler, *At Odds*, supra note 2.

53. Waite, "Women at Work," supra note 6: 9.

54. Barrett, "Women in the Job Market," supra note 34: 53.

55. Waite, "Women at Work," supra note 6: 12; but see Clair Vickery, "The Time-Poor: A New Look At Poverty," *Journal of Human Resources* 12 (1977): 27.

56. Barrett, "Women in the Job Market," supra note 34: 31, 52.

57. U.S. Department of Labor, *Perspectives on Working Women*, supra note 39:10.

58. Cynthia Fuchs Epstein, *Woman's Place: Options and Limits in Professional Careers* (Berkeley: University of California Press, 1970), 16.

59. Waite, "Women at Work," supra note 6: 24. Twenty percent of the women between the ages of twenty-five and fifty-four, but just 2 percent of the men in this age bracket, work part-time.

60. These data are drawn from Pamela Spratlen, "Work Time Options and Government Policy" (unpublished master's thesis, University of California, Berkeley, 1981).

61. See Mary Jo Frug, "Securing Job Equality for Women: Labor Market Hostility to Working Mothers," *Boston University Law Review* 59 (1979): 55, 98.

62. A study by the Massachusetts Department of Social Services revealed that half-time social workers carried 54% of an average case load and had a much lower attrition rate than full-time workers. *Exploitation from 9 to 5: Report of the Twentieth Century Fund Task Force on Women and Employment* (Lexington, Mass.: Lexington Books, 1975).

63. Arlie Hochschild, "Inside the Clockwork of Male Careers," in Florence Howe, ed., *Women and the Power to Change* (New York: McGraw-Hill, 1975); see also Robert Lekachman, "On Economic Equality," *Signs* 1 (1975), 93.

64. Hochschild, "Male Careers," supra note 63: 49.

65. Ibid., 73.

66. Gilder, *Wealth and Poverty*, supra note 22: 131–32.

67. See, e.g., Phillips v. Martin Marietta Corporation, 400 U.S. 542 (1971); Diaz v. Pan American World Airways, 442 F. 2d 385 (5th Cir. 1971).

Sexual harassment too is covered by equal opportunity laws. See, e.g., Barnes v. Castle, 561 F. 2d 983 (D.C. Cir. 1977); Catherine MacKinnon, *Sexual Harassment of Working Women* (New Haven: Yale University Press, 1979).

68. See Nijole Benokratis and Joe Feagin, *Affirmative Action and Equal Opportunity* (Boulder, Colo.: Westview Press, 1978).

69. In 1975, the EEOC spent over $56 million to bring over 33,000 actionable charges of race discrimination and over 20,000 actionable charges of sex discrimination. In the same year, over $26 million of wage underpayments were disclosed. See Burstein, "Equal Employment Opportunity Legislation," supra note 18:380.

70. See Nadine Taub, "Keeping Women in Their Place: Stereotyping Per Se as a Form of Employment Discrimination," *Boston College Law Review* 21 (1980): 345; Rhonda R. Rivera, "Our Straight-Laced Judges: The Legal Position of Homosexual Persons in the United States," *Hastings Law Journal* 30 (1979): 799; Herma Hill Kay, *Sex-Based Discrimination* (St. Paul: West Publishing, 1981), 484–535.

71. Quoted in *Congressional Quarterly*, 12 September 1981, 1749.

72. Quoted in Lester Sobel, ed., *Quotas and Affirmative Action* (New York: Facts On File, 1980), 5.

The literature on affirmative action is voluminous. Philosophical treatments include Robert Fullinwider, *The Reverse Discrimination Controversy* (Totowa, New Jersey: Rowman and Littlefield, 1980); Alan Goldman, *Justices and Reverse Discrimination* (Princeton: Princeton University Press, 1979); Marshall Cohen, Thomas Nagel, and Thomas Scanlon, eds., *Equality and Preferential Treatment* (Princeton: Princeton University Press, 1977); Barry Gross, *Discrimination In Reverse* (New York: New York University Press, 1978). Political and economic analyses include Richard Lester, *Reasoning About Discrimination* (Princeton: Princeton University Press, 1980) and Nathan Glazer, *Affirmative Discrimination* (New York: Basic Books, 1978).

73. See, e.g., William Bennett and Terry Eastland, *Counting By Race* (New York: Basic Books, 1979); John Livingston, *Fair Game* (San Francisco: W. H. Freeman, 1979).

74. See, e.g., Carl Hoffman and John Shelton Reed, "The XYZ Affair," *Public Interest* 62 (Winter 1981): 21.

75. Francine Blau Weiskopf, "Women's Place in the Labor Market," *American Economic Review* 62 (1972): 161–66.

76. Estelle James, "Income and Employment Effects of Women's Liberation," in Lloyd, *Sex, Discrimination,* supra note 13: 379.

77. Alfred Blumrosen, "Quotas, Common Sense and Laws in Labor Relations: Three Dimensions of Equal Opportunity," *Rutgers Law Review* 27 (1974): 675.

78. See Department of Labor Regulations in Federal Register, Vol. 36, No. 234, 6 December 1971: 10, 60–62.

79. Stanley Pottinger, "The Drive Toward Equality," *Change* 4 (October 1972): 24, 27.

80. Leonard Reed, "When Fairness Turns Unfair: Are Quotas Edging Out Quality," *This World,* 1 February 1981, 1.

81. See Sobel, *Quotas,* supra note 72: 115, 134, 176–78.

82. EEOC v. AT&T, 365 F. Supp. 1105, 1108 (E. D. Penn, 1973).

83. The AT&T case has been discussed in Phyllis Wallace, ed., *Equal Employment Opportunity and the AT&T Case* (Cambridge: MIT Press, 1976); Herbert Northrup and John Larson, *The Impact of the AT&T-EEOC Consent Decree* (Philadelphia: The Wharton School, University of Pennsylvania, 1979); and Robert Fullinwider, "The AT&T Case and Affirmative Action," (College Park, Maryland: Center for Philosophy and Public Policy, University of Maryland, 1981).

For background on the company, see Elinore Langer, "Inside the New York Telephone Company," *New York Review of Books,* 12 March 1970.

84. Fullinwider, "AT&T Case ," supra note 83: 4.

85. Northrup, "AT&T-EEOC Consent Decree," supra note 83: 41–44.

86. Fullinwider, "AT&T Case," supra note 83: 6.

87. Northrup, "AT&T-EEOC Consent Decree," supra note 83: 52.

88. Ibid., 58–60.

89. Ibid., 78.

90. Fullinwider, "AT&T Case," supra note 83: 9.

91. Northrup, "AT&T-EEOC Consent Decree," supra note 83: 3.

92. Ibid., 232.

93. Louis Ferman, *The Negro and Equal Employment Opportunities: A Review of Management Experiences in Twenty Companies* (New York: Praeger, 1968), makes this point with respect to race.

94. Aaron, *Politics and the Professors,* supra note 51: 48.

95. Ruth Shaeffer and Edith Lynton, *Corporate Experiences in Improving Women's Job Opportunities* (New York: The Conference Board, 1979).

96. Barrett, "Women in the Job Market," supra note 34: 52.

97. U.S. Department of Labor, "Trends in Women's Employment and Training in Selected Professions" (February 1976).

98. Shaeffer and Lynton, *Corporate Experiences,* supra note 95: 21.

99. Sidney Hook, *Philosophy and Public Policy* (Carbondale: Southern Illinois University Press, 1980), 145.

100. See, e.g., Barbara Bergmann and Jill King, "Diagnosing Discrimination," in Wallace, *Equal Employment Opportunity,* supra note 83: 49; Kanter, *Men and Women of the Corporation,* supra note 50.

101. See James Rachels, "What People Deserve," in John Arthur and William Shaw, eds., *Justice and Economic Distribution* (Englewood Cliffs, New Jersey: Prentice-Hall, 1978), 155; see generally Joel Feinberg, *Doing and Deserving* (Princeton: Princeton University Press, 1970).

102. Gross, *Discrimination in Reverse,* supra note 72: 121.

103. Benokratis and Feagin, *Affirmative Action,* supra note 68: 211. Compare Janet Richards, *The Sceptical Feminist* (London: Routledge & Kegan Paul, 1980), 111–12, who argues unpersuasively that quality should sometimes be sacrificed in order to improve the position of women; Richards picks the particularly unfortunate example of medicine to make her point.

104. See generally Goldman, *Justices and Reverse Discrimination,* supra note 72.

105. Carol Krucoff, "Money: The Question of Men, Women, and 'Comparable Worth'," *Washington Post,* 13 November 1979.

106. Christensen v. Iowa, 563 F. 2d 353 (1977).

107. Carolyn Powers, "The Same Pay for Different Jobs," *Washington Post National Weekly Edition,* 6 August 1984, 9.

108. See Treiman and Hartmann, *Women, Work, and Wages,* supra note 49.

109. Eleanor Holmes Norton, ex-chairman of the EEOC, quoted in the *Wall Street Journal,* 15 September 1981.

110. Christensen v. Iowa, 563 F. 2d. 353, 356 (8th Cir. 1977).

111. County of Washington v. Gunther, 452 U.S. 161 (1981).

112. American Federation of State, County and Municipal Employees v. Washington, 578 F.Supp. 846 (W.D., Washington, 1983).

113. Ernest McCormick, "Minority Report," in Treiman and Hartmann, *Women, Work, and Wages,* supra note 49: 115, 118.

114. Adam Smith, *The Wealth of Nations* (London: Book I, C.V. 1776), quoted in George Milkovich, "The Emerging Debate," in Robert Livernash, ed., *Comparable Worth: Issues and Alternatives* (Washington, D.C.: Equal Employment Advisory Council, 1980), 25, 34.

115. Treiman and Hartmann, *Women, Work, and Wages,* supra note 49.

116. Lee Smith, "The EEOC's Bold Foray into Job Evaluation," *Fortune,* 11 September 1978, 59, 60.

117. See, e.g., Robert Lucas, "Hedonic Wage Equations and Psychic Wages in the Returns to Schooling," *American Economic Review* 67 (1977): 549; Robert Smith, "Competing Wage Differentials and Public Policy: A Review," *Industrial and Labor Relations Review* 32 (1979): 339.

118. George Hildebrand, "The Market System," in Livernash, *Comparable Worth,* supra note 114: 81, 95. As Blumrosen, "Wage Discrimination," supra note 17, points out, this difficulty may be finessed by erecting a legal presumption that the fact of lower wages in a female-dominated field reveals discrimination, but that lawyers' gambit substitutes *force majeur* for analysis.

119. "The New Pay Push for Women," *Business Week,* 17 December 1979, 69.

120. Only if the principle of equal pay for work of comparable worth became a truly national norm might some of these consequences be alleviated, but that prospect evokes its own nightmarish implications. The price tag for implementing comparable worth across the board by levelling up, conservatively estimated at 150 billion dollars, should give one pause; so too should the nature of the regulatory apparatus required to implement this policy. A mammoth federal bureaucracy would have to be installed to administer a costly and inefficient scheme.

121. U.S. Department of Labor, *Perspectives on Working Women,* supra note 39.

122. Nearly half the students in the Reform Jewish Seminaries are women; until the late 1960s, there were no female rabbinical students. Andrea Altschuler, "Women and the Formulation of Gender Policy in Five Organizations" (unpublished manuscript, 1981).

123. Corcoran and Duncan, "Work History," supra note 32. But compare Duncan, *Years of Poverty*, supra note 29.

Chapter 8

1. Quoted in Barbara A. Burnett, "Family Economic Integrity Under the Social Security System," *New York University Review of Law and Social Change* 7 (1978): 155.

2. See Gilbert Steiner, *The Futility of Family Policy* (Washington, D.C.: Brookings, 1981). Compare Steiner's earlier, more optimistic assessment of family policy, *The Children's Cause* (Washington, D.C.: Brookings, 1976).

3. Jessie Bernard, *Women and The Public Interest* (Chicago: Aldine, 1971), 57.

4. See Sheila B. Kamerman and Alfred J. Kahn, eds., *Family Policy: Government and Family in Fourteen Countries* (New York: Columbia University Press, 1978); Judith Stacey, "When Patriarchy Kowtows: The Significance of the Chinese Family Revolution," in Zillah Eisenstein, ed., *Capitalist Patriarchy and the Case for Socialist Feminism* (New York: Monthly Review Press, 1979).

5. Halcyone Bohen and Anamarie Viverds-Long, *Balancing Jobs and Family Life* (Philadelphia: Temple University Press, 1981), xi.

6. The data are drawn from Bureau of the Census, *Population Profile of the U.S.: 1980* (Washington, D.C.: Department of Commerce, 1981). See also Sar A. Levitan and Richard S. Belous, *What's Happening to the American Family?* (Baltimore: Johns Hopkins University Press, 1981).

7. The phenomenon of the woman-headed household may not represent a choice made by the woman, particularly when the proportion of such households is as high as it is in the black community, where 41.7 percent of all family heads are female. U.S. Bureau of the Census, *Statistical Abstract of the United States: 1982–83* (Washington, D.C.: Government Printing Office, 1982), table 73.

8. Social scientists have traditionally treated living alone as psychologically harmful, but recent evidence is to the contrary. See Michael Hughes and Walter R. Grove, "Living Alone, Social Integration, and Mental Health," *American Journal of Sociology* 87 (1981): 48.

9. See, e.g., Emile Durkheim, *Suicide* (New York: Free Press, 1966).

10. See David A. J. Richards, "The Individual, The Family, and The Constitution: A Jurisprudential Perspective," *New York University Law Review* 55 (1980): 1.

11. See David A. J. Richards, "Sexual Autonomy and the Constitutional Right to Privacy: A Case Study in Human Rights and the Unwritten Constitution," *Hastings Law Journal* 30 (1979): 957.

12. Compare Bellotti v. Baird, 443 U.S. 622 (1979); H. L. v. Matheson, 450 U.S. 398 (1981). See Nanette Dembitz, "The Supreme Court and a Minor's Abortion Decision," *Columbia Law Review* 80 (1980): 1251; Note, "Parent vs. Child: H. L. v. Matheson and the New Abortion Legislation," *Wisconsin Law Review* (1982): 75.

13. See generally Leo Kanowitz, *Women and the Law: The Unfinished Revolution* (Albuquerque: University of New Mexico Press, 1969).

14. Blair v. Blair, 199 Md. 9, 14; 85 A. 2d 442, 445 (1952); see generally, Kanowitz, *Women and the Law*, supra note 13: 46–52.

15. See generally Kenneth Karst, " 'A Discrimination So Trivial': A Note on Law and the Symbolism of Women's Dependency," *Ohio State Law Journal* 35 (1974): 546.

16. Compare Walter Barnette, *Sexual Freedom and the Constitution* (Albuquerque: Uni-

versity of New Mexico Press, 1973), with J. Harvie Wilkinson, III and G. Edward White, "Constitutional Protection for Personal Lifestyles," *Cornell Law Review* 62 (1977): 563.

17. See Marjorie Maguire Schultz, "Contractual Ordering of Marriage: A New Model for State Policy," *California Law Review* 70 (1982): 204; Lenore J. Weitzman, "Legal Regulation of Marriage: Tradition and Change," *California Law Review* 62 (1974): 1169.

18. Schultz, "Marriage," supra note 17: 209. Compare Gary Becker, *A Treatise on the Family* (Cambridge: Harvard University Press, 1981).

19. See generally Isaiah Berlin, "Two Concepts of Liberty," in *Four Essays on Liberty* (Oxford: Oxford University Press, 1969).

20. Compare Schultz, "Marriage," supra note 17: 213–19.

21. Kenneth Karst, "The Freedom of Intimate Association," *Yale Law Journal* 89 (1980): 624, 640.

22. Lynne Carol Halem, *Divorce Reform* (New York: Free Press, 1980), 238–69.

23. Herma Hill Kay, "A Family Court: The California Proposal," in Paul Bohannan, ed., *Divorce and After* (Garden City, New York: Doubleday, 1970), 243, 279.

24. See Robert Mnookin and Lewis Kornhauser, "Bargaining in the Shadow of the Law: The Case of Divorce," *Yale Law Journal* 88 (1979): 950.

25. Arthur Norton and Paul Glick, "Martial Instability: Past, Present and Future," *Journal of Social Issues* 32 (1976): 5.

26. Doris Freed and Henry Foster, "Divorce in the Fifty States: An Overview," *Family Law Quarterly* 14 (1981): 299.

27. See Henry Foster, "Alimony Awards," in *Economics of Divorce: A Collection of Papers Prepared by the Section of Family Law, American Bar Association* (Chicago: American Bar Association, 1978).

28. See Orr v. Orr, 440 U.S. 268 (1979).

29. Lenore Weitzman and Ruth Dixon, "The Alimony Myth: Does No-Fault Divorce Make a Difference?" *Family Law Quarterly* 14 (1980): 141, 150, 166.

30. Ibid., 170, 164.

31. Stuart S. Nagel and Lenore J. Weitzman, "Women as Litigants," *Hastings Law Journal* 23 (1971): 171.

32. See, e.g., In re Marriage of Morrison, 20 Cal.3d 437, 573 P.2d 41 (1978), Lash v. Lash, 307 So.2d 241 (1975).

33. An alimony system that gave divorcing spouses "drawing rights" on social insurance to which everyone contributed, proposed by Jessie Bernard, *Women, Wives, Mothers: Values and Options* (Chicago: Aldine, 1975), 273–76, exaggerates this tendency to subsidize a preference for dependency, and so has little to commend it.

34. But compare Gary Becker, *Treatise on the Family*, supra note 18.

35. See Mnookin and Kornhauser, "Bargaining," supra note 24.

36. In re Marriage of Brantner, 67 Cal. App. 3d 416, 420 (1977).

37. Compare Nancy Chodorow, *The Reproduction of Mothering* (Berkeley: University of California Press, 1978) with Alice Rossi, "A Biosocial Perspective on Parenting," *Daedalus* 106 (Spring 1977): 1.

38. See James Levine, *Who Will Raise the Children? New Options for Fathers and Mothers* (Philadelphia: Lippincott, 1976).

39. See, e.g., Salk v. Salk, 385 N.Y.S. 2d 1015 (1976); Henry Foster and Doris Freed, "Life with Father: 1978," *Family Law Quarterly* 11 (1978): 321, 330; Freed and Foster, "Divorce," supra note 26.

40. Lenore Weitzman and Ruth Dixon, "Child Custody Awards: Legal Standards and

Empirical Patterns for Child Custody, Support and Visitation After Divorce," *University of California Davis Law Review* 12 (1979): 472, 504–507. Compare Nancy Polikoff, "Gender and Child Custody Determinations: Exploding the Myths," in Irene Diamond, ed., *Families, Politics and Public Policy* (New York: Longman, 1983), 183.

41. Arends v. Arends, 30 Utah 2d 328, 329, 517 P. 2d 1019, 1020 (1974).

42. U.S. Bureau of the Census, *Population Profile of the United States: 1980* (Washington, D.C.: Department of Commerce, 1981), 20.

The fledgling men's liberation movement is part of this transformation. See Ira Victor and Win Ann Winkler, *Fathers and Custody* (New York: Hawthorne, 1977), 74–77.

43. Weitzman and Dixon, "Child Custody Awards," supra note 40: 518–19.

44. See, e.g., Nan Hunter and Nancy Polikoff, "Custody Rights of Lesbian Mothers: Legal Theory and Litigation Strategy," *Buffalo Law Review* 25 (1976): 691.

45. Robert Mnookin, "Child Custody Adjudication: Judicial Functions in the Face of Indeterminacy," *Law and Contemporary Problems* 39 (1975): 226; Laurence Tribe, "Childhood, Suspect Classification, and Conclusive Presumptions: Three Linked Riddles," *Law and Contemporary Problems* 39 (1975): 8.

46. See Joseph Goldstein, Anna Freud, and Albert Solnit, *Beyond the Best Interests of the Child* (New York: Free Press, 1973).

47. George Cooper, *A Voluntary Tax: New Perspectives on Sophisticated Estate Tax Avoidance* (Washington, D.C.: Brookings, 1979).

48. Harvey Rosen, "Is It Time to Abandon Joint Filing?" *National Tax Journal* 30 (1977): 423; Pamela Gann, "Abandoning Marital Status as a Factor in Allocating Income Tax Burdens," *Texas Law Review* 59 (1980): 1.

49. See generally Boris Bittker, "Federal Income Taxation and the Family," *Stanford Law Review* 27 (1975): 1389.

50. Married persons may file individual returns but these are treated differently from returns filed by the unmarried. These separate returns have a rate schedule higher than the joint schedule.

51. See generally Joint Committee on Taxation, 96th Congress, 2d Session, Staff Report, *The Income Tax Treatment of Married Couples and Single Persons* (Washington, D.C.: Government Printing Office, 1980).

The tax law gave some couples a marriage bonus—24 million joint returns enjoyed a $19 billion bonus—even as it penalized other couples—16 million joint returns were out of pocket $8.3 billion.

52. See Clair Vickery, "The Time Poor: A New Look at Poverty," *Journal of Human Resources* 12 (1977): 27.

53. Lynda Sands Moerschbaecher, "The Marriage Penalty and the Divorce Bonus: A Comparative Examination of the Current Legislative Tax Proposals," *Review of Taxation of Individuals* 5 (1981): 133, 135.

54. See generally *Report of the Royal Commission on Taxation* (Ottawa: Queen's Printer, 1966).

55. This burden was eased but not eliminated by the 1981 amendments to the tax code.

56. Compare Glen G. Cain and Harold W. Watts, eds., *Income Maintenance and Labor Supply* (Chicago: Rand McNally, 1973) with Masao Nakamura, Alice Nakamura, and Dallas Cullen, "Job Opportunities, the Offered Wage, and the Labor Supply of Married Women," *American Economic Review* 69 (1979): 787.

57. See Gann, "Marital Status," supra note 48: 32–39.

58. See Carol Jaffe, "Why the United States Has No Child Care Policy," in Diamond, *Families,* supra note 40: 128.

59. Alice Rossi, "Equality Between the Sexes: An Immodest Proposal," *Daedalus* 93 (Spring 1964): 607, 633.

60. Linda Waite, "U.S. Woman at Work," *Population Bulletin,* 36 (May 1981): 2, 7.

61. Susanne H. Woolsey, "Pied Piper Politics and the Child-Care Debate," *Daedalus* 106 (1977): 127.

62. Shelia B. Kamerman, *Parenting In An Unresponsive Society* (New York: Free Press, 1980).

63. Mary Jo Bane, et al., "Child-care Arrangements of Working Parents," *Monthly Labor Review* 102 (October, 1979): 50, 54.

64. U.S. Senate, Senate Committee on Finance, *Child Care: Data and Materials* (Washington, D.C.: Government Printing Office, 1974).

65. See Shelia Kamerman and Alfred Kahn, *Child Care, Family Benefits and Working Parents* (New York: Columbia University Press, 1981).

66. "Statement of the National Women's Conference: National Plan of Action," reprinted in Stevanne Auerbach, *Confronting the Child Care Crisis* (Boston: Beacon Press, 1979), 99–100.

67. Woolsey, "Child Care Debate," supra note 61: 141.

68. Richard Nixon, "The President's Message to the Senate Returning S. 2007 Without His Approval," 9 December 1971, *Weekly Compilation of Presidential Documents VII* (1971): 1634.

69. Selma Fraiberg, *Every Child's Birthright: In Defense of Mothering* (New York: Basic Books, 1977); Alice Rossi, "Parenting," supra note 37.

70. Woolsey, "Child Care Debate," supra note 61: 142.

71. Ibid., 134.

72. Kamerman and Kahn, *Child Care,* supra note 65: 48.

73. Meredith Larson and James Marver, "Public Policy Toward Child Care in America: A Historical Perspective," in Philip K. Robins and Samuel Weiner, eds., *Child Care and Public Policy* (Lexington: D.C. Heath, 1978).

74. Brigette Berger, "The Helping Hand Strikes Again," *Public Interest* 65 (Fall 1981): 113.

75. Betty Friedan, *The Second Stage* (New York: Summit, 1980); Jean Bethke Elshtain, *Public Man, Private Woman* (Princeton: Princeton University Press, 1981).

76. See, e.g., Shulamith Firestone, *The Dialectic of Sex* (New York: Morrow, 1970); Mary Daly, *Gyn/Ecology* (Boston: Beacon Press, 1978).

77. See, e.g., Carol Lopate, "Pay for Housework?" *Social Policy* 5 (September/October, 1974): 27; Myra Marx Ferree, "Housework: Rethinking the Costs and Benefits," in Diamond, *Families,* supra note 40: 148.

78. Sir Henry Maine, *Ancient Law* (1861; reprint, Boston: Beacon Press, 1963) traces the progression of societies from status-based to contract-based.

79. For a history of the social security system, see George E. Rejda, *Social Insurance and Economic Security* (Englewood Cliffs, New Jersey: Prentice-Hall, 1976).

80. For examples illustrating this and other inequities, see Grace Gan Blumberg, "Adult Derivative Benefits in Social Security," *Stanford Law Review* 32 (1980): 233.

81. Ibid., 243–46.

82. In addition to the unfairnesses chronicled above, the benefit calculation can produce irrational results. For instance, a woman who married a worker three years before he dies is as eligible for retirement or survivor benefits as someone who has been living with her spouse for twenty years. The system extends benefits to those who may have had no relationship with the worker for some time: for instance, to a wife who has not lived with her husband for many

years, but who never went through a formal divorce. If the worker has since lived with a woman who is dependent on him when he dies—or worse, who has married him, thinking that he had divorced his first wife—she will have no claim for entitlement.

See Peter W. Martin, "Social Security Benefits for Spouses," *Cornell Law Review* 63 (1978): 789.

83. This point ignores the problem of women earning less, on average, than men.

84. For descriptions of typical income splitting schemes, see "Men and Women: Changing Roles and Social Security," *Social Security Bulletin* 42 (May 1979): 25; Martha Derthick, *Policymaking for Social Security* (Washington, D.C.: Brookings, 1979); Advisory Council on Social Security, *Social Security Financing and Benefits* (1979); Blumberg, "Derivative Benefits," supra note 80: 279–80. Blumberg points out the problem with tying splitting to the filing of a joint tax statement, namely, that one spouse will refuse to file.

85. Perhaps a simpler solution than income splitting is to base benefits on fewer years of earnings—for instance, on the twenty years with the highest earnings.

86. Blumberg, "Derivative Benefits," supra note 80: 261–64.

87. Pension systems have inequities of their own, which have only recently been addressed. The Retirement Equity Act, passed by Congress in 1984, requires the consent of the dependent spouse before pension survivors' benefits can be waived by a worker, and allows employees to take time off from work without losing pension credit for earlier service.

88. For historical and crosscultural discussions of the family, see, e.g., William Stephens, *The Family in Cross-Cultural Perspective* (New York: Holt, Rinehart, & Winston, 1963); Carl Degler, *At Odds: Women and the Family in America from the Revolution to the Present* (New York: Oxford University Press, 1980); Edward Shorter, *The Making of the Modern Family* (New York: Basic Books, 1975); Lawrence Stone, *The Family, Sex and the Marriage in England: 1500–1800* (New York: Harper & Row, 1977).

89. Degler, *At Odds,* supra note 88: vi–vii.

90. This discussion draws on Lionel Tiger and Joseph Shepher, *Women in the Kibbutz* (New York: Harcourt Brace Jovanovich, 1975), and Melford Spiro, *Gender and Culture: Kibbutz Women Revisited* (Durham: Duke University Press, 1979).

91. Spiro, *Gender and Culture,* supra note 90: 56.

92. Ibid., 31.

93. Kenneth Kenniston, et al., *All Our Children: The American Family Under Pressure* (New York: Harcourt Brace Jovanovich, 1977); Mary Jo Bane, *Here To Stay* (New York: Basic Books, 1976); Christopher Lasch, *Haven In a Heartless World* (New York: Basic Books, 1977).

94. Daniel Yankelovich, *New Rules* (New York: Random House, 1981), 100.

Index

Abortion, 2, 108–11; and Hyde Amendment, 220 n.100
Adkins v. Children's Hospital of the District of Columbia, 39, 119–20
Affirmative action, 25, 233 n.72; process, as focus of, 159, 162, 164–65; as result oriented, 160, 167; consent decrees, 161; AT&T case, 161–66
AFL-CIO, 40–41, 168
Aid to Families with Dependent Children (AFDC), 192
Alimony, 94, 177, 181–83, 199, 237 n.33; and gender justice, 89; women-only rule, 102
Arendt, Hannah, 29
Authority: decision-making, and collective good, 33; of husband over wife, 32–33; of laws and institutions, 14; J. S. Mill on, of state, 32; and paternalism, 34; systems of, 73; and tradition, 29; women in positions of, 148, 150
Autonomy, 101, 111; children's claims to, 176; and choice, 13, 16, 69, 80; and equal liberty, 105; and gender policy, 124; and individuals, 15, 98, 113; in public vs. private spheres, 27; and quotas, 166; in society, 14, 87–88

Barber, Benjamin, 61, 76–77
de Beauvoir, Simone, 9, 20, 51–53; *The Second Sex,* 47
Bell, Daniel, 76

Benokratis, Nijole, 167
Bentham, Jeremy, 117
Berlin, Isaiah, 42, 64, 134
Bernard, Jessie, 2
Blackstone, Sir William, 31, 34, 85
Bradwell, Myra, 118
Breckenridge, Sophonsiba, 40
Brownmiller, Susan, 49
Burke, Edmund, 15, 57, 74, 124

Califano v. Webster, 102–3
Carpenter, G. Russell, 63
Carter, President Jimmy, 168, 174
Chafe, William, 40
Children: child care, 1, 2, 4, 126, 189–94; child custody, 177, 180–81, 183–86; and paternalism, 30–31, 42–44, 59; as public concern, 17; child rearing, 20, 108, 137, 188; child support, 89, 126
Children's allowance, 191–92, 194–95
Chisholm, Congresswoman Shirley, 159
Chodorow, Nancy, 59
Choice, 73, 110, 138; and government intervention in matters of, 133, 135–36; individual, 16, 22, 23, 26–28, 64; and values of liberty, 13, 131–34, 139; and microeconomic theory, 113; and paternalism, 31; and policy-making, 11, 12, 14, 90, 125; process of, 23, 27–28, 136; and self-segregation, 106; and work-time options, 155
Citizenship, and civic obligations, 103–5

Civil Rights Act (1964), 126, 144–45, 158–59
Collectivity: and choice, 15, 24; individual responsibility to, 88; and sexual freedom in, 75; task of, 77–78
Collective will, 22, 134
Community, 67–81; disintegration of monolithic, 68–69; and the individual, 70, 74–75, 89
"Comparable worth," 168, 170–72, 235 n.120
Congregationalist Ministers of Massachusetts, 34
Constant, Benjamin, 76
Contracts, liberty to make, 118. See also Marriage, contracts
Coons, John, 70
Craig v. Boren, 93–95, 98–99, 218 n.48
Crozier, Blanche, 119

Daly, Mary, 48, 127
Day care, 1, 51; government provision of, 123, 128, 192–94
Decter, Midge, 3, 65
Degler, Carl, 199
Determinism: biological, 203; economic, 17; vs. free will, 14, 63–66, 69; of leftist feminism and naturalism, 48
Dinnerstein, Dorothy, 59
Discrimination, 3; against fathers, 185; benign, 100, 107; racial vs. gender, 44–45; sex, 99, 132, 143–45
Divorce, 1, 32, 174, 180–82; rate of, 19, 174, 183, 198
Domicile, law of, 177–78
Dostoevsky, Fyodor, 23
Douglass, Frederick, 60
Draft registration, 95, 108, 115. See also Military service
Dual labor market, 149
Due process, 119, 222 n.133
Durkheim, Émile, 73

Education, and women, 33, 137
Eisenstein, Zillah, 51
Elshtain, Jean Bethke, 80
Emerson, Thomas, 90

Ephron, Nora, 138
Equal: choice, 174; employment opportunities, 1–3, 172; liberty, 4, 97–98, 100, 110–16, 122, 203–5; opportunity, 167; pay, 4, 26, 168; protection, 87, 107, 117–20; respect, 112; rights, 39–40, 87; treatment, 36
Equal Credit Opportunity Law (1974), 126
Equal Employment Opportunity Commission (EEOC), 144, 158, 168, 233 n.69
Equal opportunity legislation, 146, 148
Equal Pay Act (1963), 126, 143–44, 158
Equal Protection clause. See Fourteenth Amendment
Equal Rights Amendment, 2, 4, 40, 90, 127, 139
Equality, as sameness vs. as liberty-securing, 90, 97
Erickson, Nancy, 101
Establishment Clause, 123

False consciousness, 69
Family: assault on, 2, 19–20; changing demographics of, 126; vs. communal approaches to child rearing, 193; effects on the, of women working, 151, 172, 190; feminist view of, 17, 199; income of, 142; patriarchal, 59; "family policy," 173, 175, 195; as private institution, 58, 173, 199, 200; roles of men and women in, 140–41; and social order, 69, 74; and the state, 58, 110, 174–201; as ultimate welfare state, 19
Family Protection Act, 128, 201
Feagin, Joe, 167
Feminism, 2, 13, 17, 31, 34, 39–40, 60–61, 98, 127; and the draft, 104–5; and formal equality, 47
Feminism, Leftist, 53, 67, 127, 203–4; and American radical politics, 61; and free will, 65; vs. liberal feminism, 48; Marxist, 48–50, 72, 145; and oppression, 51, 71, 73; paradigm of, 58–61, 63; policy aspirations of, 125; positions of, 47–49; radical, 48–49, 71–72, 127, 148; socialist, 50–51, 72
Fichte, Johann, 32–33

Firestone, Shulamith, 49–50, 58
Fitzhugh, George, 43
Flammang, Janet, 62
Flex-time, 154–56
Ford, President Gerald, 191
Fourteenth Amendment, 224 n.143, 225
  n.145; and Civil War, 116; Due Process
  clause, 118; Equal Protection clause,
  86–87, 89–90, 98, 107, 116–18, 120,
  222 n.133, 226 n.154; standard of re-
  view, 91–97
Fox, Robin, 54–55
France, Anatole, 134
Frankfurter, Felix, 39–40
Free will vs. determinism, 63–66
Friedan, Betty, 36, 53, 61, 72, 139
Friedrich, Carl J., 29
Frontiero v. Richardson, 91–94, 97, 99,
  114–15. *See also* Military service

Galbraith, John Kenneth, 23
Galanter, Marc, 122
Garside, Christine, 26
Gay couples, 174
Geertz, Clifford, 66
Gender: biological differences, 25–26, 53–
  55, 62; changing social conceptions of,
  66; and determinists, 73; and public and
  private spheres, 18–19; psychodynamics
  of, 59; relevance of, in society, 22, 24,
  79
Gender equality, 86–123
"Gender gap," 2, 60, 213 n.68
Gender justice, 1, 68, 97, 125, 205; and
  affirmative action, 167; and individual
  choice, 16–17, 67
Gender litigation. *See individual cases*
Gender policy, 2, 12, 125, 130, 135; and
  autonomy, 124, 186; and liberty, 131,
  133
Genovese, Eugene, 44
Gilder, George, 145, 157–58
Gilligan, Carol, 70–71
Gilman, Charlotte Perkins, 36
Ginzberg, Eli, 137
Goesart v. Cleary, 120
Goldberg, Steven, 54

Government: and basics of life, 21; central,
  and open community, 79; intervention
  by, 10, 14–16, 129, 133; laissez-faire
  approach to families, 176; nonintervention, 32, 205; support for religious
  groups, 123
Greer, Germaine, 59, 75
Grimke, Sarah, 35–36
Gross, Barry, 167

Hag/ocracy, 71, 127. *See also* Daly, Mary
Hare, R. M., 135
Hartmann, Heidi, 145
Hatch, Senator Orrin, 159
Head Start program, 191
Health benefits, 1, 108
Hildebrand, George, 170
Hochschild, Arlie, 156–57
Homans, C. G., 67
Hook, Sidney, 166
Hoover, President Herbert, 153
Househusbands, 144
Housewives, 195–96
Housework, and competing demands, 142

Illich, Ivan, 74–75
Income splitting, 198–99
Individualism, 68–69, 79, 214 n.4; vs.
  communitarianism, 77
Individual preference, 15, 78–79, 136, 150.
  See also Choice
Industrial Revolution, 74
Information, as necessary element for liber-
  ty, 131, 134–35
Internal Revenue Code, 1, 4, 186–90, 204,
  238 n.51

Jaggar, Alison, 26, 50
James, Estelle, 160
Jencks, Christopher, 76
Jim Crow laws, 44, 86
Job segregation, 147–53, 169, 171
Job-sharing, 154–55
Jury duty, 103–4, 115
Justice, 12–13, 21–22, 61, 69; individualist
  vs. communitarian ideas of, 80–81

Kant, Immanuel, 13–14
Keynes, John Maynard, 67
Kibbutz, Israeli, and sexual equality, 200–
    201
Kirchberg v. Feenstra, 96
Kristeva, Julia, 61
Kuhn, Thomas, 51–52

Labor laws, 30; discriminatory to men, 89;
    feminist objection to, 40–41; maximum
    hours law for women, 119, 210 n.43;
    and paternalism, 36–39
Labor unions, and women, 143, 148. *See
    also* AFL-CIO
Langer, Susanne, 66
Laws, 13–14, 16, 34, 117; common law,
    29–30, 32, 36–37; family law, 174; and
    individual autonomy, 89; and marriage,
    31, 33; and women, 21, 30, 100, 203
Leisure time, and working women, 142–43
Lesbianism, 49, 71, 185
Levy, Jerre, 53–54
Lewis, Oscar, 69
League of Women Voters, 138
Liberalism, 67, 76, 214 n.4; classical, 21,
    113
Liberty, 15, 16, 19, 21, 27, 32, 79, 116;
    and choice, 134, 202; elements of, 131;
    individual, 134, 158; nondiscrimination
    essential to, 203; positive and negative,
    112, 175, 179; religious, 122–23. *See
    also* Mill, John Stuart
Life expectancy rates, and insurance pre-
    miums, 3–4. *See also* Pension plans
Lippmann, Walter, 173
Lochner vs. New York, 37–38

Macaulay, Thomas Babington, 124
MacKinnon, Catherine, 49
McMichaels, James, 202
Marriage, 31, 137, 174; contracts, 178–81
Marx, Karl, 140
Massachusetts Bureau of Labor Statistics,
    38
Maternity benefits, 1, 41, 191
Mead, Margaret, 47
Medicaid legislation, 110

Men, 70; and labor force, 141–42, 146,
    152; and parenting roles, 101–2, 184;
    victims of laws, 30
*Michael M. v. Superior Court of Sonoma
    County,* 95–96
Military service, 1, 4, 103–5, 111, 219
    n.81
Mill, John Stuart, 14, 16, 22, 34–35, 89,
    133; *On Liberty,* 32; *The Subjection of
    Women,* 31
Millett, Kate, 52
*Mississippi University for Women v.
    Hogan,* 107
Mitchell, Juliet, 58–59
Mott, Lucretia, 35
Muller v. Oregon, 38–39, 118–19

Naipaul, V. S., 46
National Academy of Sciences, 169
National Consumer League, 38, 40
National Women's Conference, (1978), 125
Naturalism, 13, 53, 67, 73, 76; and free
    will, 65; paradigm of, 56–57, 62–63;
    resembling paternalism, 54–56; and the
    Right, 47–48; and the wage gap, 145
New Right, the, 2, 73, 128
Nineteenth Amendment, 119
Nisbet, Robert, 73
Nixon, President Richard M., 128, 191
Nondiscrimination, and choice, 158–59,
    205
Nozick, Robert, 16, 64

Objectivity, and liberal legalism, 98
Occupational patterns, 160
Open community, 76–81
Oppenheimer, Valerie, 143
Oppression, paradigm of 52, 145. *See also*
    Feminism
Organizational dynamics, and job choices,
    149–50

Parenting leave, 191
Parsons, Talcott, 144
Part-time employment, 154–56
Paternalism, 29–45, 88, 92, 176, 203
Pension plans, 1, 4, 102–3, 113; and Re-

tirement Equity Act (1984), 126, 240 n.87

People v. Williams, 37

Piercy, Marge, 140

Plato, 15, 23

Polanyi, Michael, 63–64

Pole, David, 28

Policy, 1, 2, 11, 14, 21–25, 30, 167; child care, 191, 193; choice-promoting, 125, 134, 139; family policy, 19, 174, 186; and gender, 29, 41–43, 47, 165; government-set outcomes for, 136; and judiciary, 130; and leftist feminism, 56–60; outcome vs. process oriented, 4, 10, 11; private, and behavior in marketplace, 144; social, 12; social welfare, 112; and workplace flexibility, 153

Positive and negative liberty. *See* Liberty, positive and negative

Power: feminist theories of, 62; and men, 32, 148, 150; of state, 16, 37; and women, 34, 52

Pregnancy, 93, 108–9, 126

Property rights, 174, 180

Property tax relief, 94

Public and private spheres, 17–19, 44–45, 70, 80–81, 89, 111, 153, 179, 203

Queen Victoria, 34

Quotas, 136, 139, 153, 164–67, 172

Race-sex analogy, 3, 24–25, 29, 86–88, 106; and paternalism, 43–45; and preferential policies, 137; and wage discrimination, 146

Rape, 49, 51, 78, 95–96

Rawls, John, 14, 79

Reagan, President Ronald, 2, 133, 167, 191

Reed v. Reed, 90–92, 96, 97, 120

Rehnquist, Justice William H., 94–96, 99

Religion, and gender, 120–23

Rich, Adrienne, 173

Roe v. Wade, 109–10

Rousseau, Jean-Jacques, 74

Rossi, Alice, 190

Rostker v. Goldberg, 95

Rowbotham, Sheila, 51

Rubin, Gayle, 57

Sartre, Jean-Paul, 46, 140

Sayers, Dorothy, 9

Schaar, John, 85

Schlafly, Phyllis, 106, 127

Segregation, by gender, 106–8, 112

Self-determination, 12, 136

Selznick, Philip, 76

Seneca Falls Convention of 1848, 60; Declaration of Sentiments, 31

Service sector, women in, 143, 147–53

Sex, defined as class, 49, 50, 60

Sex discrimination, 126, 158, 225 n.145, 226 n.154, 233 n.69

Sexism, 49, 57, 98; feminism as inverted, 61

Sexual freedom, 75

Sexual harassment, 2, 233 n.67

Sexual identity, 79

Sexual parity, 160, 162

Sexual preference, 1

Sexual privacy, 3, 105

Sexual roles, 4, 18–19, 21, 60, 69, 74, 76, 108, 102, 201

Simmel, George, 28

Skinner, B. F., Utopian vision of, 23

Smith, Adam, 140, 169

Social order: and determinism, 69; and paternalism, 32

Social policy, 12; and the Supreme Court, 85–90. *See individual cases*

Social Security Act (1935), 101–3, 196

Social security system, 1, 115, 239 n.82; and divorced spouses, 197; and married women, 196–97; vertical vs. horizontal equity, 196

Social tolerance, 28, 65, 144; as element of liberty, 131, 135–36

Stanton, Elizabeth Cady, 60

Stanton v. Stanton, 96

Stewart, Justice Potter, 86, 105

Suffrage, 32–33, 118–19

Sugarman, Stephen, 70

Swisshelm, Jane, 35

Tax benefits, and family, 175, 186
Taylor v. Louisiana, 103–4
Tiger, Lionel, 54–56
Tocqueville, Alexis de, and open community, 76
Tribe, Laurence, 27–28

Unger, Roberto, 76, 80
U.S. Supreme Court, 1, 29, 33–34. *See individual cases*
Utopianism, 23–24, 204; and leftist feminism, 61; and Owenites, 74

Wages: comparable worth and scheme for setting, 171; discrimination, 144, 169; setting of, 169, 170; women earning lower, 143–47, 172, 231 n.26
Walzer, Michael, 68, 76
Wasserstrom, Richard, 24–25
Weber, Max, 76
Weinberger v. Wiesenfeld, 101–2
Weiskopf, Francine, 160
Williams, Bernard, 63

Williams, Raymond, 76, 78
Wilson, E. O., 56
Wolgast, Elizabeth, 25
Women in the Year 2000, 126
Women: and access to credit, 1, 177; ethic of care, 70; exodus of, from the home, 142; exploitation of, 29, 39, 101; female self-identity vs. social identity of, 80–81; as heads of households, 137, 236 n.7; important political force, 2, 50, 60; increased respect for, 129; legal rights of, 30–31; as marginal citizens, 89; morality of, 35–36; and paternalism, 30–33, 35, 53; and preferential treatment, 93; as workers, 37–38, 41, 137, 140–44, 147, 171–72
Women's movement, 47, 144, 190
Women's Party, 39, 60
Woolf, Virginia, 1
Work-time options, 153–57

Yankelovich, Daniel, 201